THE BEST LITTLE
BASEBALL TOWN
IN THE WORLD

Praise for
The Best Little Baseball Town in the World

"Wow, how exciting to read about the rich tradition of pro baseball in my hometown! Thank you, Gaylon White, for a book that encapsulates a small town's baseball history with comical, emotional, and thrilling storytelling!"
> —Alyson Habetz, associate head softball coach, University of Alabama, and the first female to play prep baseball in the state of Louisiana, at Notre Dame High School in Crowley

"Gaylon White's latest book is a great read about the game that has been so good to me. The Evangeline League provided southwest Louisiana with unique entertainment at a time when other sports weren't present."
> —Ron "Louisiana Lightning" Guidry, three-time winner of 20+ games with the New York Yankees and 1978 American League Cy Young Award winner

"This book is full of interesting stories. Baseball in Crowley was special in the 1950s and is worth revisiting."
> —Eddie Robinson, four-time American League All-Star and former coach, farm director, general manager, scout, and consultant

"This book shares a time in the history of Acadia Parish and Acadiana that many of us have forgotten or never knew. Thank you, Gaylon White, for bringing to life a great time in our history."
> —Lewis Cook, legendary football coach for Notre Dame High School in Crowley, Louisiana, and member of the Louisiana Sports Hall of Fame

"Crowley, Louisiana, has produced national political figures and personalities on every level and world-class athletes in every sport, along with many other interesting and successful people. This book reveals how minor league baseball in the early 1950s was another piece of Crowley's colorful history."
> —John Brady, head basketball coach for Crowley High School (1977–82), Samford University (1991–96), Louisiana State University (1997–2008), and Arkansas State (2008–16)

"In *Field of Dreams*, character Terence Mann famously said, 'But baseball has marked the time.' It's true, and yet again Gaylon White is here to chronicle what happened, this time in *The Best Little Baseball Town in the World*. White brings to life the glorious, unknown stories of America's pastime."
> —Preston R. Scott, host of *The Morning Show with Preston Scott*, WFLA-FM, Tallahassee/Panama City

"Gaylon White's great book brings back memories of my childhood and how much minor league baseball meant to large and small communities all over the country. White paints such a great picture of the Evangeline League and Crowley, Louisiana. All of us owe him a debt of gratitude for keeping alive the great names and memories of minor league baseball."
> —Dave Smith, host of SportsMap radio network

"The wild and raucous Evangeline League in Louisiana survived swarming mosquitos, an outrageous gambling scandal, crooks, crazies, a deadly lightning strike, riots, torrential rain, floods, sweltering heat, and humidity, but in the end it couldn't overcome the Bermuda triangle of television, integration, and Hurricane Audrey. Gaylon White looked at this mess and saw Crowley, Louisiana—the best little baseball town in the world."
> —Bill Swank, baseball historian and author of *Echoes from Lane Field: A History of the San Diego Padres 1936–1957*

"Very interesting read, and very nice to bring out athletic heroes in small towns!"
> —Eric Hetzel (Crowley born and bred), pitcher for the Boston Red Sox and 1985 first-round draft pick from Louisiana State University

THE BEST LITTLE BASEBALL TOWN IN THE WORLD

The Crowley Millers and Minor League Baseball in the 1950s

Gaylon H. White

ROWMAN & LITTLEFIELD
Lanham • Boulder • New York • London

Published by Rowman & Littlefield
An imprint of The Rowman & Littlefield Publishing Group, Inc.
4501 Forbes Boulevard, Suite 200, Lanham, Maryland 20706
www.rowman.com

6 Tinworth Street, London SE11 5AL, United Kingdom

British Library Cataloguing in Publication Information Available

Library of Congress Cataloging-in-Publication Data

Name: White, Gaylon H., 1946–, author.
Title: The best little baseball town in the world : the Crowley Millers and minor
    league baseball in the 1950s / Gaylon H. White.
Description: Lanham : The Rowman & Littlefield, [2021] | Includes bibliograph-
    ical references and index. | Summary: "This book tells the fun, quirky, story
    of a minor league baseball town in Louisiana that was the talk of the baseball
    world in the 1950s. Written by respected minor-league baseball historian
    Gaylon White, this book will be of interest to baseball and Louisiana histo-
    rians alike"—Provided by publisher.
Identifiers: LCCN 2020035838 (print) | LCCN 2020035839 (ebook) | ISBN
    9781538141151 (cloth) | ISBN 9781538141168 (ebook)
Subjects: LCSH: Baseball—Louisiana—History—20th century. | Minor league
    baseball—Louisiana—History—20th century. | Baseball—Social aspects—
    United States—History—20th century. | Minor league baseball—Social as-
    pects—United States—History—20th century.
Classification: LCC GV863.L82 W45 2021 (print) | LCC GV863.L82 (ebook) |
    DDC 796.35709763—dc23
LC record available at https://lccn.loc.gov/2020035838
LC ebook record available at https://lccn.loc.gov/2020035839

♾ ™ The paper used in this publication meets the minimum requirements of
American National Standard for Information Sciences Permanence of Paper for
Printed Library Materials, ANSI/NISO Z39.48-1992.

In memory of my beloved father, Rev. Hooper Walker White, and uncle, Herbert Hoover White, and in recognition of two visionaries: Richard Pizzolatto and Isabella de la Houssaye, former mayor of Crowley.

CONTENTS

FOREWORD

Hy Cohen

I grew up in Brooklyn, New York, dreaming of pitching in the big leagues, won exactly 100 games in the minors, struck out Willie Mays in the majors, and, then, taught history and coached for 30 years.

All these things flashed through my mind as I read about baseball in Crowley, Louisiana, and realized once again how the history of the sport and America are intertwined like the rubber cork, yarn, and horsehide cover of a baseball.

The Best Little Baseball Town in the World puts you in the shoes of the players and gives you a sense of what it was like in the lower minors in the '50s. The book captures the innocence of the era, as well as the bigotry that prevented blacks from playing alongside whites in the South.

I'm Jewish, but I can relate to Tony Taylor, a dark-skinned Cuban, breaking the color barrier in the Evangeline League and Felipe Alou being let go because supposedly he wasn't good enough. Both went on to star in the majors.

Black and Jewish ballplayers were favorite targets for the haters.

At New Orleans in 1956, I struck out and someone yelled, "Hitler had the right idea! He killed all the Jews."

My manager, Andy Cohen, also a Jew, was coaching at third base. He turned around and ran into the stands to grab the idiot and get him kicked out of the ballpark.

By the end of my half-season at New Orleans, I had 11 wins and the loud-mouth rednecks in right field near the bullpen were my friends. The mayor of New Orleans even gave me the key to the city.

The name-calling wasn't confined to the South.

At Muskegon, Michigan, an opposing player called me "kike" and "Jew bastard" during a game. The next time the culprit came to bat, I put him on his ass all four pitches. He didn't let out a peep after that.

My father, Joseph, immigrated to the United States from Poland. One day he told me a man with a big, black cigar would sign me to a baseball contract. I thought my dad was smoking something much stronger than a cigar until New York Yankees super scout Paul Krichell showed up with a big, black cigar at New York City's Polo Grounds for an all-star sandlot game and watched me strike out four batters in two innings.

"You're going to be the next Hank Greenberg," Krichell said as he signed me for a $750 bonus plus $175 a month.

Krichell signed the great Lou Gehrig but lost out to the Detroit Tigers on the legendary Greenberg, the first Jewish superstar in American professional sports.

The Yankees sent me to LaGrange, Georgia, in the Class D Georgia–Alabama League, where I spent two years, posting a 7–5 won–loss mark in 1948, and 11–15 in 1949.

Playing in the South was a culture shock for a 17-year-old kid from Brooklyn, especially one named Hyman. A young boy in LaGrange figured out I was Jewish and wanted to know where my horns and tail were. It was my first teaching assignment.

In my second year at LaGrange, I faced Rudy York, player-manager of the Griffin Pimentos but no relation to Tony York, the Crowley Millers' player-manager in 1953–54.

Rudy was Greenberg's fence-busting buddy with the Tigers, leading the American League in home runs one year and slamming 277 in the majors overall. He stepped to the plate with the bases loaded. I struck him out swinging.

"Holy cow!" I said to myself. "I think I can make it."

The Chicago Cubs obviously agreed. They selected me in the minor-league draft at the end of the 1949 season and assigned me to their Class A farm club in Grand Rapids, Michigan.

The local newspaper reported that the Cubs envisioned me staring down the mound at Stan "The Man" Musial.

That happened in my big-league debut five years later, but it didn't turn out the way I wanted. I threw Musial three different pitches, and he got three hits—a triple and two singles.

I fared better against three other Hall of Famers—Willie Mays, Roberto Clemente, and Monte Irvin. I whiffed Willie, got Roberto to pop out, and coaxed Monte into grounding into a double play. Altogether I pitched 17 innings for the Cubs, allowing 28 hits and 15 earned runs for a 7.94 earned run average (ERA). This got me a one-way ticket to Los Angeles, where I played for the Angels of the Pacific Coast League (PCL).

The best part of my time in L.A. was marrying a local girl, Terry Davis, at the end of the '55 season and having two wonderful kids, Jeff and Jill. The worst was being demoted in early '56 to Class AA despite a perfect 5–0 record, tops in the PCL. The reason given was my ERA of 5.70 was too high.

"You scared every pitcher in the league that year when you were sent out 5–0," another pitcher in the league told me at a PCL Historical Society reunion 45 years later. "When I heard that, I thought, 'What the hell, 5–0. What more could a man do?'"

I was wondering that, too. So I went to college, got a master's degree, and became a teacher-coach.

Even with the ups and downs, playing pro baseball was a wonderful experience that helped me personalize history for my high school students.

The reference to Fidel Castro in chapter 18 reminded me of the game I was pitching in Havana in 1958, while Castro and his guerilla rebels were getting ready to take over the city. In about the fourth inning I heard a loud, gunshot-like pop. My teammates sprinted from the field into the dugout. I was left standing alone on the mound unsure whether to fall flat on the ground, duck, or run for cover. It's a story I shared with my students many times to make the Cuban Revolution more real and meaningful.

One day a student came up to me and said, "Coach, I want to go to college and be a history teacher because I enjoyed your class so much."

To me, that was like pitching a no-hitter.

About Hy Cohen

Born in Brooklyn on January 29, 1931, Hy Cohen is featured in Gaylon White's book *The Bilko Athletic Club*, published by Rowman & Littlefield. In nine minor-league seasons, Cohen had a 100–77 record. Three times he won 16 games, 15 once. He led two leagues with the lowest

ERA. In the seven games he pitched for the Cubs in 1955, he had no decisions. After pro baseball Hy taught history and coached baseball, football, and tennis at Birmingham High School in Van Nuys, California. He is a member of the Southern California Jewish Sports Hall of Fame in recognition of his teams winning 18 league titles. He also was honored in 1995, as an outstanding educator by the Los Angeles Dodgers.

PREFACE

Bob Pacanowski has been to the *Field of Dreams* movie site in Dyersville, Iowa, 31 times and counting.

On different occasions Bob took his wife and kids, brother, sister, mother, and several other relatives and friends to the cornfield-turned-ballfield and had sales meetings there for the sporting goods company he represents. He has sat on the tractor that actor Kevin Costner used to clear the corn off the field and enjoyed a beer on the front porch of the nearby farmhouse.

"It all goes back to the simplicity of going out in the backyard or onto a field and bringing out some baseballs and taking a little batting practice and just playing like kids," Bob said.

Unfortunately, Bob never got to do that at Dyersville with his father, Art, an infielder patted on the head by a dream like Archie "Moonlight" Graham, the film's central character.

Unlike Moonlight, who played two innings of a game for the New York Giants in 1905, Art never made it to the "Big Show." The closest he came was the Class C Evangeline League, playing briefly for the Crowley Millers in 1952, and the Lafayette Oilers in 1954.

Art was typical of most minor leaguers at the time in that he chased his dream from one small town to another, ending up as obscure as when he started.

Prior to Crowley, Art hopscotched from Lexington, North Carolina, to Waycross, Georgia, to Leesburg, Florida, back to Waycross, and, then, to

Crowley's Miller Stadium turned out to be Art Pacanowski's own field of dreams, as he never got any higher than the Class C Evangeline League. Art appeared in 27 games for Crowley in 1952, batting .207, with two doubles and a home run. Photo courtesy of Bob Pacanowski and the *Crowley Post-Signal*.

Hazlehurst, Georgia. After Crowley, he went from Ozark, Alabama, to Graceville, Florida, and, finally, to Lafayette, Louisiana.

The 21-year-old infielder arrived in Crowley at the same time as shortstop Mike Scivoletti and outfielder Edwin Ziencina. They were "names that could easily have been culled from the 'Fighting Irish' at Notre Dame," a *Crowley Daily Signal* columnist mused, asking, "Doesn't it remind you of the late great Knute Rockne's famous lineup?"[1]

Another writer chimed in that if Millers manager Johnny George didn't have trouble with the infield, "the scorers and newspapers might, for there is a chance of a double play that will read Pacanowski to Scivoletti to Meriwether (first baseman Conklyn Meriwether), and that's the alphabet for sure."[2]

Pacanowski wasn't around Crowley long enough for folks to learn his nickname, "Pack."

In 24 games at third base, he made 12 errors. At the plate, he batted .207, striking out 20 times in 98 at-bats. He had three hits in one game, only to get picked off third with the bases loaded and two outs in the ninth inning of a 3–2 Millers loss.

Art finished the '52 season in the Class D Alabama–Florida League, hitting a combined .293 for Ozark and Graceville. He continued at Graceville in 1953, batting .290, with nine homers.

The numbers were good enough to get Art one more shot in the Evangeline League at Lafayette. This time he hit a respectable .274, but committed 14 errors in 29 games at second base.

That was it for Art's pro baseball dream. He returned to his hometown of Chicago, got married, raised three kids with his wife, Joan, and was an insurance claims adjuster until shortly before he died in 1997, at the age of 66.

In 2000, Joan got a letter informing her the Crowley Millers were having a reunion—the first since the team disbanded in 1957. Bob and his sister, Cathy, decided to attend in their father's place.

Growing up, Bob played catch in the backyard with his dad and shared the pain of being a diehard Chicago Cubs fan, as they lost far more than they won.

Art seldom talked about his baseball career so Bob didn't know he once went 5-for-5 in a game at Graceville or that he was hit in the head by a pitch, suffering a concussion. Bob was aware his father had two stolen bases and one home run at Crowley.

"My dad didn't have much speed," he said. "That's not a Pacanowski tradition."

At 5-foot-9, 172 pounds, Art wasn't a fence-busting stud either.

The homer that sailed over the left-field fence at Miller Stadium was on Bob's mind as he stepped onto the same field at the reunion.

"I could visualize my dad, struggling as a hitter, finally getting a hold of one and running around the bases," Bob recalled. "That was probably his day in the sun in Crowley."

Standing on the outfield grass, Bob imagined what it was like to be in his father's shoes at third base. He pitched batting practice to some of Art's teammates, just like Kevin Costner did to Shoeless Joe Jackson in *Field of Dreams*. "Every time I step on the field, it's an emotional moment—lifting my head up to the sky and thinking about playing catch with Dad."

Fast forward to the seventh game of the 2016 World Series between the Cubs and the Cleveland Indians.

Bob and his wife, Beth, watched the game on television at home in Naperville, Illinois, the Cubs jumping to a 5–1 lead and, then, squandering it four outs away from winning their first World Series in 108 years. The score was tied 6-all when suddenly the rain came and delayed the game for 17 minutes.

Bob had flashbacks to infamous Cub collapses in 1969, 1984, and 2003. In each case, they snatched defeat from the jaws of victory.

"I went downstairs to my basement, picked up a photo of my dad, and brought it upstairs," Bob said. "The Cubs were his team, and we needed his help to win."

With the picture on Bob's lap, the rain stopped and the Cubs immediately scored twice in the top of the 10th inning to win the game.

Some have suggested that the showers were ordered by Cubs Hall of Famers Ron Santo and Ernie Banks looking down from above. Or, more befitting of the Cubs, maybe it was the heavenly handiwork of a long-forgotten minor leaguer from Chicago named Pacanowski.

ACKNOWLEDGMENTS

There's a Pizzolato Street in Crowley, Louisiana, but it's in the boon-docks instead of downtown where it belongs.

Richard Pizzolatto, youngest son of the street's namesake (Louis Piz-zolatto Sr.), is known around town as Coach Pizz, but as far as I'm concerned he's Mr. Crowley. Without him, Crowley's historic Miller Stadium would be long gone, the Crowley Millers and Evangeline League player reunions held from 2000 to 2010 would've never hap-pened, and there would be no book telling the amazing story of the "Best Little Baseball Town in the World."

Coach Pizz was a gang of one, connecting me with Ed "Oh Happy Day" Keim, the radio voice of the Millers, and most of the 24 players interviewed for this book—Bobby and Dickie Barras, Billy Joe Barrett, Hugh Blanton Sr., Jerry Clifford, Marland "Duke" Doolittle, Floyd "Greek" Economides, Terry Fox, Ray Hensgens, Claude Horn, Tom Jor-dan Sr., Don Keeter, Walt Laurie, Don LeBlanc, Tony Mele, Chuck Nelson, Al Ogletree, Dan Pfister, Mike Scivoletti, Jerry Simon, Mel Stein, Willard Sterling, Ray Stockton, and Leon Webrand.

He introduced me to two people instrumental in preserving Miller Stadium and the storied past of baseball in Crowley—former Crowley mayor Isabella de la Houssaye and Harold Gonzales Jr., publisher of the *Crowley Post-Signal*.

He arranged for me to tour Crowley's Grand Opera House with L. J. Gielen, the visionary who has restored the majesty of the "Jewel of the South," built in 1901.

He facilitated e-mail communication with Edwin Edwards, a four-term Louisiana governor, and Judge Edmund Reggie, a political powerhouse in the state and confidant of President John F. Kennedy. In the early 1950s, Edwards was on the Crowley city council and Reggie the youngest city judge in the United States. They were both involved in JFK's historic visit to Crowley in October 1959.

Coach Pizz helped me secure permission from Lana Keigley and Maxine Guidry to use the fabulous "portraits" their father and mother, Robert and Ninfa Guidry, took of JFK and Jackie. "Although we have visited many states since leaving Louisiana, our visit to your state was a highlight of our travels during the past few weeks," Senator Kennedy wrote in a letter thanking the Guidrys for the photographs.

Coach Pizz shared pictures of Crowley players and newspaper articles providing a game-by-game account for most of the eight years the Millers existed. He reviewed the chapters as I wrote them, providing valuable feedback.

On my first visit to Crowley in 2013, Coach Pizz showed me around town and used the recipe in this book to make "Bus Station Biscuits"—biscuits that would make any grandma a celebrity.

Twice we hooked up for dinner with Terry and Shirley Fox, and Billy Joe and Nita Barrett. Terry and Billy Joe were teammates at New Iberia in 1954–55, and are featured in chapter 11, *The Kid and the Old Pro*.

I connected with Coach Pizz through Ann Mire, head of the Acadia Parish Library at the time. Ann immediately produced relevant stories and gave me the run of the place in my search for more. Later, after she retired, Ann helped me find elusive photographs and fed me tidbits based on her excellent writings about Crowley's colorful past.

My research efforts in 2013 prompted the *Post-Signal* to do a series of articles on the Millers that, in turn, led to Bill Scholl and Rici Scholl Miller reminiscing about growing up in Crowley and the night at Miller Stadium the local Sultan of Swat, Conklyn "Conk" Meriwether, punched their father, Hirsch Scholl, in the face.

Conk left Crowley in 1954, to play for the Tallahassee Rebels in the Florida International League. There he confided in manager Duke Doolittle about the personal problems that eventually led to tragedy for Conk and his family. Duke recreates those conversations for us.

Photographer Ninfa Guidry's favorite photo of Senator John F. Kennedy may well be the one taken of her and the future president of the United States in October 1959. Photo courtesy of Lana Keigley and Maxine Guidry.

Infielder Art Pacanowski was one of the lesser-known Millers, but through his eldest son, Bob, I came up with the story about him in the preface.

Joe Chaillot, a professional storyteller, shared numerous tales about his father, Emile, leading me to repeat what Emile often said: "That's an interesting story, Joe. It could be true."

Annie Mele Mazzaro pulled photographs from the scrapbooks her late father, Tony Mele, meticulously maintained, then scanned and sent them via the same "the jolter" e-mail address that he named in honor of his boyhood hero, Joltin' Joe DiMaggio.

Steve Holleman, one of Marv "Lefty" Holleman's three sons, supplied the vintage shot of the team's "bright, dazzling, blinding, red" bus and photos of his father with fellow 20-game-winners Gil Ross and Chuck Nelson in 1953, as well as a group of Millers players in 1954, at Toler's newsstand in downtown Crowley.

Ralph Maya, a Cuban baseball historian, filled in the blanks on what happened to infielder-pitcher Juan Izaguirre after he quit pro ball in the United States to return to Cuba. He also supplied the photo of Juan in a Marianao Tigers uniform.

The late Charlotte Jeffers of the city of Crowley arranged for the scanning of the Millers player photos, which fortunately were saved in a large notebook.

The quality of the pictures is as good as it is because Rory White, my photographer-son, and Leann DeBord restored them so they look like they did when they were shot in the '50s.

Researching a book like this is impossible without the help of librarians like Tom Cole of the Mecklenburg Library in Charlotte, North Carolina, and Ammon Marshall of the main branch of the East Baton Rouge Parish Library, one of the finest in the country.

I want to recognize the hosts and producers of radio and television shows throughout the country that featured my previous books. It's an impressive list of individuals I'm grateful to for spreading the word about mostly obscure players on forgotten minor-league teams. In alphabetical order, they are as follows:

- Nestor Aparicio of WNST-FM, Baltimore, Maryland
- Ben Ball of WTKF-FM, Morehead City, North Carolina
- Ron Barr of *Sports Byline USA*
- Mike Bates and Bill Parker of *This Week in Baseball*
- John Baxter of Jefferson Public Radio, Ashland, Oregon
- Greg Berg of WGTD-FM, Kenosha, Wisconsin
- Dave Bierstein of KDUS-AM, Phoenix, Arizona
- Mark "Munch" Bishop of WTAM-AM, Cleveland, Ohio

- Todd Brommelkamp and Alex Kuhn of KGYM-AM, Cedar Rapids, Iowa
- Jordan Buscarini of KOAL-FM, Price, Utah
- Ken Cail of WTPL-FM, Bow, New Hampshire
- Mike Cameron and Matthew Laurance of WLXG-AM, Lexington, Kentucky
- Elissa Walker Campbell of *The Big E Sports Show*, Dallas, Texas
- John Clemens of the USA Radio Network
- Jeffrey Cohen and Jason Springer of WTEL-AM, Philadelphia, Pennsylvania
- Mel Crippen of KASI-AM, Ames, Iowa
- Nick Diunte of *Baseball Happenings* podcast and *Forbes* magazine
- James Ernest of the Grueling Truth Radio Network
- Al Eschbach and Matt Meyer of WWLS-AM, Oklahoma City, Oklahoma
- Paul Esden Jr. of WSKO-AM, Syracuse, New York
- Carl Falk of WHTK-AM, Rochester, New York
- Rich Fisher of KWGS-FM, Tulsa, Oklahoma
- Bruce Haertl and Shane Dennis of KFH-AM, Wichita, Kansas
- Steve Kaplowitz of KROD-AM, El Paso, Texas
- Brian Kenny of *MLB Now*
- Toby Laek of *Daytime Tri-Cities*, WJHL-TV, Johnson City, Tennessee
- Robert Land of *Houston Sports Podcast*
- Warren Lawrence and Chris Burns of WKNY-AM, Kingston, New York
- Dave Light of WKPT-AM, Kingsport, Tennessee
- Paul Linnmann of KEX-AM, Portland, Oregon
- Marty Lurie of KNBR Radio, Berkeley, California
- Todd Marino of WCCS-AM, Indiana, Pennsylvania
- Derek Martin of KMA-AM, Shenandoah, Iowa/Omaha, Nebraska
- Jeff Santos of the Revolution Radio Network
- Jeremy Schaap of *The Sporting Life*, ESPN Radio
- Preston Scott of WFLA-FM, Tallahassee/Panama City, Florida
- Gabriel Segura of KCAA Radio, Loma Linda, California
- Dave Smith of SportsMap Radio Network, Los Angeles, California
- Pete Spadora of *Spadora on Sports*
- Brian Stull of WGNU-AM, St. Louis, Missouri

- John Vorperian of White Plains, New York, Cable TV
- Pat Williams of WORL-AM, Orlando, Florida

Thanks also to faithful readers like Brandon Rose of Fort Myers, Florida.

Soon after the publication of my last book, *Left on Base in the Bush Leagues*, Brandon shared his memories of the 1963 El Paso Sun Kings. They lost more games in the Class AA Texas League than they won but made a lasting impression on Brandon, 10 years old at the time, by socking 207 home runs in 140 games. Jose Cardenal rapped 36; Dick Dietz, 35; Moose Stubing, 27; Randy Hundley, 23; and Vic Roznovsky, 13. All of them went on to play in the big leagues.

But Arlo Engel, the biggest bopper of the bunch, with 41 over-the-fence shots, never got higher than the Class AAA Pacific Coast League.

"Arlo had a huge hole in his swing," Brandon noted, citing his 205 strikeouts for two teams in different leagues in 1961. "For all I know he had fielding and/or base-running speed challenges."

Fans hollered, "Hey, Engel, you couldn't catch a beach ball!" Or, "Hey, Arlo, you run like you have a refrigerator on your back!"

So many minor-league mashers couldn't do anything except smash the ball a mile, assuming they made contact. "But at a lower level of baseball," Brandon wrote, "they were stars, beloved and adored. They were our heroes."

Hearing about these forgotten heroes keeps me going.

Meanwhile, the always-dependable Leann DeBord keeps me on track, proofreading every page, preparing the index, restoring photographs and sorting out technology glitches that leave me yearning for my old, reliable Smith-Corona electric typewriter. Leann has had my back on the five books I've had the privilege of doing with the Rowman & Littlefield team, spearheaded by acquisitions editor Christen Karniski.

Thank you, Leann.

Thank you, Christen.

Thank you, Coach Pizz.

INTRODUCTION

"**I** hate to even mention this guy to you," the old pitcher said. "Did you ever hear of Conk Meriwether?"

The only Meriwether I knew about was Lee, the 1955 Miss America and actress.

"He was one of the sorriest people that I've ever seen, but he was the greatest hitter that I've ever seen in the minor leagues," continued Hugh "Slim" Blanton Sr., a 20-game winner in three of the nine seasons he pitched during the '50s. "Nobody would put up with him."

I looked it up.

At Greenville, Texas, in 1949, Conklyn "Conk" Meriwether walloped 27 homers to top the Big State League, and at Lake Charles, Louisiana, in 1950, he socked 24 in 62 games to pace the Gulf Coast League (GCL). At Crowley, Louisiana, he was home run king of the Class C Evangeline League in 1952–53, clouting 33 and 42, respectively.

Conk played two full seasons and part of another in Crowley, the longest he lasted anywhere.

"He had trouble everywhere he went," Blanton said of his Crowley teammate in 1952. "I wouldn't walk down the street with him because I was afraid somebody would shoot at him and hit me."

This got my attention and led me to Crowley and the amazing story of *The Best Little Baseball Town in the World*, which reads more like fiction than nonfiction. It has tragedy and triumph, mystery and mayhem, good guys and bad guys, the renowned and the unknown, and even a biscuit recipe.

Babe Ruth visited the Southwest Louisiana city in 1921, and Senator John F. Kennedy in 1959, when he was thinking about throwing his hat in the ring for president of the United States.

The Crowley Millers topped the 100,000 mark in attendance three straight years, from 1951–53. The high point, in 1952, produced crowds totaling 119,333, nearly 10 times Crowley's population of 12,700.

"The most amazing baseball town in the country, not excepting Milwaukee," Associated Press sports columnist Gayle Talbot began a story in 1953, the same year the Wisconsin city set a National League attendance record of 1,826,397.[1]

"Every inhabitant of Crowley, including infants and the infirm, watched the Millers perform better than eight times," Talbot calculated. "The citizens of Crowley seem not to have been informed that minor-league ball is going to hell."[2]

Talbot sought an explanation for the "phenomenon of a community going crazy about Class C baseball at a time when most higher minors are crying like stuck pigs."[3]

He learned that the fans themselves were the owners, and the board of directors consisted of doctors, lawyers, farmers, rice millers, and merchants.

In 1948, long before the phrase "Build it and they will come" was made famous in the movie *Field of Dreams*, Crowley built Miller Stadium, and two years later, in 1950, pro baseball came to town.

The club's first player-manager, Johnny George, was a mystery man, but no one bothered to find out more about him, as the Millers were pennant winners in two of the three years he was at the helm.

The only year the Millers didn't win under George was in 1951, when Andy Strong, the team's center fielder, was struck and killed by lightning in the middle of a game. At the time of the tragedy, the Millers were in first place. They finished fifth.

Conk arrived late in the '51 season and slammed 19 homers in 38 games, a preview of 1952–53, when he powered the Millers to back-to-back Evangeline League titles.

As the number of television antennas in Crowley went up, the crowds at Miller Stadium spiraled downward, to 65,099 in 1954, 45,130 in 1955, 37,265 in 1956, and, finally, 17,779 in 1957, when Hurricane Audrey severely damaged the stadium and shut down the Evangeline League.

A working agreement with the Kansas City Athletics enabled the Millers to hang on until the end and produce big-league pitchers George Brunet and Dan Pfister.

Brunet, a hard-throwing, beer-guzzling 20-year-old, whiffed 114 batters in 87 innings for the Millers in 1956, while tossing a no-hitter and winning seven of nine decisions. By the time he retired at the age of 49, Brunet had pitched for 32 teams, winning 69 games in the majors and 244 more in the minors. "He covered more ground than a guy in front of a posse," wisecracked syndicated columnist Jim Murray. [4]

Altogether, Brunet struck out a record 3,175 in the minors, plus 921 in the majors. "There wasn't a batter in any league he played in who didn't get on his knees every night and pray that George stayed thirsty," Murray quipped. [5]

Pfister posted a 13–6 won–loss mark at Crowley in 1957, and five years later his face was on a Topps baseball card with four other rookie pitchers, including Bo Belinsky, a renowned playboy, and Jim Bouton, author of the tell-all memoir *Ball Four*.

What happened to Conk after leaving Crowley in 1954, is the stuff of front-page headlines in newspaper tabloids.

"He was one of the greatest Millers and also one of the craziest," recalled Harold Gonzales Jr., publisher of the *Crowley Post-Signal*. "He could hit a baseball with the best of 'em, and off the field, you didn't know what was coming next.

"You read and hear about these stories of eccentric people that actually have the world and go do something crazy. On a more local and smaller scale, that's how Conk seemed to be. He owned the baseball world of the Millers, and yet he couldn't prosper with it because of his attitude and his actions."

The story of baseball in Crowley goes beyond any one player.

The Millers played in the Evangeline League, also known as the Tabasco and Pepper Pot League. It survived a world war, a game-fixing scandal, and a racial ban, only to be done in by Mother Nature—Hurricane Audrey.

Players from other Evangeline League teams are part of the Crowley story.

Terry Fox, a kid pitcher who went on to star for the Detroit Tigers, and Billy Joe Barrett, an old pro who never made it to the big leagues, reminisce about their baseball careers and how their team, the New Iberia Pelicans, replaced the Millers at the top of the standings in 1954–55.

Bob Riesener had a 20–0 won–lost record for Alexandria in 1957, something no one has ever done before or since. A game-by-game log kept by Riesener to track and improve his performance lets you relive the remarkable season with him.

Going into 2021, minor league baseball will be trying to recover from a double whammy, a season-long shutdown caused by the COVID-19 pandemic and a drastic restructuring imposed by Major League Baseball that threatens the future of teams in dozens of cities and entire leagues such as the Appalachian, which has been around since 1911. Pro baseball's retreat from small-town America is nearly complete.

When Crowley fielded its first pro team in 1950, there were 58 minor leagues. By the end of the decade, there were 21. The passion that made Crowley the "Best Little Baseball Town in the World" was gone.

The minors are the lifeblood of baseball. They produce both future big-league players and fans. They often account for our first memories of attending a game with a parent, brother, sister, or friends.

Folks in Crowley latched onto Johnny Pfeiffer, a shortstop for the Millers in 1950–51, who got as high as the Triple-A International League. "Pfeiffer is drawing the raves of the Shreveport Sports fans," the *Crowley Daily Signal* reported in 1957, when he played for the Sports, a Class AA team.[6]

Millers fans paid extra attention to Brunet and Pfister because they saw them first—before big-league fans.

Today, the only link pro baseball has to Crowley is Miller Stadium.

Restored in 1998, it's a testament to one of the most successful small-town teams in Minor League Baseball history. It's a story worth celebrating and remembering.

I

ALL ROADS PASS THROUGH CROWLEY

"All roads pass through Crowley," the saying goes.

Babe Ruth passed through on his way to the National Baseball Hall of Fame in Cooperstown, New York.

Little Richard, the singer-songwriter, passed through on his way to the Rock and Roll Hall of Fame.

Edwin Edwards passed through on his way to the Louisiana statehouse in Baton Rouge, where he served four terms as governor.

Senator John F. Kennedy and his wife, Jackie, passed through on their way to the White House.

The parade of celebrities passing through Crowley started in 1908, with Colonel William F. "Buffalo Bill" Cody, legendary army scout, buffalo hunter, and showman, executing "deeds of daring horsemanship" with his "unapproachable company" of cowboys, cavalrymen, and Rough Riders.[1]

"One of the unfailing signs of good times or hard times is the crowds that attend a circus," the *Crowley Signal* pointed out.

> In hard times the crowds are small. . . . In good times everybody goes to the circus.
>
> The city is filled today with people who have come in from the surrounding country to see the Buffalo Bill show. The streets are crowded with people who appear to have money. It's a good sign.[2]

Buffalo Bill returned in 1912, on his farewell tour.

Dr. Booker T. Washington, the trailblazing African American educator, author, and founder of the Tuskegee Institute, passed through in April 1915, "to observe conditions within my race in Louisiana and then to try to offer some scheme for the betterment of these conditions."[3]

Dr. Washington died the following November.

The same month, the Liberty Bell passed through Crowley on its way home to Independence Hall in Philadelphia, Pennsylvania, from an international exposition in San Francisco. It was the famed relic's last road trip.

Approximately 5,000 people flocked to the Southern Pacific train station in Crowley to get a glimpse of the national symbol of freedom. "The vast crowd could not all get close up," the *Signal* reported, "but the Bell, mounted on an open car upon an elevated frame, was clearly seen for several blocks by the eager populace."[4]

Interstate 10 now passes through the outskirts of Crowley, the self-proclaimed "Rice Capital of America." A restaurant and casino named the Rice Palace marks the way downtown to the Grand Opera House, where world heavyweight boxing champion Jack Dempsey and flamboyant politician Huey P. Long once appeared on stage, and Babe Ruth's signature is barely legible on a wall backstage.

"All roads will lead to Crowley," the *Signal* boasted, as townsfolk eagerly awaited Babe's arrival the morning of St. Patrick's Day 1921. Babe and his New York Yankees mates stopped in Crowley on a five-day swing through southern Louisiana that started in Lake Charles and ended in New Orleans.[5]

At Crowley, they played an exhibition game against the Indianapolis Indians, a minor-league team that made its spring training home there. A baseball field was set up inside a horse-racing track at the local fairgrounds, and organizers insured the game for $2,000 to cover their costs in case it rained and had to be canceled.

"Fans galore" greeted the Yankees train, and Babe "mingled with the players and newspaper writers" until the hollering of enthusiastic fans forced his retreat to the Egan Hotel for an interview with a *Signal* reporter.[6]

"I noticed your skyscraper," Babe said, referring to a new seven-story bank building. "You can't imagine what help the signs of prosperity mean. It is all in thought, after all, think right, live right, and you get there with flying colors."

"Grit like that makes cities," he raved. "Keep it up, snap your finger at failure, and hit the ball hard."[7]

Babe already had eight home runs for the spring and was "looking to lose one of the balls" for the crowd of 2,500, nearly half of Crowley's population at the time.[8]

Stores and schools closed for the afternoon game. The train schedule was changed so fans could depart later than usual.

"People came from all nearby towns to see the wonder-man of baseball," the *New York Daily News* reported. "Automobiles came by the dozen and stretched halfway around the little track."[9]

The Grand Opera House celebrated the occasion by declaring it "Babe Ruth Day" and featuring a postgame movie, *Over the Fence*, about the record-breaking 54 homers Babe swatted the year before. Nearby, the Acadia Theatre screened another film about the slugger who would hike the single-season home run mark to 60 in 1927, and become known as the "Great Bambino."

Fans had to go to the movies to see one of Babe's four-base shots. At the fairgrounds, he was blanked in four at-bats, twice belting long fly balls that were caught because, "Indianapolis outfielders were able to play so far back that it was impossible to hit beyond them."[10]

Babe's visit "put Crowley in big display letters in the sporting world," editorialized the *Signal*. "It is the constant dripping on the stone which eventually brings results."[11]

Crowley didn't have a ballpark worthy of pro baseball until 1948, the year Babe died. Two more years passed before there was a pro team to play in it—the Millers of the Class C Gulf Coast League.

Baseball put Crowley on the map in the early 1950s. For three straight years, 1951–53, season attendance topped 100,000. One sportswriter calculated that attendance was roughly 10 times Crowley's 1950 population of 12,700, and the equivalent of the Yankees drawing "about 80 million fans."[12]

Crowley was dubbed the "Best Little Baseball Town in the World."

Folks in Crowley took their baseball as seriously as "Bus Station Biscuits" served piping hot every morning by Lillian Bartell at the Greyhound bus station coffee shop. They were "well-known from Houston to New Orleans" and the main attraction for visitors like rock-and-roller Little Richard, who satisfied his craving whenever he was in the area.[13]

**"GRIT LIKE THAT MAKES CITIES,"
SAID BABE RUTH COMMENTING ON
THE PROGRESS BEING MADE HERE**

Babe Ruth was a legend in the making when he arrived in Crowley on St. Patrick's Day 1921, his 54 home runs the year before an all-time record for a single season and five more than he had in his entire career up to that point. Babe broke his own mark with 59 in 1921, and 60 in 1927. The game in Crowley lasted just one hour and 20 minutes, and, according to the *Shreveport Times*, it was "remarkable" for Babe, as he "was without strikeouts, base on balls, and home runs"—categories in which he typically led the league. Courtesy of the *Crowley Post-Signal*.

The buttermilk biscuits were slathered with a stick of melted butter as they were pulled from the oven. Mrs. Bartell died in 1992 but different versions of her biscuits live on the internet.

"The only thing missing was a cup of my grandmother's good coffee," one man declared in a Facebook post after making a batch of the biscuits based on a recipe handed down by his Aunt Bitsy.

Using a recipe from her mother, a woman concluded they are a "cross between cookies and biscuits."

L. J. Gielen has operated the Rice Palace restaurant in Crowley since it opened in 1994.

"Everybody gives me the recipe, but I cannot duplicate those biscuits," Gielen lamented. "I come close to duplicating them, but I can't do it consistently. They were good—crumbly, almost like cake."

Dickie Barras grew up in Crowley and, in 1952, fulfilled his boyhood dream of playing for the Millers.

"Crowley was like Mayberry," he said, referring to the fictitious town that was the setting for two popular television sitcoms in the 1960s, *The Andy Griffith Show* and *Mayberry R.F.D.* "One of the worst things that ever happened was somebody jaywalking."

Freda Scholl often told her children, Rici and Bill, "They just ought to put a wall around it and keep it exactly the way it is."

Freda ran the Pelican Bag Factory with her husband, Hirsch, who also was coowner of the local radio station with Edmund Reggie, a judge of Lebanese descent.

It didn't matter that the Scholl family was Jewish in a predominantly French Catholic community.

When there was a fire at Judge Reggie's house, Hirsch Scholl crawled into the burning structure to rescue the Reggie children. Fortunately, no one was inside.

Rici attended Sunday school and belonged to the Methodist Youth Fellowship. She sang with her dad in the Easter cantata at the Baptist church. "I can sing every hymn known to the Methodists," she said.

Segregation laws kept blacks and whites separated in public places, but kids were color blind.

"Everybody was friends with everybody," Gielen said. "In the summer, you cut the grass, and, then, you made time for baseball. White, black, it made no difference. They would come from all over and we played baseball in my yard."

Blacks had their own Star Theatre, which advertised "accommodations for white patrons"—balcony seating. [14]

"That period, postwar through the '50s, was a time of possibility and innocence," said Bill Scholl. "President [Dwight] Eisenhower was sort of this uncle we were all fond of, and it was just a great time. This little town lived it."

Rici compiled a cookbook based on recipes with a Jewish twist developed by her mother and Shirley Breaux, the family's black maid. Freda didn't cook, but she could tell by tasting any dish exactly what the ingredients were and how to prepare it. She taught Shirley how to make a variety of Jewish, Cajun, French, Italian, and Mexican dishes.

"It was like eating in a fine restaurant every night," Rici recalled. "Her dinner parties were legend in a town where cooking was valued as highly as Louisiana State University football."

Hirsch Scholl set up a cot in the kitchen and baked cheesecakes around the clock so he could sell them to an upscale restaurant in Houston.

"Daddy had guests for lunch and dinner every day, and gave tea parties for children in the afternoon," Rici said.

For Rici, growing up in Crowley was all about food, family, and fun. Restaurants reflected the town's diversity.

Charlie Pizzolatto opened a café in downtown Crowley at about the time Dean Martin was crooning "That's Amore," a song with a line about the moon hitting your eye like a big pizza pie. A woman in England gave Charlie a recipe for pepperoni pizza, and, then, on his own he came up with a meat pie made from pizza dough stuffed with meat balls and deep fried.

"It was the first time that anybody in Crowley ever had pizza," Rici said. "And we thought that was the most exotic food that had ever been."

A Greek couple, Mary and George Mamoulides, ran the Rice Café, billed as "Mealtime Home of the Crowley Millers." They served a Creole-Italian salad with the politically incorrect name of "Wop Salad," but no one cared because it was considered the best in the world. [15]

The Acadia Café, owned by Albert Lopez, was popular for Mexican food and a veal cutlet dinner that cost 60 cents.

Located in the Egan Hotel building, DeRousselle's was an upscale restaurant popular for sizzling steaks and crawfish prepared any way patrons wanted.

Joe's Place was known for the best hamburgers in town, Sam's Café for biscuits and fried chicken, Keller's Café for seafood, DeLuxe Café for Harry the Greek's home cooking, and Ed's Lounge for a Lebanese dish called kibbi.

Dominic's was named after Dominic Serio, a Sicilian who specialized in French cooking and cussing out switchboard operators who placed calls for others because there were no dial phones.

"Do you have lemons?" a young caller would ask.

"Yes," Dominic replied.

"Squeeze them!" the youngster yelled before hanging up and leaving Dominic shouting, "You sonofabitch!"

The operator was still on the line and got an earful of Dominic's foul language. The telephone company threatened to cut off service to the restaurant if he didn't stop swearing.

Nearby Lafayette was three times bigger than Crowley but attracted far less attention.

Jay D. Miller produced a string of hit Cajun, country, and swamp blues songs at his recording studio in Crowley.

New Orleans–based novelist Frances Parkinson Keyes lived for nearly two years in Crowley in the early 1950s so she could use the town as the backdrop for her book *Blue Camellia.*

On his way to becoming governor of Louisiana, Edwin Edwards was a lawyer in Crowley and served on the city council for eight years. "We did not yet have dial telephones," Governor Edwards explained. "I was very instrumental in getting them installed."

He was center stage in 1959, when Senator John F. Kennedy and Jackie attended the International Rice Festival, held every October. After introducing Senator Kennedy, a band started playing "Dixie" and placards popped up in the audience. One of them read, "We like rice and gravy, strong coffee, the South, and Jack Kennedy."[16]

Senator Kennedy smiled and announced, "The South is rising again."[17]

Just as Babe Ruth did 38 years earlier, the Massachusetts senator discussed prosperity in a 10-minute speech. "We cannot be prosperous in Boston, Massachusetts, unless there is prosperity in Crowley, Louisiana," he said. "The cities and farms are bound together for their mutual well-being."[18]

The International Rice Festival takes place every October in Crowley, but in 1959, it was a once-in-a-lifetime event for the estimated 90,000 people who jammed "every nook and cranny they could find along Parkerson Avenue," the city's main thoroughfare, to see Massachusetts senator John F. Kennedy and his wife, Jackie. "I promise to eat rice the rest of my life," Senator Kennedy told the crowd, the largest to see him speak prior to his election as president of the United States 13 months later. Portraits by Ninfa Guidry/courtesy of Lana Keigley and Maxine Guidry.

The real star of the show was Jackie, who delivered her remarks in flawless French. "Bonjour, Mesdames et Monsieur," she greeted the thousands of French-speaking people in the audience.[19]

The crowd erupted with yells and cheers that "sounded like the top of the city of Crowley had exploded." Jackie went on to recall her father's description of South Louisiana as a "small corner of France."[20]

A woman columnist for the *Post-Signal* hailed Senator Kennedy as a "refreshing figure on the American scene" with "his shock of hair and boyish smile that erases the hardness and cynicism too often found among public figures." She added, "And that wife! If I were a man, I could say only, 'WOW!'"[21]

In 1960, Senator Kennedy was elected president of the United States, and three years later he was assassinated.

"To me, the point at which everything stopped going up in America and turned and began to go down was 1963, with the Kennedy assassination," said Bill Scholl. "That was sort of the end of innocence for the whole country."

A bronze plaque outside the Acadia Parish Courthouse in Crowley marks the spot where Senator Kennedy stood on the main stage and looked out at the crowd of 90,000 people. Throughout the years that number has increased to 135,000, perhaps allowing for those who later claimed they were there. Whatever the actual figure, it was the largest crowd of his presidential campaign and a powerful testament to the saying, "All roads pass through Crowley."

* * *

A century has passed since Babe Ruth visited Crowley.

Senator John F. Kennedy crowns the 1959 International Rice Queen, 17-year-old Judith Ann Haydel of Houma, Louisiana, and then poses for a shot with Jackie. Portraits by Ninfa Guidry/courtesy of Lana Keigley and Maxine Guidry.

The "skyscraper" Babe praised still stands. It belongs to the First National Bank.

The "grit" Babe mentioned led the city to restore the three-story Crowley Motor Company building, which was originally a Ford Model T dealership. It's now City Hall and houses two pristine classic Fords (a 1923 Model T and 1928 Phaeton Model A), a replica of Jay Miller's recording studio, and a Rice Interpretive Center with interactive exhibits that celebrate the history of the local rice industry. A welcome sign reads, "Crowley . . . where life is rice and easy."

The same grit inspired Crowley native L. J. Gielen to buy the Egan Hotel and the Grand Opera House. Gielen transformed the Egan into offices for his construction and real estate development business and restored the Grand to its original majesty.

It was true grit that produced the Grand in the first place.

Crowley-born Dave Lyons was a livery stable owner who couldn't read or write, but he had a fearless entrepreneurial spirit that, at age 24, spurred him to build the Grand, and later the Egan Hotel and Lyons Fairgrounds with the horse-racing track where the Yankees played in 1921.

"Mr. Lyons started in Crowley without a dollar and no backing," the *Signal* said in 1901, while the Grand was being built. "What he is and has today, he had made by his pluck and energy."[22]

The ground floor of the three-story brick structure was initially a mini-mall that throughout the years housed a pharmacy with an ice cream counter, printing press, bakery, barbershop, clothing store, pool hall, funeral parlor, café, saloon, gift boutique, and hardware store. Lyons tried unsuccessfully to lease the opera house to someone in the entertainment business.

"He never wanted to run the theater," Gielen said. "He was an entrepreneur."

A 70-foot oak and Louisiana cypress staircase climbed to the 1,500-seat auditorium on the second level. A ballroom was on the third floor.

The theater flooring was made of oak and the ceiling of pine slats, both three inches thick. The stage, measuring 20 feet high and 43 feet wide, was reportedly the largest between Houston and New Orleans.

Vaudeville and minstrel shows were featured early on, and, then, in 1909, Lyons renovated the theater so that movies could be screened. He added two box seats on each side of the stage to sell the tickets for a premium. The stage was about 40 percent less visible from these seats, but the people buying them were more interested in being seen than seeing.

Part of the balcony was designated for blacks, who entered and left the auditorium by a separate stairway.

Lyons was a bachelor and lived with his girlfriend, Eunice, on the second floor of the building until 1940, when he suffered a third stroke and died in his bedroom. The theater was immediately shut down and sealed off in 1946, from the Dixie Hardware store, which took over the ground level.

Dixie was a fixture in Crowley.

In 1921, it ran a newspaper advertisement for sporting goods that concluded, "If you want to be a second 'BABE' RUTH, get one of our bats."[23]

By 1952, the Crowley Millers were center stage, and kids wanted to be like one of the team's players.

"Baseball was a big part of everybody's life around here," Gielen said. "The Millers were a local team. They came from all over, but everybody considered them local. They were part of the community. Everybody knew them. All the young boys had their idols."

Seven-year-old L. J. idolized Willard Sterling, a 19-game winner for the '52 Millers. "I wanted to change my name to his name."

Sterling wound up marrying L. J.'s babysitter, a girl who lived a block away.

L. J. kept his name and went into business with his brother, John Daniel, building and operating a chain of convenience and discount to-bacco stores. They lost in a bid to buy the Grand in the 1980s, but L. J. and his wife, Carol "Chee Chee" Gielen, succeeded in 1999, and an-nounced plans with their daughter, Kim, to return the landmark to its original glory.

The Grand cost $18,000 to build in 1901, and $4.5 million to restore.

"When I told Chee Chee what I wanted to do, my estimate was $300,000," L. J. said. "She told me I was never good with numbers."

The original staircase was dismantled in 1946, and a freight elevator installed to access the second floor, which Dixie Hardware used as a storage area.

Uncovered during the restoration was a gun stolen from Dixie and used in a murder in Chicago. The weapon was returned to the store with a tag indicating the case number of the crime. Several items from the opera house were found, notably an electronic sign reading "Grand" that once graced the front entrance.

There were no blueprints or photographs to use in rebuilding the staircase, so a Baton Rouge architect did some research and produced a pen-and-ink drawing based on what turn-of-the-twentieth-century staircases looked like.

The Grand reopened in 2008, with *The Phantom of the Opera* performed by local high school students. "When they opened the curtains, you could hear a pin drop," Gielen said. "It was beautiful."

Today's Grand Opera House seats 400 people. It hosts plays, concerts, weddings, receptions, and a variety of special events. It's the center of entertainment in Acadia Parish, just as it was a century ago.

Tours take visitors backstage, where Babe Ruth wrote his name on a wall near the men's dressing room: George Herman Ruth—The Babe.

"That's how he signed his name," Gielen said. "Three lines. People wrote over it so many times over the years, it's hard to see."

The man who discovered Babe's signature told Gielen, "Some days it's clearer than others."

"What are you trying to tell me?" Gielen asked.

"I'm just telling you what I'm telling you," the man said.

Gielen didn't ask more questions because he knew the answer. "There are things that happen we can't explain. Some things we have to take for granted that they are here, and we can't worry about them."

One of the things that can't be explained is why George Herman Ruth's signature comes and goes.

"There are still spirits in the building," Gielen said matter-of-factly.

During demolition of the storage area, workers suddenly stopped what they were doing when the lights went off and the drawstrings Gielen used to turn them on earlier were inexplicably missing. Two workers were needed to move a red Naugahyde rocker.

"I think Dave Lyons was in the rocking chair," Gielen said. "That's why they couldn't pick it up."

A woman who claims to see and communicate with Lyons's girlfriend, Miss Eunice, says they sat next to one another in the balcony the night the Grand reopened.

Any doubts Gielen had about Lyons being in the building disappeared one sunny October day in 2010, as he was opening the door of Kim's office. Previously, it was Lyons's bedroom. "I put the key in the dead bolt. Something caught my eye."

He turned and saw a man walking toward the opening of the staircase. "I'm looking at him; he doesn't look at me. He had on a dark suit, white shirt, tie, and a dark hat with the brim pulled down in front."

Gielen left the key in the dead bolt and walked to a door where the man appeared to be headed.

"There's no outlet that way," he said.

Gielen expected to find the man at the door. "I scanned the whole second floor, and he wasn't there."

He returned to his daughter's office, removed the key, and went down the elevator to the ground floor. "When I turned the corner to go out the back, I said, 'It's all yours today; I'll be back tomorrow.'"

No one knows for sure if ghosts inhabit the Grand.

Maybe Babe Ruth is in the building and the guy sitting in the rocker that Gielen's workers struggled to lift. After all, Babe ate a lot of hot dogs and weighed as much as 260 pounds in his playing days.

Given all the celebrities that have passed through Crowley, it's not far-fetched that a few ghosts were among them and still hanging around. There are worse places to be than the historic Grand, the Jewel of the South.

2

BUILD IT AND THEY WILL COME

World War II was over. Americans were ready to have fun again.

"With the end of the war," the *Crowley Daily Signal* editorialized in October 1945, "sportsmen all over the country began to think of good baseball clubs, grid teams of prewar years, fast basketball clubs, trips to the mountains for winter sports, good golf balls that would zing down the fairway—and a complete return to a prewar sports for everybody."[1]

Free from the rationing of gas, tires, food, and clothing, people in small towns throughout the country wanted to go to the ballpark, something most of them couldn't do during the war, when the number of minor leagues plunged from 41 in 1941, to as few as nine in 1943.

The minors rebounded in 1946, with 42 leagues. By 1949, there were 59, with 447 teams, both all-time highs, attracting a record 41.7 million fans—double the attendance for the majors.

All of the lower 48 states, except Vermont and Wyoming, had cities with teams. North Carolina boasted 42 clubs; Texas, 41; New York, 28; Pennsylvania, 26; California, 25; Georgia, 24; Virginia, 22; and Alabama and Florida, 18. Louisiana ranked 16th, with 10 towns represented.

"Every town big enough to have a bank also had a professional baseball team," recalled Furman Bisher of the *Atlanta Journal*, "and the peak of excitement was reached when the bank was robbed, or the baseball team won the pennant."[2]

Crowley had a bank that towered over other buildings in Southwest Louisiana but no minor-league team.

"Crowley is starting from scratch," the *Daily Signal* acknowledged in another October 1945 editorial. "We have no grandstand, lights, or park. Every possibility should be exhausted in our effort to make the club a reality. It will pay real dividends."[3]

Some 30 Crowley baseball fans formed a corporation and sold stock at $50 a share to raise the $30,000 needed to build a ballpark and land a spot in the Class C Evangeline League. The Evangeline was a wartime casualty, shutting down on June 1, 1942.

"Those fans were crazy about any kind of sport, but baseball was their great love, and the rivalry between the towns was as keen as any Dodger–Giant feud," a former Evangeline League player said. "I wonder what they're going to do for their baseball down there now. I don't think they can get along without it."[4]

The top two pitchers for the world champion Detroit Tigers in 1945 were Hal Newhouser and Virgil Trucks, graduates of the Evangeline.

"The Evangeline has sent many famous ballplayers into the big leagues," the *Daily Signal* chortled. "That's why the towns in South Louisiana keep baseball seething. They keep close tabs on their former stars."[5]

The reorganized league was Crowley's best chance to get a pro team in 1946, but the bid failed, supporters blaming a shortfall in funds raised and the "unavailability of materials with which to construct stands and erect flood light[s]."

The *Daily Signal* questioned whether they tried hard enough. "Somebody is getting some lumber somewhere, and other cities have secured fine lighting system[s] disposed of by the army."[6]

Build a ballpark with lights and a minor-league club will come, the newspaper concluded in a page-one editorial. "If we lose the chance of a franchise this year, it will be lost to us next year—and all the rest of the years."[7]

Crowley baseball fans were left to dream.

"Of course, we dream all the time that Crowley might someday have an Evangeline team," a *Daily Signal* editorial writer admitted in October 1947. "We dream of seeing the people served up with a type of enjoyment that reaches the humble and mighty alike, regardless of job, position, or reputation."[8]

A team in the Evangeline meant publicity for the city, the Crowley name mentioned frequently on the radio and appearing daily on sports pages in the state throughout the season. "Being realistic," the editorial continued, "we know that 1948 will certainly not see Crowley in the Evangeline loop, but we can dream, can't we?"[9]

What happened next was a nightmare for Crowley boosters.

Natchez, Mississippi, dropped out of the Evangeline, creating an opening. Club owners snubbed Crowley in favor of Lafayette and, then, slammed the door shut for 1948 by voting down a proposal to increase the league from eight to 10 teams.

Undaunted, Crowley joined a new Class D circuit, the Louisiana–Texas League, made up of teams from two other Louisiana cities, Lake Charles and Opelousas, and three from Texas—Galveston, Orange, and Port Arthur. The league was quickly approved by George Trautman, head of the National Association of Professional Baseball Leagues (NAPBL).

This led to the creation of the Crowley Baseball Association and a quickie campaign to sell stock in the team for $25 a share. Stockholders would have a say in the management of the team. "Buy a share of fun, recreation, and good times by buying a share of the Crowley Baseball Association," Harold "Red" Mitchell urged readers of his *Daily Signal* sports column. "It's an investment, not a donation."[10]

The campaign was a success, but the Louisiana–Texas League never got going. Two of the six clubs were unable to complete their ballparks in time for the 1948 season, so the league was placed on the backburner for a year.

Crowley Baseball Association stockholders still didn't have a team, but work on a stadium was underway. They voted overwhelmingly to continue and be ready for 1949.

Meanwhile, semipro baseball in South Louisiana was booming, with the 10-team Teche League often drawing bigger crowds than the pro clubs. Games were played on Sundays, enabling players to work other jobs during the week.

Roy "Lefty" Price was a train conductor for Southern Pacific when he wasn't firing bullets for Crowley's Teche League entry, the Millers.

The 6-foot-3 Price pitched in the Evangeline League before and after the war.

In 1941, he posted a 13–10 record and a 2.86 earned run average (ERA) for his hometown of Lafayette, leading the league in strikeouts (171) and walks (153). In 1946, he notched a 12–12 mark and 3.20 ERA for Abbeville, whiffing 167 and walking 136. He played semipro ball most of the next three years and then won 35 games for three different Evangeline teams from 1950–52. At Houma, Louisiana, in 1951, he twice whiffed 23 in a game, while striking out a league record 344 for the season.

"I hear he was born BC, but I still like him," one manager said in selecting Price in the minor-league draft following the 1951 season. [11]

Price kept hitters off-balance with a blazing fastball and a big round-house curve that had them bailing out to the next parish as the ball sailed over the plate.

"When he mixes them up, he's a rough person to do business with, as any Teche Leaguer will plainly say," one scribe wrote. [12]

Price's numbers for Crowley in 1948 were spectacular: 11–3 won–loss record and 206 strikeouts in 122 innings, for an average of 1.69 per inning, or 15.2 per game. He limited foes to 4.7 hits and 2.4 runs per nine-inning game as the Millers captured the Teche League title.

The opening of Miller Stadium during the playoffs in late September pitted Price against another storied southpaw—38-year-old Sam "Lefty" Tarleton of Opelousas. It was a showdown of contrasting lefties, the powerful and sometimes erratic tosses of the ponderous Price versus the diminutive Tarleton, a so-called "nothing ball pitcher." [13]

"They broke the mould [sic] when they made Sam Tarleton," according to Red Mitchell. [14]

Tarleton was injured twice during World War II, ending any hopes of a pro baseball career.

"Sam imagined himself to be a pitcher," Mitchell said, noting he "could read the trademark on the baseball as it eased its way to the plate." [15]

When he wasn't on the mound for the Opelousas semipro team, Tarleton was a newspaper columnist.

"The old southpaw had a thing about him," Mitchell explained. "Everything he wrote was controversial to some respect. And his readers gobbled it up. Sam could create a rhubarb at a quilting bee if he put his mind to it." [16]

Tarleton wrote about putting America first long before it became a political campaign slogan.

"What about America?" he asked in a column published in 1947. "Are we supposed to support a universe of nations and peoples by giving them anything they seem too lazy to accumulate for themselves?"[17]

The matchup of lefties filled the 2,200 seats in the new, all-steel ballpark, fans spilling onto outer edges of the outfield. It was the first of many capacity crowds to come.

Going into the 1949 season, Crowley had a ballpark that still lacked lights, a roof over the stands, and a pro team. By year's end, the Millers had another Teche League crown, and the team was entertaining an offer to join the Gulf Coast League (GCL), a new Class C circuit that strongly resembled the Louisiana–Texas League, which had folded two years earlier before a single game was played.

Townsfolk had their hearts set on playing the nearby cities of Lafayette, Abbeville, and New Iberia in the Evangeline League.

"Being realistic," the *Crowley Daily Signal* editorialized, "we know that 1948 will certainly not see Crowley in the Evangeline loop, but we can dream, can't we?" The dream started with the building of the 2,200-seat Miller Stadium the same year, the birth of the Crowley Millers pro baseball team in 1950, and the team's entry into the Evangeline League in 1951. It was a dream come true for the Southwest Louisiana city of 12,700 people. Photo courtesy of Richard Pizzolatto and the *Crowley Post-Signal*.

The GCL cities of Crowley and Lake Charles in Louisiana and Port Arthur, Galveston, Jacksonville, and Lufkin in Texas were scattered across a 600-mile radius.

The Crowley Baseball Association was "cold" toward the league, a spokesman pointing out that Jacksonville and Lufkin "were too far removed from Crowley to make the loop workable and practical."[18]

"The very act of bringing such an unlikely circuit into being at all was a piece of promotional midwifery unparalleled in baseball annals," declared a Louisiana sportswriter, expressing the view of many of his colleagues.[19]

The most vocal critic was Tarleton, who repeatedly clashed with Howard Green, the president of the league and a former sportswriter.

Green touted the loop as the "best Class C league in the country."[20]

Tarleton, now writing for the *Beaumont Enterprise*, predicted, "A foul ball will never be hit in the Gulf Coast League."[21]

Green threatened to ban Tarleton from Gulf Coast press boxes for a "defeatist" attitude.[22]

Crowley fans had nowhere else to go. It was take it or leave it.

The Crowley Baseball Association launched another drive to sell stock so lights, a grandstand roof, bleacher seats, sunken dugouts, and player dressing rooms could be added to the ballpark.

"Not owning shares of stock in the Crowley Baseball Association is like a South Louisianan not eating rice," one writer observed.[23]

Some 400 fans paid $25 per share to become stockholders.

The search for a player-manager to build and run the team led to the selection of an obscure catcher from Alabama named Johnny George.

"To put it plainly, George was low man on the totem pole for the manager's post," Mitchell acknowledged in the *Daily Signal*. "There were several who, for a period of time, came ahead of him."[24]

In fact, George invited himself to Crowley for an interview.

"When deal after deal with the bigger wigs fell through, George's proposition sounded better and better," Mitchell reported. "He didn't possess the tag of having been a former big-leaguer, but he did possess the background of having been around plenty in the minor loops. His knowledge of minor-league play and of minor-league players was abundant."

On hiring George, Crowley Baseball Association president R. E. Schlicher quipped, "It's our club while we're winning, but it's yours when we're losing."[25]

It was intended as a joke, but the message was clear—win or else.

3

JOHNNY ON THE SPOT

Who Was Johnny George?

No one really knew the answer to that question until long after the 29-year-old George was named playing manager of the Crowley Millers, and even then, there were missing pieces to the mysteries that shrouded his nomadic baseball career.

In announcing George's signing in January 1950, the *Crowley Daily Signal* reported he was married with a six-month-old son, served a hitch in the U.S. Marines during World War II, and was a gangly 6-foot-3, 180-pound catcher as obscure as the small-town teams he toiled for in 12 minor leagues.

"I've played in all of 'em below the Mason–Dixon line but none above it," George quipped, to a Baton Rouge sportswriter. [1]

The *Daily Signal* article listed nine clubs, leaving out the Andalusia Arrows in Alabama, where he made his managerial debut in early 1948. He lasted a month.

According to Emile Chaillot, a boyhood friend and a Crowley team-mate in 1950, George made a deal with an Andalusia banker and club official to live in a vacant mansion his bank had foreclosed on.

"I've got a brother who is a big contractor," George told the banker. "I can get him down here, and he can really develop this area. But I'd like to live in that house."

"Go ahead and move in," the banker said.

George called his brother and said, "Get the yard man, put him in a chauffeur's uniform, rent a Cadillac, and come on down here."

Johnny George, center, built the Crowley Millers into a Class C powerhouse, winning league titles two of the three years he was player-manager. Flanking George are Al Ogletree (left) and Frank Brown, backup catchers on the 1952 team. Ogletree also played for the Millers in 1955, and went on to become one of the winningest college baseball coaches in history. In 29 seasons at Pan American University, his teams compiled a record of 1,084–618–1. Photo courtesy of Richard Pizzolatto and the *Crowley Post-Signal*.

They had some lumber and other building supplies placed on a lot and went to see the banker.

"It was just a con," Chaillot said. "When the banker found out he was being shysted, they were run out of town."

The local newspaper, the *Andalusia Star*, ignored George's departure except for an editorial titled "Dim Horizons for Baseball," which lamented, "Never before has the Andalusia ball park been so noticeably empty of fans," and stated the difficulty in hiring a new manager willing to "stick his neck out in accepting the job of bringing some semblance of a baseball comeback to the town."[2]

The Arrows were in the midst of a 13-game losing streak at the time. Without mentioning George by name, the *Star* cited the "disillusioning job" he did, leading to fans telling one another, "I told you so."[3]

"Johnny George could always talk himself into things," Chaillot later confided to his eldest son, Joe. "But it got kind of seamy when he couldn't talk his way out."

George wound up in Arkansas, piloting the Pine Bluff Cardinals for two months. Then he moved to North Carolina in 1949, to guide the Reidsville Luckies for just nine games. Altogether, his teams won half as many games as they lost—37–74.

The officers and directors of the Crowley Baseball Association represented a cross section of the city—rice millers, car dealers, and accountants, plus a banker, barber, newspaper editor, truck-line operator, furniture store owner, and city clerk. The stockholders they served were "high on spirit and enthusiasm but short on shekels."[4]

George was a slow talker because as a kid, a schoolteacher had him speak slowly to make it easier to understand the heavy Irish brogue he picked up from his parents. He joked about it with a story about charging out of the dugout to argue an umpire's call. "George, I don't mind you arguing," the ump said, "but you talk too darned slow and you'll never get it out and it's late enough already. G'wan back to the bench."[5]

In discussions with Crowley officials, George pointed to his seven years of wandering through the baseball wilderness as proof he had the connections needed to assemble a winning team at an affordable price. It was music to the ears of his new bosses.

Each Gulf Coast League (GCL) team was allowed 16 players—three "class men" with more than three years in pro ball; six "limited service men" with one to three years' experience; and seven rookies.

One of the veterans was Chaillot, a first baseman-pitcher who grew up with George in Mobile, Alabama, and two years earlier was pictured on a *Life* magazine cover showing "550 fresh-faced young Americans, supercharged with ambition to play baseball for the Brooklyn Dodgers."[6]

George broke in with the Dodgers in 1939, a big believer in the team's aggressive style of play at the time. "We don't care if we aren't fast, we'll run. When you're running, you'll get your share of breaks," he said.[7]

He signed three former teammates—second baseman Ray Smerek and pitcher Oscar Johnson at Pine Bluff, and outfielder Jim Howell at Andalusia and Reidsville.

"I'm willing to go along with inexperienced men in the other positions as long as my old hands can get those runs," George said.[8]

George was an "old hand" behind the plate, and he let his pitchers know it.

"He didn't take any crap off anybody," said Willard Sterling, who won 19 games as a rookie for the Millers in 1952. "I shook him off one time. He came out on the mound and said, 'Look, Rookie, you don't shake me off. You throw what I tell you.'"

If a pitcher got wild, he'd step five feet in front of home plate and hum a fastball back to the mound. "Get the ball over the plate," he yelled. He did this to Sterling, and the pitcher ducked as the ball shot past him into center field.

George schemed with pitcher Oscar "One Eye" Johnson to scare new players in the league. Totally blind in one eye, Johnson would intentionally fire a pitch to the backstop, followed by George warning, "You'd better watch it, he's only got one eye."

Sometimes George shucked his catcher's gear to pitch. In 1952, he won four games in nine days and seven overall, despite a 7.13 earned run average (ERA), highest in the league.

"Every time I'd throw the ball back to him, he'd kick a little dirt on the pitching rubber," said Al Ogletree, a backup catcher to George in 1952. "He'd cover it up. After three or four pitches, he'd be three or four feet in front of the pitching rubber."

"Winning wasn't everything to Johnny, it was the only thing," said Tony Mele, a third baseman on the '52 team.

"If you missed a signal, you got fined $5," Ogletree noted. "That was a lot of money then."

Long before it was common, George juggled pitchers and position players to gain a strategic advantage. He switched his first baseman, Chaillot, with two different pitchers in the same game so he could get the matchup of lefties he wanted.

"Johnny was the kind of manager that would rather win with strategy than for his team to go out there and kill somebody," said Hugh Blanton, a 21-game winner for Crowley in 1952. "He loved to be smart."

He outsmarted himself in a game Blanton was within one out of winning, 2–0. He removed the pitcher with two runners on base, and the Millers ended up losing, 3–2, in 10 innings.

"He came into the clubhouse raging mad because his strategy had backfired," Blanton said. "The veins in his neck looked like they had pencils stuck in 'em."

George hurled a ball through the clubhouse door, which was slightly ajar. A young boy retrieved the ball and asked if he could have it.

"Keep it!" George grumbled.

Oscar Johnson combined a knuckleball and a sidearm cross-fire pitch with plenty of "zip and dipsy-doodle" to win 16 games for the Millers in 1950, and 11 in 1951. On leaving pro baseball he stayed in Crowley to start various youth sports programs as a volunteer and guide the city's recreation department for 28 years as its director. The street that runs through Crowley's recreation area is named after him. Photo courtesy of the *Crowley Post-Signal*.

He grabbed a ball bag and heaved it out the door. "Take these balls, too. I don't have anybody that can do anything with them."

Next, he picked up the bat bag and tossed it. "Get you a bat. Nobody on this team can use them."

George didn't have anything else to throw so he hollered, "If you want any of these lousy players, you can take some of them."

The following morning at practice, George couldn't find his favorite black bat because it was in the bag he gave away. He got mad all over again.

George wasn't pleased to see one of the Millers' directors hop on the bus for the team's next road game.

"Why are you traveling with us, Joe?" a player asked Joe Dore Jr.

"To protect our equipment," he said.[9]

George's strategizing knew no boundaries.

Late in the 1950 season, the legendary Vallie Eaves was scheduled to pitch both games of a Sunday doubleheader against the Millers. Described by one former manager as "part Indian by birth and part Scotch by midnight," the 38-year-old Vallie was the most promising hurler in baseball—always promising not to show up at the ballpark drunk again, punch another stranger, or threaten any more bartenders with a knife.[10]

"Vallie had a friendly little habit of pulling a knife when they shut him off," explained Bill Veeck, one of the many bosses Vallie had while racking up 227 victories in the minors.[11]

George ordered Chaillot and Smerek to get Vallie drunk in a card game the night before he was to try the iron-man stunt. Vallie was still drinking when the pair called it quits around one o'clock in the morning.

That afternoon the first of the two seven-inning games was about to start when Vallie stumbled out of the dugout to take the mound. He went the distance in both games to beat the Millers 6–1 and 5–2, allowing five hits in the first and seven in the second.

The losses left George fuming. He took a bat and pounded a 10-gallon water jug to smithereens. On the way back to Crowley he stopped the team bus at a restaurant. "Not one of y'all get off the bus," he announced prior to going inside and eating by himself.

"He was one of the hot-headedness guys you've ever seen," Blanton said. "Despite all his ranting and raving, he made a pretty good manager."

The GCL was envisioned as a rookie circuit that would become a "breeding ground for future big-leaguers instead of a home for has-beens."[12]

In 1950, George transformed a bunch of "never-beens" into pennant winners.

Pitcher G. T. "Rusty" Walters went from being a flop with a career mark of 16–29 to being the only 30-game winner in Organized Baseball. Bill Simon improved his record from 3–4 in 1949, to 21–9, and Oscar Johnson's 16 victories were two more than the previous two years combined.

"Rusty had the best knuckleball I've ever seen," Blanton said.

It was so good that the Washington Senators gave him a tryout. He was pitching in an exhibition game against the New York Yankees and threw Joe DiMaggio six straight knuckleballs. Washington catcher Al Evans signaled for a fastball, and Rusty threw it. Joltin' Joe knocked the ball out of the park.

Afterward, Evans went up to Rusty and said, "Son, I wasted six pitches settin' him up for a fastball and, then, find out you don't have one."

Rusty's knuckleball baffled hitters in the GCL. At mid-season he had a 22–2 record and was well on his way to 30 wins before losing four straight. He ended up with 33, counting three playoff victories.

"Rusty's best pitch is the one they're not looking for," George said of the right-hander. "He has a good curve and knuckleball, and can poke a fast one in there when he's ready. But the best part of his pitching is his ability to change speeds and styles and keep 'em guessing."[13]

Chaillot poked 21 home runs and won 10 games as a starter-reliever, both career highs. He was voted the team's most valuable player.

A close second to Chaillot in popularity was the hard-nosed Smerek.

"We'd hope he'd get to first and they hit a ground ball double play cause whoever covered the bag was going into the outfield," recalled one of his fans.

Smerek made it to first base often, batting .331.

The best of the Millers rookies, sawed-off third baseman Bill Turk, was the team's top hitter, with a .340 average. The 5-foot-6 Turk never got past Class B, but 18-year-old rookie shortstop John Pfeiffer, a .275 hitter, made it to the Class AA Texas League and lasted three years.

More than half of Rusty Walters's 58 wins in the minors came with the Crowley Millers in 1950, when he posted a 30–7 won–loss mark and 3.15 ERA. Rusty had a 22–2 record mid-season before losing four straight. He ended up with 33 victories, counting the playoffs. Photo courtesy of the *Crowley Post-Signal*.

One rookie George tried to get rid of but couldn't was John "Medicine Man" Lormand, a far better pool hustler than pitcher.

"Every time Johnny George wanted to release him, Lormand would get him to play pool," Chaillot said. "Needless to say, he was never released."[14]

Lormand wound up carrying the team's medicine kit.

It was a colorful bunch.

Chaillot had the unusual nickname "Smut." As a teenager, he was a grease monkey for the railroad, working in a pit under the locomotives being lubricated. It was dirty work that made his olive skin even darker.

Smerek was an accomplished artist who spoke Russian and German fluently. At the end of World War II, he went to Germany for *Stars and Stripes*, the official newspaper for the U.S. military, to sketch what was left of the war-ravaged country. A book of the drawings was later published.

The Millers took over first place in mid-June and got a hero's welcome at the Rice Café in downtown Crowley.

"The boys and I have talked it over a lot of times, and we want you all to know that Crowley is a swell place," George told the fans. "We've never been treated better anywhere, and we're going to keep on playing the best baseball we know how for you all."[15]

The Millers rolled to 96 victories, 90 in the regular season and six more in the playoffs, which they lost in the final round.

Paid attendance for regular-season games was 84,180—an average of 1,588 per game, or roughly one out of eight Crowley residents. If 19 games hadn't been rained out and rescheduled as doubleheaders, it's likely the Millers would have topped the 100,000 mark.

"With costs as they are today, a town that can't draw 100,000 attendance in a season can't make a riffle," the Associated Press reported.[16]

Sam Tarleton of the *Beaumont Enterprise* suggested one GCL club "could reap a nice profit by rolling some of their paychecks into little balls and peddling them to golfers . . . they'd bounce further than most golf balls anyhow."[17]

The Millers finished the season in the black, a rarity for minor-league teams in 1950.

From the beginning, cynics dismissed the GCL as a "'rump circuit'—a temporary refuge for cities who couldn't get into older, established leagues."[18]

Crowley already was being touted as the best little town in baseball. The Evangeline League just so happened to have an opening in 1951.

Johnny was on the spot more than ever.

As Red Mitchell pointed out in the *Crowley Daily Signal*, the Evangeline "has proved time and again to be as hot as some of the Tabasco sauce brewed along its circuit. It is a question of being on the hot seat of the hottest Class C professional baseball loop in Minor League Baseball."[19]

If George felt the heat, he was cool about it. "They'll know we're in the league," he promised.[20]

4

THE PEPPER POT LEAGUE

A calculator is almost needed to count the ways the Evangeline was different from other minor leagues.

For starters, the league was named after the epic Henry Wadsworth Longfellow poem *Evangeline*, which chronicles the Acadian heroine's search for her lover from Nova Scotia in Canada to southern Louisiana. The name often was shortened to Vangy in newspaper headlines.

The Evangeline had three nicknames that captured the flavor and spirit of the region where most of the league's teams were located—"Tabasco," "Hot Sauce," and "Pepper Pot."

"Some of the wildest games in the history of baseball were played in stadiums around South Louisiana," wrote Fred Bandy, a columnist for the *Daily Iberian* in New Iberia, Louisiana, home of the world-famous Tabasco sauce. "That's why it was called the Pepper Pot League."[1]

A Sunday doubleheader in 1939, between the Jeanerette Blues and Rayne Rice Birds, left two umpires bloodied by irate fans, one struck on the mouth by a flying pop bottle and the other whacked from behind by a baseball bat.

The league was once described as a "circuit that just about meets the dreamed-of condition where every game will be a home game because in most of the jumps, a team's followers can hop in a car and within an hour be in the 'enemy' town where their heroes are playing."[2]

Fans harassed umpires and sometimes one another in Cajun French.

"The stands were almost always filled to capacity with the wildest, screamingest bunch of fans anybody ever had to play before," one player recalled.[3]

Ballparks could easily be found by following the smoke from fires used to dry out a rain-soaked infield or "keep the bugs of summer off of the boys of summer."[4]

One evening in Texas City, Texas, mosquitoes were feasting on New Iberia outfielders Billy Joe Barrett and Remy LeBlanc. Remy set a pile of dead grass on fire in center field to keep the mosquitoes off him between pitches. After an umpire stomped out the fire, Remy started another one.

"The umpire came out there again and threatened to run Remy off the field," Barrett laughed. "It was the damnedest thing I've ever seen."

Surrounded by swamps in southern Louisiana, the city of Houma had the reputation for having the biggest mosquitoes in the league.

"They were huge, and they'd bite you through your uniform," said Chuck Nelson, a pitcher for Crowley in 1952–53.

Crowley center fielder Jimmy Moore stopped one game, hollering, "Time out, time out!"

One of the umpires rushed to where Moore was standing and pointing at the sky. "What is it, Jimmy?" he asked.

"A mosquito is going across the field with a chain around his neck," Moore answered.

Weird and the wacky was the norm in the Evangeline, as common as snakes in the Louisiana bayou.

"We used to go out and shoot snakes in the bayou," Nelson said. "Have something to do during the day."

In a game at Crowley's Miller Stadium, two umpires rushed toward the outfield with players from both teams in hot pursuit. Fans expected a fight to break out. Instead, they watched as the umps, armed with bats, clubbed to death a cottonmouth water moccasin.

Another snake story involved Art Visconti and Al Alonso, teammates at Alexandria, Louisiana, in 1950.

Alonso was talking with some girls in the stands when Visconti snuck up from behind and dangled a rubber snake over his shoulder. The startled Alonso darted away and ran smack dab into a telephone pole, ending up with a knot on his head the size of a silver dollar.

"He was scheduled to pitch that night and, because of the knot, took the mound without a cap," Visconti explained.[5]

Alonso was cruising along with a shutout in the third inning when the opposing manager insisted that the umpire make him wear a cap. So the pitcher put his cap on sideways with the bill facing first base and went on to toss a three-hitter to win the game.

"Al was right-handed, and as he turned to make his delivery, his cap pointed toward home plate," Visconti added. "This drove the hitters crazy."[6]

It wasn't unusual for teams in the lower minors to use local semipro players to fill in for a few days, but the New Iberia Pelicans raised eyebrows when they put their bus driver on the roster temporarily to meet the league's minimum requirement for rookies.

"He had a beard so he had to shave it," said Terry Fox, a pitcher for the Pelicans in 1954–55.

The Pelicans had a big lead in a game so the bus driver was sent to home plate with a bat and instructed not to swing. He walked, and the next batter singled.

"The bus driver didn't go to second," Fox said. "He cut across the mound from first to third. He slid about three feet short of the bag and, then, got up and walked the rest of the way. We laughed and we laughed and we laughed."

Road trips in the Evangeline were shorter than other leagues but no less eventful.

The Pelicans were traveling to Alexandria when their bus ran out of gas, and manager Billy Adams ordered a rookie catcher to hitch a ride to a nearby town and get some fuel. The catcher returned with the manager of the station where he got the gas. Adams rolled down his window to tell the manager, "He's a baseball rookie, and we're going to let you have him for that gasoline."

The rookie looked on in shock as the driver started the bus and went about a hundred yards down the road before stopping to let him back on.

What really made the Evangeline a league of its own was the slot machines with names and pictures of such players as Billy Joe Barrett, who starred for the Thibodaux Giants in 1951–52.

Slot machines were everywhere in Thibodaux, and profits from one of them at a local nightclub helped the pennant-winning Giants pay Barrett's monthly salary of $400.

"I knew where that money was coming from," Barrett said. "It was coming out of that slot machine."

The practice ended in 1953, with a statewide war to confiscate and destroy slot machines.

The Evangeline League was established in 1934, and operated 21 years—nine before World War II and 12 afterward.

The prewar years earned the Evangeline the reputation as the "biggest little league in baseball" by producing some of the biggest stars in the big leagues.[7]

Pitchers "Prince Hal" Newhouser and Virgil "Fire" Trucks were teammates at Alexandria in 1939. In the majors, Newhouser won 207 games to earn a plaque in the National Baseball Hall of Fame, while Trucks racked up 177 victories, including two no-hitters in the same season (1952).

Tom Jordan, a catcher who caught the legendary "Bullet Bob" Feller, batted against both hurlers in the Evangeline and the majors when they were mowing down hitters for the Detroit Tigers.

"Trucks was a lot easier to hit in Detroit than he was in the Evangeline," Jordan said. "Same way with Newhouser. They threw harder, and they were a little bit wilder in the Evangeline."

Jordan was 18 years old in 1938, the first of two seasons he played in the Evangeline for the Abbeville A's. At the time of his death in 2019, at age 99, he was still in awe of the talent in a Class D circuit.

"Probably 20 pitchers out of that league went to the majors," Jordan said. "Every club had one or two, and some had four or five."

He rattled off the names of Newhouser, Trucks, Eddie Lopat, Howie Pollet, Ed Head, and Johnny Beazley.

Lopat compiled a 166–112 won–lost record in the majors, spearheading the New York Yankees to five straight World Series titles.

Pollet was a three-time National League All-Star with the St. Louis Cardinals, posting a 131–116 mark in 14 seasons.

Beazley won 21 games for the Cardinals in 1942, and two more in their conquest of the Yankees in the World Series.

Head won just 27 games in five years with the Brooklyn Dodgers, but one of them was a no-hitter.

"It was a great league," Jordan concluded.

Another twirler who made it to the majors was the aptly named Ace Adams, the first to pitch in as many as 70 big-league games in a single year. In five full seasons with the New York Giants (1941–45), Ace led the National League in games pitched three times and saves twice.

During a game early in the '46 season, Giants manager Mel Ott was looking for his star reliever: "Adams! Adams! Where in the hell is Ace Adams?"

A Giants coach found him collecting his belongings in the clubhouse. "Where you been Ace?" the coach said.

He explained that Mexican multimillionaire businessman Jorge Pasquel phoned just as he was leaving for the ballpark and invited him to his hotel room. "So, I got to his room and there on the bed are these bundles of bills, hundred-dollar bills. He says to me, 'They are all yours, Ace. All you gotta do is sign with me.'"[8]

Ace stuffed about $15,000 worth of cash into his pockets, played in the Mexican League a year, and returned to the United States banned from Organized Baseball.

The Evangeline sent several other standouts to the big leagues: catcher Clyde McCullough; infielders Don Kolloway, Emil Verban, and Les Fleming; and outfielders "Pistol Pete" Reiser and Al Zarilla.

McCullough caught 15 years for the Chicago Cubs and Pittsburgh Pirates, and Verban batted .272 in seven seasons with the St. Louis Cardinals, Philadelphia Phillies, and Cubs. Both were two-time National League All-Stars.

Kolloway batted .271 in 12 years in the majors, mostly with the Chicago White Sox and Tigers, and Fleming posted a .277 average in seven seasons, playing primarily for the Indians.

Injuries prevented Reiser from realizing his potential greatness, although the Brooklyn Dodgers got a glimpse in 1941, when he led the National League in four categories—batting average (.343), triples (17), doubles (39), and runs scored (117).

Playing for the lowly St. Louis Browns in 1948, Zarilla hit .329, to make the American League All-Star Team.

The biggest Evangeline League star didn't last with the Dodgers past spring training at Bear Mountain, New York, in 1943.

Roy Sanner, a pitcher-outfielder also known as the "Houma Houdini," was released after he got into a fistfight with Dodgers manager Leo Durocher. Described by one Brooklyn sportswriter as a "ridge runner from the Arkansas Ozarks," Sanner was "skeered" to ride New York City subways, pointing out, "Those trains run underground."[9]

On touring Radio City Music Hall for the first time, Sanner made news nationally by observing, "Sure would hold a lot of hay."[10]

He made a lot of hay at Houma in 1948, compiling a 21–2 won–lost record and winning the league's Triple Crown with a .386 batting average, 34 homers, and 126 runs batted in.

Altogether, 74 players advanced to the majors from the Evangeline prior to World War II, a lofty number for a Class D league. At the time the highest classification in the minors was AA. Eventually the war took its toll on the minors, shutting down 23 of the 41 leagues in 1942, including the Evangeline.

"We are saying au revoir and not good-bye," explained Judge Wilmot Dalferes, the loop's president, "because after the war is over you'll find the Evangeline League, about the finest little league, back in baseball."[11]

When the Evangeline returned in 1946, *New Orleans Times-Picayune* columnist Bill Keefe reminded readers that the "brand of baseball played in the Evangeline League of old, while rated as Class D, was not far removed from Class A."[12]

In the early years, Evangeline teams frequently used "ringers"—old pros that played a few games using aliases. Rosters are dotted with the last names of players followed by a question mark. Shoeless Joe Jackson may well have been one of them.

Banned for life from Organized Baseball because of his alleged role in the 1919 Black Sox Scandal, Shoeless Joe supposedly used different names so he could pick up $100 for playing weekends in the Evangeline.

The circuit was recovering from its own "Little Black Sox" scandal when catcher Floyd "Greek" Economides joined the Houma Indians in 1948.

"I just started dating my wife-to-be," Economides recalled, "and her mother says, 'You going out with a baseball player? Didn't you read the paper?'"

Shortly after the 1946 season ended, five Evangeline League players, including four from Houma, were suspended indefinitely for conspiring with New Orleans bookies to fix playoff games.

"The long-smoldering fire of scandal finally has burst into leaping flame in the Evangeline League," Keefe wrote in the *Times-Picayune*.

> An example should be made of these contemptible culprits. Their names should be published so that all honest employees will shun them. You'd think that the miserable lives eked out by men who were in the Black Sox Scandal would serve as an eternal warning to young

men to keep themselves clean and keep above suspicion the great sport that gives them a livelihood. [13]

The "Little Black Sox" also were charged with constant betting on horse races through bookies.

"They turned one bookie's clock back 30 minutes and bet on a horse that had already won," Economides said.

The skullduggery earned the players $185, as the bookie didn't know his clock had been tampered with or that the race was over before the bet was placed. One of the accused, Houma outfielder Leonard Pecou, didn't see anything wrong with this because "bookies were crooked." He dismissed a muffed fly ball in the championship series against Abbeville as a "case of bad judgment and not intentional." [14]

Paul Fugit, Houma's manager-first baseman, said that some of his players had to work for bookies in New Orleans so they could afford to play baseball.

Veteran Houma pitcher Bill Thomas, winner of 35 games in the regular season and five straight in the playoffs, admitted to shooting dice and betting on racehorses but pointed out that there were gambling devices throughout the area. "Everybody in Louisiana gambles," he asserted, "including stockholders of clubs." [15]

"Americans had money stuffed out their ear after World War II because of rationing," explained Paul Leslie, a retired professor of American history at Nicholls State University in Thibodaux who has researched and written about the Evangeline League extensively. "Gambling in South Louisiana was rampant. They bet on every pitch. They bet on everything."

The banishment of the players coincided with a crackdown on New Orleans gambling houses that was failing miserably.

"Dominoes continued to gallop, roulette balls to click, and slot machines to whir as resort operators flouted reported 'word' that they close," the *Times-Picayune* reported. One operator was quoted as saying, "We'll be open tonight, tomorrow night, and every other night, and you can put that into your pipe and smoke it." [16]

Evangeline League president Walter Morris declared, "Fighting the gamblers is like fighting roaches. You have to keep at it all the time." [17]

The Evangeline weathered the storm, attendance climbing to nearly 700,000 in both 1947 and 1948. The league was reclassified from "D" to

"C" in 1949, and two of the five players expelled in the "Little Black Sox" scandal were reinstated—Pecou and Thomas.

Like Shoeless Joe Jackson before him, Thomas always insisted he was innocent. He declared, "Every manager I ever played for will tell you that I play to win—every time."[18]

Unlike Shoeless Joe, Thomas found redemption. After a nearly three-year suspension, he returned to the Evangeline at the age of 44, to win three games in 1949, and 23 more in 1950. He retired two years later with minor-league career records for most games and innings pitched (1,016 and 5,995), most wins and losses (383–347), and most hits and runs allowed (6,721 and 3,098).

Johnny George and the Crowley Millers entered the Evangeline League in 1951, looking for respect. They were champions of a league, the Gulf Coast, that got no respect. As one pundit put it, "Crowley was a rookie in a rookie loop."[19]

The Evangeline was an established league with a colorful history and rich tradition of grooming future big-leaguers. To get the respect they wanted, the Millers had to prove they could handle the heat in the Pepper Pot League.

5

"LIGHTNING HAS HIT THIS BALLPARK"

Andy Strong was on cloud nine; Ed Keim wasn't far below.

Nineteen days after leaving a high school coaching job to play pro baseball, Strong was hitting .347 and performing flawlessly in center field for the Crowley Millers. He was 25 years old, a college graduate, and happily married with a six-month-old son.

Keim was in his first season as play-by-play announcer for the Millers, calling the games for KSIG radio in Crowley. He was one of the lucky ones to survive the bloody Battle of the Bulge during World War II, and now he was living the dream of a boy who grew up on the North Side of Chicago watching the Cubs play at Wrigley Field. He loved his job, especially when the Millers won and he could delight listeners with variations of his signature phrase, "Oh, happy day!"

Andy was virtually unknown when he signed with the Millers in late May. The *Crowley Daily Signal* referred to him only as "Strong" because the team's president "didn't know his full name or the club he last played with."[1]

When his full name first appeared in print, it was wrong—"Eddie Strong."[2]

By the third week, people were getting it right, as they could see the athleticism that attracted the Millers and made Andy a baseball and basketball star at Centenary College in Shreveport, Louisiana.

Almost every day was a happy one in early June 1951, as the Millers won 11 in a row to take over first place.

Ed Keim was the play-by-play announcer of Crowley Millers baseball, his signature victory signoff, "Oh, Happy Day!" eagerly anticipated by his KSIG radio audience. Listeners were shocked to hear Keim shout during the sixth inning of a game in Alexandria, Louisiana, "Lightning has hit this ballpark!" Photo courtesy of the *Crowley Post-Signal*.

The streak began with Ray Hensgens, an 18-year-old pitcher who grew up on a rice farm just outside Crowley, tossing a two-hit shutout in his first pro start.

"You're going to start the game tonight," Crowley manager Johnny George informed Hensgens earlier in the day.

The opposing pitcher was Houma's Roy "Lefty" Price, the league's strikeout king and a local legend Hensgens faced many times as a semi-pro.

"I can't beat him," Hensgens said.

"If you think you can't beat him," George bristled, "hang up your uniform and get out of town. We don't need you."

Hensgens accepted the challenge.

"I can do it," he said to himself. "If he wants me to do it, I can do it."

Beating Price sparked the entire team.

"Oh, Lord," Hensgens said, "I thought I was on top of the world."

So did Andy Strong after his three hits rallied the Millers to their seventh straight win.

When the streak reached nine, the Crowley Baseball Association announced plans for "Johnny George Night."

"If any one baseball person in Crowley is deserving of a 'night' it is George," Red Mitchell penned in his *Daily Signal* column. "It was George who gathered the players together. It is George who still scouts them out today. He is player, manager, scout, and partway business manager. And he is one of the keenest and hardest baseball competitors we have ever seen."[3]

The Millers opened the year with nine holdovers from the 1950 season. Missing was Emile Chaillot, the team's top home run hitter, drafted by the U.S. Army, and Rusty Walters, the ace of the pitching staff, taken in the minor-league draft by the West Palm Beach Indians, a Class B team.

"Solving problem after problem," Mitchell wrote, "he has worked his charges into first place with a 4½-game edge on the field."[4]

The lead was up to five and the streak at 10 going into a game Saturday, June 16, against the Alexandria Aces in Alexandria, Louisiana.

On Saturday morning, the players gathered after breakfast on the huge veranda of the Bentley Hotel in downtown Alexandria, where they were staying.

"We were all shooting the breeze," Keim said.

All except Andy. He was by himself in a corner of the veranda. Ed went over to chat. "He wasn't his usual bubbly self. He had something on his mind, or it appeared that way."

Keim cut the conversation short by saying, "I'll see you at the ballpark tonight."

The next day was Father's Day. Andy was anxious to see his wife, Merle, and son, Danny, and take them to Crowley for the rest of the summer. He traveled to Alexandria in his own car so he could drive to his home in Doyline, Louisiana, and pick them up.

Andy and Hensgens were roommates on the road.

The pitcher took Andy to Alexandria's Bringhurst Field Saturday afternoon to show him the way from the hotel to the ballpark and, then, to the Shreveport highway.

"We came back to the ballpark later, got dressed and went out, and the rest is history," Hensgens said.

Keim was still thinking about Strong when he got to the ballpark. Rain was forecast. Off in the distance, there was thunder and lightning. Perhaps Andy was worried about a storm disrupting the 125-mile drive to Shreveport and the even longer trek to Crowley.

As Keim was getting the starting lineups from George, he spotted Andy standing at the end of the dugout, one foot up on the railing and staring into space. Ed moved closer. "Well, Andy, in two or three hours you'll be on your way to Shreveport to get the family. We'll see you back in Crowley."

"Yeah, if I make it," Andy said.

The subdued tone of Andy's voice and the detached look on his face was the same as earlier in the day. It was disturbing to Keim, but he wasn't sure why.

The game started and, then, was halted by rain and lightning in the fifth inning with the scored tied 1–1.

"Looks like I'll get an early start tonight," Andy said to a teammate.[5]

When play resumed about 30 minutes later, Andy told a park attendant, "I sure hate to go back out there in that lightning."[6]

The Millers' starting pitcher, Oscar Johnson, took the mound. Hensgens began loosening up on the sidelines just in case he was needed.

Every out took on greater importance. Andy was particularly excited by a Miller double play in the bottom of the sixth inning.

"That's two away," he shouted to Walt Lamey in left field. "Only need one more now."[7]

In the press box, Keim looked down at his scorebook to see who was batting next. "I looked up to see how the outfield was setting up."

That's when Keim heard "this God-awful rumble" shake the ballpark and saw a "sharp crack of lightning hit" and light up the outfield.

"Lightning has hit this ballpark!" Ed announced to his radio audience back in Crowley.

Listeners heard a "tremendous crackling sound followed immediately by the high-pitched scream" of shortstop John Pfeiffer's pregnant wife sitting next to Keim in the press box. [8]

In the stands, fans yelled as they ran for cover.

"Some of them wandered around for over an hour before departing from the park, unbelief written all over their faces," wrote Mack Owens, sports editor of the *Alexandria Town Talk*. [9]

On the field, the force of the lightning shoved Hensgens several feet. "Just blew me up. Pushed me," he recalled.

Players frantically took off their gloves, spikes, and caps so the metal wouldn't attract the lightning.

Keim tried to make sense of the chaos but decided it was better to sign off and go down on the field to find out exactly what happened.

"What about Andy?" he asked.

"He's gone," said George, shaking his head in disbelief.

From his left-field position, Lamey "saw flames all around. It was like opening a furnace door." [10]

Lamey was the first to reach Andy. "I hollered to him several times, but I knew he was dead. His hair was smoking and was straight out. He was laying half on his face. His pants and sock were all torn, like it blew off. His hat was about three feet away." [11]

Hensgens rushed to where his roommate was standing in center field. "Andy's shoes were kicked off; the button from the top of his cap was lying off on the side. It was the worst smell I've ever run across—burnt human flesh. It was terrible."

"It just seemed all night that somethin' was going to happen," George said. "Both teams were trying for that one run. Everybody was swingin' on the first pitch, and it looked like we were all hurrying." [12]

Keim went back on the air to tell listeners that Andy was hit by the lightning strike and died instantly. He described the bedlam caused by the lightning and how it hit the light post in right-center field and, then, shot through the metal button in Andy's cap and down his body to the wet ground.

"The impact of the sudden tragedy left hundreds of Crowley baseball fans stunned beside their radios," the *Daily Signal* reported. [13]

"I was listening to the game on the radio when the lightning struck," recalled L. J. Gielen, who was six years old at the time. "It was devastating."

Crowley Daily Signal

VOLUME XI   CROWLEY, LOUISIANA, MONDAY, JUNE 18, 1991   NUMBER

LIGHTNING KILLS YOUNG CROWLEY BASEBALL PLAYER IN ALEXANDRIA

Andy Strong, 23-Year-Old Rookie Centerfielder With Miller Club, Killed In Saturday Night Game

EDITOR'S NOTE: Forty years ago today, a bolt of lightning took the life of a fine young baseball player for the Crowley Millers. Andy Strong, a 23-year old centerfielder for the Evangeline League Millers struck dead by a bolt of lightning during a game against the Alexandria Aces played at Bringhurst Field in Alexandria. A number of Crowley fans were either on hand or at home listening to the radio when the tragic death occurred. Here is an account of the accident in the Crowley Daily Signal forty years ago.

Andy Strong

A lightning bolt that crackled out of Alexandria skies at 9:10 o'clock Saturday night brought sudden death to Andy Strong, 23 year-old rookie baseball player of the Class C Evangeline League, as he was playing his position in centerfield in the sixth inning of a scheduled game with the Alexandria Aces.

The impact of the sudden tragedy left hundreds of Crowley baseball fans stunned beside their radios where they had been listening in a broadcast of the game.

There who were listening heard a tremendous crackling sound followed immediately by the high-pitched scream of a woman in the stands at Bringhurst Field. Shortly thereafter, the sportscaster Sid Kern, said that Strong was dead, having been struck by the lightning bolt.

Members of both teams, many of them stunned and shaken by the suddenness of the flash, rushed to centerfield where the stricken player lay prone, his face into the ground. An ambulance and a policeman were ordered immediately but the unidentified doctor pronounced Strong dead.

Smoke arose from the dead player's body. His shattered cap was also three feet away. One shoe ripped and lay to the side and his trousers were smoking on the left side were ripped and torn.

Strong had left Crowley for Alexandria in his own automobile with intentions of driving to his home in Doyline, La., near Shreveport, to retain his wife and infant child at Crowley. After the tragedy, state policemen were asked to locate Mrs. Strong.

The body was taken to the Hickman Funeral Home in Alexandria pending arrival of relatives. B.W. Pentland of Crowley, who was in the stand remained in Alexandria with the body of Strong. Pentland is a member of the board of directors of the Crowley Baseball Association.

With the baseball game immediately postponed, Manager George reserved his stricken players in Crowley.

Shock and despair ruled in the clubhouses of both the Millers and Aces immediately after the tragedy struck. Men of both teams watched with tears filled eyes on the body of the player was removed from the field.

Rites for Strong went to be held at 2 p.m. today in Doyline. The young player is survived by his widow, the former Merle Oldham of Pittsburg, Texas, and an infant son, Dewey, not quite a year old, his parents, Mr. and Mrs. O.L. Strong of Doyline, a brother and three sisters.

Strong, a basketball and baseball football coach at Pittsburg High School in Texas, had joined the Millers on May 28 in Baton Rouge after his school season had ended. He was a rookie player and was playing his first professional of baseball.

Strong attended Centenary College in Shreveport on an athletic scholarship from 1946-49, lettering three times in baseball and basketball there.

Crowley Millers center fielder Andy Strong was killed by lightning during a game at Alexandria on June 16, 1951. The *Crowley Daily Signal* marked the 40th anniversary of Andy's death by reprinting the story of the tragedy, a defining moment in the team's eight-year history. The 23-year-old Strong was scheduled to drive home to Doyline, Louisiana, the next day, Father's Day, and take his wife and infant son to Crowley for the rest of the summer. Photo courtesy of the *Crowley Post-Signal.*

"The outfield was lit up by this light that I had never seen before, it was so bright," Keim said 62 years later.

It seemed there was a speck—a dark speck—about in the center fielder's position where Andy was. Some of the guys were yelling, "Andy!" They shed their gloves, their spikes, their caps and started to run out to center. And while they were running out there, I'll swear on a stack of Bibles, it looked to me like a puff of smoke was going up off of where Andy was laying. And the weirdest thought crossed my mind: There goes his soul.

Eventually, Keim realized his encounters with Andy on that fateful Saturday were eerily similar to one he had with an army major on a troop ship going to Europe during World War II. The major was leaning over the deck railing, watching the propeller churn the water as the shoreline got smaller and smaller. There was no one else on deck, so Ed struck up a conversation. "He had a faraway look in his eyes that I'll never forget."

They talked for a while and, then, went their separate ways—the major to a signal battalion and Ed to a combat military police platoon. A few months later Nazi Germany aircraft bombed the mess hall in the camp where he was stationed.

Ed was in the mess hall having a midnight snack about five minutes before the attack. Now, his platoon was checking the carnage. One of the dead soldiers was slumped over the table Ed had sat at moments earlier. It was the major he befriended on the ship.

At first Keim didn't link the two incidents. They became inseparable, the odd look in the eyes of Andy and the major, the subdued tone of their voices, and their tenuous words forming a bond that etched the Andy Strong tragedy in his mind forever. "I will never, ever forget that," Ed said.

"I think about it every day," Hensgens said shortly before he died in 2013, at the age of 81.

Andy's death cast a pall of gloom over the Millers.

Johnny George Night, set for two days later, was postponed indefinitely.

In the Millers' first game after the incident, George fractured an ankle bone that prevented him from catching for a week. Soon after returning to the lineup, he broke a bone in a finger on his throwing hand.

"You couldn't stop him from playing," Keim said. "He played when he was banged up and other people would prefer to be in a hospital or in a wheelchair. But he's out there catching. He was tough as nails."

The Millers were 11–31 during one stretch, plunging them into seventh place. One of the defeats was the completion of the June 16 game suspended when Andy was killed by lightning. Alexandria won, 3–2. Andy's name is listed in the box score with one hit in two at-bats.

Oscar Johnson, who had a 10–4 won–lost record going into the Alexandria game, was 1–8 thereafter.

"It took the fight out of everybody," Hensgens said. "It just stayed on your mind all the time. You couldn't shake it. The team just deteriorated, and we couldn't do a thing right."

At one point, George took the players to Hester's, a local supper club.

"Any man who doesn't get drunk tonight will be fined $100," he said. "We've got to loosen up. We've got to start over."

In late July, George overhauled the roster with eight new players. Two of the additions were Conklyn "Conk" Meriwether, a husky power-hitting first baseman, and outfielder Art Edinger, the Gulf Coast League (GCL) batting champion and top rookie the year before. In just 38 games, Conk clouted 19 homers and batted .373. Edinger chipped in with nine dingers and a .325 batting average.

The changes helped the Millers get back on track in mid-August with an eight-game winning streak that they took into Johnny George Night.

The *Daily Signal* praised George's "determination to win" and "utter disregard for his own physical condition" by playing "night after night behind the plate with a fractured ankle bone."[14]

A truck loaded with gifts from fans rolled onto the field just before the game. One gift was a spade for George to use the next time he covered home plate with dirt to show his disgust with an umpire's call. The spade also could be used to bury memories of the lightning strike that killed Andy Strong and the team's pennant hopes.

The Millers wound up in fifth place with a 70–70 mark, seven games out of first.

The highlight of the season was a record crowd of 2,550 jamming Miller Stadium on "Andy Strong Night" to raise nearly $5,000 toward an educational endowment fund for Andy's son and help his 19-year-old widow return to college for a teaching degree.

"Crowley takes a back seat to no other baseball town in the land," *Beaumont Enterprise* columnist Sam Tarleton proclaimed.[15]

Season attendance was 100,595.

"Most remarkable of all is the fact that when the Millers *were* leading the league and riding high, they drew an average of 1,407 fans per game," Tarleton added near the end of the season. "And now, while struggling in the second division, attendance goes *up* to an average of 1,481. Crowley is our nomination for the title of 'America's best little baseball town.'"[16]

"The community was all behind us," Hensgens said. "People would line up all around the field, standing room only."

Hensgens ended his only season in pro ball with a 3–6 record and one complete game—the win over Lefty Price, the pitcher he didn't think he could beat.

The following summer, Hensgens returned to Alexandria's Bringhurst Field with a semipro team. He walked out to the spot in center field where

Ray Hensgens was 18 years old in 1951, when he tossed a two-hit shutout for the Crowley Millers in his first pro start. "I thought I was on top of the world," he said. The world turned upside down after roommate Andy Strong was killed by lightning during a game. "I think about it every day," Hensgens said shortly before he died in 2013, at the age of 81. Photo by the author.

he last saw Andy. "Both footprints were there. The grass was still dead where the lightning struck," he said.

It was a grim reminder of the chain of events that led up to the disaster.

George tried to get Jack Doland, a part-time player for the Millers in 1950, to fill in for Andy that night. George arranged for Doland to travel by bus from Lake Charles to Alexandria, but he missed his connection in Krotz Springs, Louisiana, by 15 minutes.

"Look, Jack didn't get here," George informed Andy. "You're going to have to stay."

Andy stayed and played the final game of his life.

Doland went on to a distinguished career as a college football coach, athletic director, and president before his election to the Louisiana state senate.

Fifteen minutes changed the lives of two young men and the course of the Millers' first season in the Evangeline League.

6

THE CONKER HITS TOWN

Just before Babe Ruth stepped foot in Crowley in 1921, legendary sports-writer Grantland Rice penned this poem for the *New York Tribune*:

> The game is full of subtlety
> Of science and of art,
> Where mind and brain,
> Beneath the strain
> Must carry out their part.
>
> But when it comes to climax stuff
> Beyond the final scoff,
> Give me the bloke
> With mighty poke
> Who tears the cover off. [1]

The poem was inspired by Ruth, described by Rice as a "cave man who can crack out 54 home runs, where no major leaguer before his day had ever gathered more than 25."[2]

Babe was a pitcher for the Boston Red Sox before he became the "Great Bambino" and his trade to the Yankees, a curse that plagued the Red Sox for nearly a century.

The deal that brought pitcher-turned-slugger Conklyn Wells Meriwether to Crowley from Galveston, Texas, in late July 1951, was a big one by minor-league standards.

The Millers paid $2,250 for the husky 6-foot, 210-pounder and even hatched a plan, "Operation Meriwether," to get him in a Millers uniform quicker. A rice truck and car were dispatched to Galveston for his family and belongings while another car was ready in Crowley to take Meriwether to Thibodaux, Louisiana, for the Millers' next game.

The 33-year-old Meriwether played in 18 cities before arriving in Crowley. He started his pro baseball career in 1939, at Easton, Maryland, a New York Yankees farm club in the Class D Eastern Shore League. He was signed by the Yankees after talking himself into a trial with their Newark Bears farm club, which was staying at a Sebring, Florida, hotel where he worked as an elevator boy.

"Meriwether is a finished twirler in every sense," a local sportswriter reported after his first two starts at Easton.[3]

The reviews got even better the next month, the same writer raving, "When this flinger is right the opposition has little chance to win."[4]

He lost more games than he won at Easton (7–12) and the next year at Amsterdam (6–10) because, as another reporter put it, "he was wild as a hawk."[5]

The blond-haired Meriwether was nicknamed "Lefty" early in his career and "Conk" or "The Conker" later on. He also was eccentric—a "story for a book," said Eddie Sawyer, his manager at Amsterdam, who went on to guide the Philadelphia Phillies to the National League pennant in 1950.[6]

"The day it was his turn to pitch, he would enter the park near the center-field gate and turn cartwheels all the way to the pitcher's mound," Sawyer recalled. "He was an acrobatic dancer with a band during the winter, and that was his way of warming up before pitching."[7]

One day Meriwether was bragging about his ability as an acrobat and swimmer when some kids dared him to dive into a swimming pool with about a foot of water in it.

"He took the challenge without looking," Sawyer said, "and skinned his nose, his chest, his legs, and his feet—and I mean skinned, like you would skin a rabbit."[8]

A telephone call tipped off Sawyer on what happened, but he was curious to hear what Meriwether had to say about the incident, which sidelined him for 10 days.

"Well, I'll tell you what happened, Skipper," Meriwether said. "I bought a new radio today and started to string some wire cross the room. The chair fell from underneath me, and I took a shaking up."[9]

On another occasion, Meriwether claimed he was sick and couldn't pitch the second game of a doubleheader at Oneonta, New York. After-

Conk Meriwether once was described as a "story for a book" by Eddie Sawyer, manager of Philadelphia Phillies from 1948–52 and 1958–60. Sawyer managed the eccentric Meriwether at Amsterdam, New York, in 1939, and had no idea his left-handed pitcher would become a dangerous minor-league slugger feared on and off the field. Photo courtesy of the *Crowley Post-Signal*.

ward, Sawyer and the team's road secretary, Spencer Fitzgerald, went to his hotel room to see how he was doing, and he wasn't there. "I think I know where he is," Sawyer said as they headed to a nearby dance hall. [10]

"There's Conklyn, and he's really dancin' it up," Fitzgerald said. [11]

Fitzgerald's wife, Hilda, recalled Meriwether going with them to downtown Amsterdam one evening, and the entire way "he was yellin' at all the girls. He just wanted to have a good time; he wasn't like any of the others." [12]

Meriwether opened the 1941 season at Joplin, Missouri, and quit after five games because of a contract dispute. He returned to Easton.

"I struck out 18 men in the second game, and during the innings I have pitched I fanned on an average one each inning," Meriwether said, explaining his 4–1 record and 36 strikeouts in 37 innings at Joplin. "I am trying to get reinstated, and that is why I'm here." [13]

At Easton, he whiffed twice as many as he walked (94–45) to post a 9–7 record and 2.46 earned run average. He continued to impress at Sanford, North Carolina, in 1942, with a 10–5 mark and 2.63 ERA.

Meriwether served in the U.S. Coast Guard from October 1942 until his discharge for medical reasons in July 1944. A St. Louis Cardinals scout found him "cavorting with the Sebring, Florida, firemen." [14]

The scout arranged a tryout with the Allentown Redbirds, the Cards' affiliate in the Class B Inter-State League. At Allentown, he went from being a pitcher called "Lefty" to an outfielder-first baseman worthy of the nickname "Conk."

In his first start, he pitched a 16-hitter to win, 12–7, and had three hits in as many at-bats. He went on to notch an 8–4 won–lost record and hit .314, earning a promotion to the Rochester Red Wings in the Class AA International League.

In 1945, he played for Rochester, Columbus, and Allentown, pitching 46 innings and losing all seven decisions. Meanwhile, he pounded other pitchers at a combined .359 clip, nearly half of his 98 hits for extra bases.

A defining moment was a mid-August doubleheader in Allentown, when he hammered three home runs, one soaring over the left-field scoreboard and two over the right-field fence. It was a power display reminiscent of another left-handed pitcher-turned-position player—Stan Musial.

The Cardinals added Conk to their 40-man roster and invited him to spring training in St. Petersburg, Florida, to learn how to play first base.

A headline in the *St. Louis Star and Times* heralded his arrival: "Conklyn Wells Meriwether Really 'Conks' 'Em."[15]

Asked about the "collection of zeroes appended" to his winless 1945 record, Conk replied, "Gosh, I don't know what happened to my pitching. I guess I should have made the change to first base long ago."[16]

He explained Conklyn was his dad's family name, Wells someone else's family name, and Meriwether the name of his adopted family. The *Star and Times* article concluded, "The Cardinal front office says Conklyn Wells Meriwether, 'The Name,' hits a baseball harder than a gentleman bearing the simple moniker of Ruth. Babe Ruth, that is."[17]

Conk needed experience playing first base, so the Cards assigned him to their Houston farm club in the Texas League.

"Card scouts and managers of clubs where Meriwether has played are confident the distance slugger will make the Texas League grade," the *Houston Post* reported.[18]

Conk was in limbo most of the spring because of a ruling that required the Cardinals to keep him on their roster well after he was sent to Houston. As the *Post* pointed out, "Meriwether's case is undecided, and it is no cinch he will wear a Buff uniform this season."[19]

Conk was in the lineup on opening day, ripping three hits. He had two more three-hit games and was batting .333 (10-for-30) when he virtually disappeared for a week because of an undisclosed illness. Soon after returning to Houston, the Buffs demoted him without explanation to Lufkin, Texas, in the Class C East Texas League.

In 110 games at Lufkin, he hit .319, walloped 21 homers, and batted in 96 runs, the first step in becoming one of the minors' most feared hitters. He continued to pitch, compiling a 4–1 record and 1.90 ERA.

"Conk Meriwether firmly established himself as the best pitcher in the East Texas League," one writer declared.[20]

The Dallas Eagles of the Texas League selected Conk in the minor-league draft and, at the beginning of the 1947 season, optioned him to their Lubbock, Texas, farm club in the home run–happy West Texas–New Mexico League. Injuries to both ankles limited the damage Conk did in nine games—a .367 batting average that included five doubles, three triples, and a home run.

He finished the year at Texarkana, Texas, in the Class B Big State League, where he was primarily used as a pitcher, posting a 9–5 record and 4.28 ERA. He stepped to the plate a mere 76 times, hitting .303, with five homers.

Conk asked to be traded so he could play every day. Another Big State team, the Greenville Majors, granted that wish, and he delivered 31 homers and 151 runs batted in 1948, and a league-best 27 round-trippers and 108 RBIs in 1949.

He earned a share of the Gulf Coast League (GCL) home run title at Lake Charles, Louisiana, in 1950, by blasting 24 in only 62 games. Fourteen of the four-base blasts came in the first month, leading to a newspaper advertisement for a bread company, the nickname "Meal Ticket," and a special night honoring him as the team's most popular player.

Conk was well liked by Johnny George, too.

The Millers' catcher-manager pulled Conk aside before a game against Lake Charles and said, "Look, we're going to throw it fat. You go ahead and knock them out."

Conk was battling Galveston's Elwood Grantham for the home run crown, and George didn't want Grantham to win. He had his pitchers throw the ball right down the middle each of the three times Conk batted. He looked at nine straight strikes, never lifting the bat off his shoulder.

Conk joined Galveston in 1951, and had 25 home runs and 112 RBIs in 111 games when Crowley acquired him and put "Operation Meriwether" into effect. At Crowley, he slugged 19 homers and batted in 51 runs in 38 games, to give him 44 circuit blasts and 163 RBIs for the season.

The outfield fences at Miller Stadium almost begged for Conk to knock one over them, as they were 340 feet from home plate all around, even deepest center field.

Crowley fans eagerly awaited Millers broadcaster Ed Keim announcing Meriwether stepping to the plate: "Here comes the Conker!"

Keim's memories of "The Conker" never faded.

> He had the most unorthodox batting stance I've ever seen in my life. He'd choke up a couple or three inches from the knob and stand there. The bat was parallel to the button holes on his uniform. He held it down around the waist, and he'd wait for the pitches. When the pitch came in, the only thing you'd basically see move is his wrists would come around and snap the bat. And that ball took a ride. It was unreal the power he had in his wrists.

As the ball rocketed off the bat, Keim exclaimed, "Here goes another one!"

"It was blunt, matter-of-fact, and people knew exactly what I meant," Keim said, explaining his call of a Conk home run. "The crowd went bananas. Conk had kind of a shuffled gait—short, mincing steps. Made sure that each base was touched properly. He'd have a great big smile on his face and tip his cap. Home plate got an extra hard stomp when he crossed it. It was just a sight to see."

It was a familiar one, too, as he topped the Evangeline League in home runs the next two years, conking 33 in 1952 and 42 in 1953.

Conk used a yellow Babe Ruth model Louisville Slugger bat 35 inches long and weighing 33 ounces.

"It was more like a softball bat," said Chuck Nelson, a pitcher for the Millers in 1952–53, who sometimes used the bat in practice. "I had to choke up on it about halfway."

Conk stood at the back of the batter's box, dragging his massive bat back slowly while warning the catcher to watch out and not get hit when he swung.

"The catcher would have to back up about three feet from his normal position," said Alan Siff, a pitcher who played with and against Conk, causing low breaking pitches to bounce in the dirt before reaching the catcher. "This gave Meriwether a distinct advantage as he could always feed on the fastball or a high curveball, pitches he could hit with power."[21]

Millers infielder Dickie Barras often caught batting practice.

"When Conk hit the ball, I think I could smell the bat burn," he said. "His home runs were never a question mark. The ball cleared the fence by a hundred feet. And he did it all with his wrists—just a snap of the wrists."

The joke in the Millers locker room was that Conk would drive in 30 runs and let in 29, so you've got to keep him. Conk committed a league-leading 28 errors at first base in 1953. He was runner-up in 1952, with 24 miscues.

As Nelson found out in his first start for the Millers, catching a routine pop fly was a challenge for Conk.

"I was going to catch it—just stick my glove up and catch the thing," Nelson said of a popup that landed untouched about halfway between home plate and first base. "But Conk's hollering, 'I got it! I got it!' He didn't get within 10 feet of the ball."

"He could move about two steps to his left and two steps to his right, and that was it," noted Mel Stein, a first baseman-turned-outfielder on the '53 Crowley team. "He was not very mobile. But it didn't make any difference. He could catch balls thrown from the infield and hit 42 home runs."

"He was an affable, likeable guy with a good sense of humor," Keim said. "His mind was filled with baseball. He'd spend a lot of his spare time visiting people downtown. They liked to be around him."

Conk usually wore a stylish hat, dress shoes, and a sports coat over working coveralls.

"He dressed the same way pretty much all the time," said Crowley-born Don "Boo" LeBlanc, a Millers pitcher in 1955. "To me, it just didn't fit. I heard other people say the same thing. There was something just not right."

Tony Mele joined the Millers nearly two months into the 1953 season.

"People said he was crazy, but I didn't think he was crazy or off-the-wall," Mele said. "He just didn't care."

Actually, he cared a lot about baseball and fishing.

"Oh, he loved fishing," Keim said. "It might've been a close toss on where he would be happier, on the ball field or fishing. He loved them both."

Conk was an expert fly fisherman and took his fishing pole with him on road trips. "I want to go see how the water is," he'd tell a teammate.

"I was born and raised in Brooklyn, and never went fishing in my life," Mele said. "He took me fishing for the first time."

Hugh Blanton, ace of the Millers pitching staff in 1952, also fished with Conk. "He was the best I've ever seen with a fly rod. He could make that fly go in places that nobody else could."

There was a dark side to Conk that some of the Miller players knew about but didn't discuss until years later.

"He was the most foul-mouthed individual I've ever known," Stein said. "If the people of the town could hear what he said, he wouldn't have been quite the hero that he was."

Outfielder Ray Stockton played for the Millers in 1952, the memory of lightning striking Andy Strong dead still vivid.

"He [Conk] was one of the most ungodly persons I've ever played with," Stockton said. "I've seen him stand in front of the dugout and when a cloud would come up, lightning flashing, he'd hold his hands up in the air and dare God to strike him. It would just make your blood curdle."

"If he liked you, he'd do anything for you," explained Donald Keeter, the Millers' catcher in 1953. "If he didn't like you, you might have a broken arm by the time he got through with you."

That's what almost happened to Mike Scivoletti, a pint-sized shortstop for Crowley in 1952–53. Conk took exception to something Scivoletti said, so as they were walking down the street one day, he grabbed his arm, swung his body around, and tossed him to the ground.

"Conk, you're going to hurt him!" Keeter shouted.

"I mean to hurt him," Conk yelled back.

A local drugstore gave Conk a box of chocolates for every home run he hit. Shortly after the incident, Conk told Scivoletti to pick up the chocolates and keep for himself. "I got quite a few boxes of chocolates from him," Scivoletti chuckled.

"He was one way one day and some other personality the next day," Keeter said.

The first sign of Conk's erratic behavior was after the 1951 season, when he had a leading role in the play *Born Yesterday* at the Crowley Little Theater, the pride and joy of its founders, Hirsch and Freda Scholl.

According to the *Crowley Daily Signal*, Conk's opening night portrayal of a bumbling multimillionaire swindler "entertained the audience through the entire three acts, and the prolonged laughter held up the performance at many points of the play."[22]

There was no mention of Conk refusing to go onstage unless he was paid.

"We had to pass the hat among the other cast members," an angry Hirsch Scholl told his son, Bill, when he got home that night. "We couldn't go on without him."

Conk appeared in the next three performances, but Hirsch made sure he wasn't in another play at the Little Theater.

Prior to a game at Miller Stadium the following spring, Hirsch was standing by his box seats near the team's third-base dugout.

"Conk walked over to him and knocked him cold as a cucumber," Blanton said. "Hit him right in the face with his fist."

Conk Meriwether took a shot at acting his first winter in Crowley, portraying an unscrupulous multimillionaire in a local theater production of *Born Yesterday*. At far right, Conk is being interviewed by Judge Edmund Reggie, playing the role of a newspaper reporter. Conk refused to go onstage opening night until he got paid by other cast members. Photos courtesy of the *Crowley Post-Signal*.

"Daddy wasn't the only one he hit," said Rici Scholl Miller.

Hirsch Scholl was Jewish, just like another victim.

"Conk and this Jewish fellow had done some business together, and I don't think it turned out really well," Chuck Nelson said.

One night the Millers' batboy rushed into the locker room to inform Conk there was a man waiting outside to talk to him. Conk sent the batboy back with a warning to leave or get his butt stomped.

"When we got dressed and went out, the guy was still there," Nelson said. "Conk walked up and hit him in the face, and knocked him down and just went right on and got in his car."

Nelson was with Conk at Johnson's Drive-In, a restaurant with car hops where the players liked to eat and hang out after games.

"Conk got to mouthin' off to this guy in a car beside us," Nelson began.

Conk got mad and jumped out of the car. He ran to the other vehicle and started yanking on a winged glass window that was open on the driver's side.

"He got his fingers into the thing and just pulled the glass part out of the frame," Nelson said. "He reached in and unlocked the door from the inside. He drug the guy out; hit him several times, knocking him to the ground; came back to the car, sat down; and, then, continued our conversation as if nothing had happened."

Conk popped another man standing in line outside a movie theater.

Rici remembers thinking, "Why does he always hit people?"

Conk was placed on a pedestal, isolated from any wrongdoing or bad publicity by business leaders and Red Mitchell, sports editor of the *Daily Signal*. "There's no way he (Red) would put anything negative about a Crowley Miller in the paper," said Harold Gonzales Jr., publisher of the *Crowley Post-Signal*.

"People took him as their hero," said Billy Joe Barrett, a star for three different teams his five years in the Evangeline League. "He was hitting home runs and winning ballgames. They didn't think about what was going on with the rest of his life."

Grantland Rice's ode to home run hitters turned out to be an apt description of Conk—the bloke with the mighty poke who tears the cover off the ball. He was the center of attention on the field, but off it, everyone looked the other way as he swung away.

7

OH, HAPPY DAY!

Mike Scivoletti had a last name that was difficult to pronounce, and Anthony Mele went by Tony because no one called guys Anthony in his neighborhood. They were from Brooklyn, New York, with accents foreign to Southwest Louisiana.

"All I ever heard," Mele would later write about growing up in Brooklyn, "was 'doity doid street, tree balls, and two strikes, earl, deez, dem, doze, nuttin."[1]

There was a common saying in the lower minors that "if you can't give them a winner, at least give them new names and faces."[2]

The boys from Brooklyn were new and different, as well as sure-handed infielders that Crowley manager Johnny George needed to make the Millers winners again. They were part of the rebuilding of the Millers that started the last month of the 1951 season and continued in 1952, with the addition of outfielders Jimmy Moore and Ray Stockton, and pitchers Hugh Blanton, Chuck Nelson, and Roy Niccolai.

If holdovers Conklyn Meriwether and Art Edinger were the power and pop of the revamped Millers, Scivoletti and Mele were the pep and piz-zazz. They were talented rookies others overlooked. They grew up within four blocks of one another, attended the same public school two years apart, and learned how to play baseball on the sandlots. They were fans of the game as much as they were players.

"I can't remember not loving baseball," Mele said. "I lived across from the schoolyard, and I was there playing ball all day long."

The Crowley Millers infield of 1952, with, left to right, Conk Meriwether at first base, Ray Smerek at second, Mike Scivoletti at shortstop, and Tony Mele at third, was sure-handed, with one big exception—Conk. He committed 24 errors, second highest in the league for first sackers, despite playing in only 116 games. In 1953, he led the loop with 28 miscues. Photo courtesy of Annie Mele Mazzaro and the *Crowley Post-Signal*.

Scivoletti was a diehard Brooklyn Dodgers fan and Mele a New York Yankees booster.

"I was no potential major leaguer," the 5-foot-11, 175-pound Mele conceded. "I didn't have the scouts hovering over me."

It didn't matter in Crowley.

"People treated us like we were major leaguers," Mele said. "In fact, what the Crowley Millers were to Crowley, the Yankees were to New York. We would walk the street and they would greet us, invite us to cookouts, and ask for autographs. They had a radio station where they had calls dedicating songs to Tony Mele or Jimmy Moore."

Sometimes the fans were the 10th man on the field. One night, 7,381 people jammed Miller Stadium. They filled the stands and were five-and-six deep behind ropes along the outfield and both foul lines.

"I'm playing third base," Mele said. "The fans are six feet in foul territory from third base. A pop foul was hit to me, and the crowd moved back so I could catch the ball. Now, one of our guys hit a ball to the same spot. The other team's third baseman went into foul territory, and the fans didn't move at all."

Scivoletti spent the entire '52 season with the Millers while Mele joined the club around the half-way mark.

On stepping off the train in Crowley, Scivoletti asked himself, "What the hell am I doing out here?"

"It looked deserted," he recalled.

Scivoletti's journey to Crowley began in the U.S. Army at Fort Monmouth, New Jersey. He tried out for second base, the position he played in high school.

The Fort Monmouth manager was hitting infield grounders, and when it was Scivoletti's turn, he ripped a line drive over second base. "I lunged for it, backhanded the ball on the short hop, and in the same motion flipped it to second base," Scivoletti said.

"Hold it!" the manager bellowed, dropping his bat. "I don't believe that! Let me see you do that again."

Scivoletti did it again, and walking off the field he was told to pick up his uniform the next day. "But you didn't see me bat," he demurred.

"That's all right," the manager said. "I've seen enough."

Scivoletti played second base three seasons in the army, his performance described by one sportswriter as "steady as the Rock of Gibraltar both at bat and in the field."[3]

One of his teammates his last year in 1951 was Yankees pitcher Whitey Ford. As a rookie the year before, Whitey had a spectacular 9–1 won–lost record and 2.81 earned run average. He would go on to win 236 regular-season games and 10 more in the World Series to make it into the National Baseball Hall of Fame.

On meeting Whitey for the first time, Scivoletti introduced himself as a Dodgers fan, adding, "I hate the Yankees, and I'll never ask you for your autograph."

They became good friends, Whitey insisting Scivoletti travel with him to road games in his new 1951 Pontiac.

During a game at Sing Sing prison in Ossining, New York, they conspired to put on a hit-and-run play without the permission of the team's manager.

Scivoletti was the leadoff hitter, batting behind Whitey in the ninth spot.

"I was praying he wouldn't get on base," Scivoletti said. "I was so nervous, I didn't know what to do."

Whitey singled and then flashed the hit-and-run sign. Scivoletti swung, and instead of hitting the ball behind Whitey sprinting to second, he knocked it over the left-field wall. As he trotted around the bases, Whitey stood at home plate, yelling, "I said, 'Hit and run, not hit and walk!'"

Another army teammate was Emile Chaillot, the Millers' most valuable player in 1950. He was aware a New York Giants scout wanted to sign Scivoletti, but his boss deemed the 5-foot-7, 150-pounder too small. "I'm going to have Johnny George call you," Chaillot said.

That's how Scivoletti wound up in Crowley.

He assumed he would be used at second base, the position he always played. But when he took the field the first day of spring training, George sent him to shortstop.

"I want you to concentrate on defense," he told the surprised Scivoletti. "I don't care if you bat zero."

"So I took him at his word," Scivoletti quipped. "I batted .217."

In a speech to the team, George said, "I don't expect Conk to hit no 60 homers or Rusty to win no 30 games."

Rusty Walters, a 30-game winner in 1950, was back with the Millers.

"Coming from New York, I know major leagues," Scivoletti said. "I thought to myself, 'This guy is talking major leagues.'"

Conk totaled 14 round-trippers in spring training and, after going hitless in the season opener, homered in six straight games. He was up to 14 home runs through 28 games and on track for 70.

"He was in a groove," Blanton said, noting the left-handed Conk didn't hit a ball to the left of second base the entire '52 season. Almost everything he hit was a line drive, and he rarely struck out—once in every 10 at-bats.

Just before facing the league's best southpaw pitcher, Conk told Blanton, "First pitch he's going to throw is a fastball. I'm going to take it. And the next pitch he's going to throw is a curve, and I'm going to hit it out of here."

That's exactly what happened.

Blanton asked Conk why he didn't hit the first pitch if he knew it was going to be a fastball.

"Well," Conk said, "I wasn't exactly sure he would throw the fastball, but I knew if he did, he'd throw a curveball the next pitch."

"He hit that thing over the lights in right field," Blanton marveled.

Every time Conk homered at Miller Stadium fans passed the hat, filling it with anywhere from $25 to $50 in bills and coins.

The speedy Scivoletti was a singles hitter, many of them coming on bunts.

"I'd almost rather see Mike bunt than swinging away," said Ed Keim, the Millers' play-by-play announcer. "He was the best bunter that I ran across in the years I did baseball, and that includes guys up in the majors. He was fast, and he got away from home so quick. It was just a treat."

He once bunted and ran around the bases to score without stopping.

"The third baseman charged, picked up the ball, and threw it over the first baseman's head down into the right-field corner," Scivoletti explained.

> So I went to second. The right fielder picked up the ball and threw it over the shortstop's head into the left-field corner. I went to third. The left fielder picked up the ball and threw it wild to third. I'm running home, and I'm going to be out by at least 10 feet when the catcher dropped the ball.

After the game Scivoletti was eating at Johnson's Drive-In when a Millers fan walked up to him with a hat full of money. "Here, Mike," he said, "we know you ain't ever going to hit the ball out of the park. So we decided to take up a collection for you."

The Millers were in second place, three games behind the league-leading Lafayette Bulls, when Mele joined the club on June 9. He began the season as the Bulls' starting shortstop.

Neither Mele nor Scivoletti knew the other was in the Evangeline League until their teams played the first time.

"Tony, what are you doing here?" Scivoletti asked.

"Mike, the same thing you're doing here."

Mele homered and singled in the game.

"You know that fellow?" George asked Scivoletti afterward.

"Yeah, I've known him since public school," Scivoletti said.

"Can he play third base?"

"He sure can," Scivoletti said, even though Mele always played short-stop in Brooklyn.

Third base was true to its nickname, the hot corner, as three players, plus George, a catcher, took a crack at the position before Mele was acquired from Lafayette.

It turned out to be a big deal—the "silver lining" in a cloud that hovered over the Millers after a leg injury sidelined Conk briefly and, then, nagged him the rest of the summer.[4]

Conk was hitting .404, with 23 homers and 78 runs batted in, at the end of the first week in June. He went nearly six weeks without a four-bagger, his batting average dropping 45 points.

Meanwhile, Edinger and Moore picked up the slack in the power department, each socking seven homers. Mele hit in 10 straight games, batting .361 (13-for-36), while the rest of the team slumped to .210.

The Millers, minus Conk, took over first place in mid-June.

"Oh, happy day!" Keim gleefully announced to his radio audience.

"They Love BASEBALL in Crowley," proclaimed a headline in the *New Orleans Times-Picayune* Sunday magazine, *Dixie.*[5]

"Crowley is the kind of place baseball promoters dream about," the story gushed.[6]

An opening night crowd of 5,763, almost half the town's population, was larger than the curtain-raiser in Boston, Massachusetts, between the Dodgers and Boston Braves. Two weeks later, the Millers attracted 3,611 fans, two-thirds of them black.

The *Times-Picayune* article pointed out that Crowley's average attendance of 1,600 was the equivalent of the hometown New Orleans Pelicans drawing 62,000 fans per game instead of their usual 5,000.

Conk admitted that "he goes to the plate to knock the ball over the fence rather than just get a hit."[7]

Second sacker Ray Smerek was praised as a "local Ty Cobb" who "plays hard" and "never lets up."[8]

George was quoted as saying, "I've got a tight infield and one of the best outfields I have seen in C ball."[9]

Pitching was his biggest concern. "You have to sacrifice something to have a well-rounded ballclub," George said. "If my pitchers just hold up, we will do all right."[10]

A sore-armed Walters won two of three decisions but was a shadow of the 30-game winner he was two years earlier. He was released so Smerek could return to Crowley.

Pitching turned out to be a strength for the Millers, with Hugh Blanton posting a 21–10 mark and Sterling 19–12 to rank one–two in the league in wins. Sterling topped the loop in complete games and was second in innings pitched and strikeouts. Blanton was third in all three categories.

Sterling lost his last three starts by scores of 1–0, 4–3 in 13 innings, and 3–1.

"He should've won all three," said Mele, who committed a two-run error in one of the games. "I not only lost the game and kept Willard from winning 20, I also made him lose a $500 bonus."

Hugh Blanton topped the Crowley Millers pitching staff in 1952, with 21 wins, followed by Willard Sterling, with 19. Sterling led the team in innings pitched (258), strikeouts (164), and ERA (3.10). Left to right are Roy Niccolai, 6–6; Chuck Nelson, 8–8; Blanton, 21–10; Cassius Clay, 15–10, at Lafayette and Crowley; Bill Hurley, 5–5; and Sterling, 19–12. Photo courtesy of Richard Pizzolatto and the *Crowley Post-Signal*.

Mele didn't know about the bonus clause in Sterling's contract until they met at a reunion of Millers players in 2000.

"He asked me for that $500 plus interest for the last 48 years," Mele joked.

George rejected a plan by Blanton to get Sterling his elusive 20th win.

"I'll pitch four innings," he said to the Millers manager prior to starting the final game of the regular season, "and if we're ahead, bring Sterling in to finish the game. That way we'll have two 20-game winners."

"I don't play that way," George snapped.

Blanton was the winning pitcher, leaving the game after five innings and the Millers leading 3–0.

The Millers won the pennant with an 81–59 record and won all eight playoff games.

Conk slugged a league-high 33 home runs, including three grand slams, despite missing 22 games. His .335 batting average was second best in the circuit and his 123 RBIs fourth.

Art Edinger and Jimmy Moore were almost as potent, with averages of .329 and .317, respectively, 24 and 17 homers, and 105 and 128 RBIs.

The hottest hitter the last month of the season was Ray Stockton, who batted a sizzling .413 to finish with a .320 mark.

Scivoletti led all shortstops in fielding, making the fewest errors and taking part in the most double plays. Mele ranked near the top of the league's third basemen on defense.

Ironically, the most attention the hard-hitting Edinger got was for stepping to the plate seven times in a 10-inning game without being charged a single at-bat. He was hit by a pitched ball, drew five walks, and sacrificed. This oddity was featured in a nationally syndicated cartoon titled "Strange as It Seems."

Moore was involved in a couple of strange incidents himself.

The night before he and Sterling were to play in the league all-star game, they were in a car driven by teammate Pat Patrick that knocked down two trees and crashed into a house. On the eve of the playoff finals, Moore and Patrick got into more mischief and were kicked off the team.

"The two players were entirely in the wrong," *Crowley Daily Signal* columnist Dud Wilkins reported without mentioning any specifics. "It was not their first offense. Neither was it the second or the third."

Nothing stopped the Millers.

Art Edinger played in the shadow of Conk Meriwether and Jimmy Moore his three-plus years (1951–54) at Crowley despite hitting a combined .315, with 89 homers and 352 RBIs. The most attention Edinger got was for a game on July 2, 1952, when he stepped to the plate seven times in a 10-inning game without being charged a single at-bat. Illustration courtesy of Richard Pizzolatto.

"The team was absolutely terrific," Mele said. "And the fans were unbelievable."

Attendance for the season, including four playoff games, was 119,933—nearly 10 times Crowley's population. Someone figured out that it was roughly the same as the Yankees drawing 80 million fans through the turnstiles at Yankee Stadium.

One wag suggested that if you live in Crowley, "you either pull for the Millers or pull out."[11]

By the end of the season, a Crowley girl had taught Mele how to drive a car. He was eating grits; drinking the mud-like coffee; and saying, "Y'all," like the locals. He was best man in Sterling's wedding and, 50 years later, attended his golden anniversary party.

The Brooklyn Boys personified the Tabasco League. They oozed enthusiasm for Crowley baseball and basked in the laughter they produced wherever they went.

"Mike should've been a comedian instead of a baseball player," Blanton said.

A fan in Lafayette once told him, "Scivoletti, I'd like to buy you for what I think you're worth and sell you for what you think you're worth."

Scivoletti didn't hit a home run in 1952. "They used to play me in close all the time," he said.

In a game against the Lafayette Bulls, he fouled off a pitch attempting to bunt. Lafayette manager Earl Caldwell hollered at his pitcher, "Throw at the foreign bastard's head."

The next inning, Caldwell was coaching at third base when Scivoletti took the field to play shortstop.

"What's the idea throwing at the foreign bastard's head?" Scivoletti asked.

"You're trying to show us up," Caldwell said.

Later in the game, one of Caldwell's players, a Puerto Rican, tried to bunt.

"Hey, what about him?" Scivoletti inquired.

"He's a foreign bastard, too," Caldwell said.

Scivoletti also played for the Millers in 1953, hiking his batting average to .269, and even hitting a home run. He was sitting behind home plate at Crowley's Miller Stadium watching the Evangeline League all-star game when shortstop John Millard of New Iberia bobbled a ground ball for an error.

The Crowley Millers dominated the Evangeline League in 1952, capturing both the regular-season and playoff titles, and placing six players in the circuit's all-star game. Kneeling, left to right, are left fielder Art Edinger, pitcher Willard Sterling, and first baseman Conk Meriwether. Standing, left to right, are catcher-manager Johnny George, right fielder Jimmy Moore, and pitcher Hugh Blanton. Photo courtesy of Richard Pizzolatto and the *Crowley Post-Signal*.

A Millers fan stood up and shouted, "That wouldn't have happened if Scivoletti was there!"

When Millard belted a grand-slam homer, Scivoletti jumped to his feet and yelled, "And that wouldn't have happened if Scivoletti was there."

"The ballplayers were heroes," Mele explained.

Mele's hero growing up was "Joltin' Joe" DiMaggio.

In an instructional book published in 1949, Joltin' Joe wrote, "My advice to a boy in C or D ball who doesn't move up at the end of the season is to get out of baseball and look for another career."[12]

With a .243 batting average and five homers for a Class C team, Mele moved out, not up. He spent the next two years in the U.S. Army and, then, returned to Crowley to play one more season. He couldn't get enough of hearing Ed Keim say, "Oh, happy day!"

8

MISSED OPPORTUNITY

In just three years, Johnny George transformed Crowley from a town with no professional baseball team into the model for success in the minor leagues.

When Crowley Millers president Monte Loving was introduced to Joe Cronin, a Boston Red Sox star-turned-executive, at baseball's winter meetings in December 1952, Cronin said, "Crowley, eh! Everybody in baseball knows about Crowley."[1]

Loving shared a sign showing Crowley's population and attendance figures to communicate "what a real baseball town could do."[2]

There were 43 minor leagues in 1952, down 15 from 1950, when Crowley entered pro ball. Attendance in the minors dropped 9 million during the same period. Driving this downward trend was what one writer referred to as the "distraction of the Korean War" and the "growing counterattraction of television and radio."[3]

The classification of a league was determined by the total population of its member cities. The minimum requirement was 150,000 for Class C leagues, 1.75 million for Class AA, and 3 million for Triple-A.

Of the 80 Class C clubs, only five topped Crowley's regular-season attendance of 110,814, and they represented cities at least three times larger. The Millers drew better than San Antonio and Beaumont in the Class AA Texas League, and two Triple-A clubs, Columbus, Ohio, and Springfield, Massachusetts.

A San Antonio newspaper even tried to stimulate its readers by print-ing the Crowley attendance of the previous night alongside the figure for the hometown Missions. The number for Crowley was usually higher.

After the Millers wrapped up their second league title in three years, a *Crowley Daily Signal* editorial suggested that it could've been three straight, except the 1951 team was "torn to pieces by misfortunes and an act of God." The newspaper concluded, "The baseball world knows Crowley is a good baseball town and that we take the great American game seriously."[4]

The question going into the 1953 season was whether Crowley could remain the poster child of Minor League Baseball without George, who guided the Millers to a 255–185 won–lost record, including playoffs.

In mid-January, George informed the Millers' board of directors that he was going to buy the Dublin, Georgia, team in the Class D Georgia State League. He offered to continue as manager of the Millers through the '53 season if they wanted him to remain.

"We don't want to hold Johnny back in bettering himself in his chosen career, and if he feels he would rather be 'on the spot' to direct his own club then I feel we should agree to let him go," one of the directors said.[5]

They voted unanimously to accept his resignation.

"I have never played ball in a city where I was treated as well as I have been here," George said. "For the first time in my baseball career, I feel lost. I know that I will never be as happy anywhere as I have been here, but I feel that I must take this opportunity to further my position in the baseball field."[6]

George's departure coincided with the discharge from the army of Emile Chaillot, the Millers' most popular player in 1950. He returned to Crowley with his wife, Jane, and their 16-month-old son, Joe.

Emile grew up three blocks from downtown Mobile, Alabama, near the black section called Plateau. The baseball field at a nearby park was along the demarcation line between the black and white neighborhoods, and the one place in Mobile where kids could mix freely without worry-ing about the color of their skin.

Emile was a precocious baseball player. At age 12, he showed up at the park to play with boys bigger and several years older.

"You're not playing with us," one of the boys said. "You're too small."

"Let me hit and then you can tell me if I can play," Emile replied.

Emile "Smut" Chaillot pulled double duty for the Crowley Millers in 1950, pitching and playing first base. Fans rewarded his 10–6 won–lost record and team-high 21 home runs by voting him the Millers' most valuable player. Emile was one of three finalists interviewed in 1953 to replace Johnny George as manager. Photo courtesy of the *Crowley Post-Signal*.

The left-handed Emile stepped to the plate and smashed the ball out of the park.

"You can stay," Emile was told.

Emile was one of the big boys at the park when a skinny black kid named Henry Aaron knocked the cover off the ball just like he did.

"Dad was very popular with the blacks," Joe said. "Because of his dark skin, many blacks thought he was one of them."

He often was a ringer for black teams in exhibition games.

"Dad was actually darker than two or three players on the black teams," Joe Chaillot said. "If anyone was going to be challenged, it wasn't going to be him."

Emile's swarthy looks enabled him to blur the color lines in the segregated South.

"He had a Mediterranean complexion," Joe said. "He'd pass for black or white. It didn't matter to him."

Emile married a local girl, Jane Alice "Sis" Bernard. He was a favorite of Crowley fans and players alike.

Tony Mele considered Emile "Brooklyn's ambassador to Crowley," because he started his pro baseball career with the Dodgers and he "speaks with a southern drawl with a lot of Brooklynese mixed in."[7]

Emile applied for the Millers' managing job and was one of three finalists interviewed by the team's directors.

The other candidates were Joe Powers, a veteran Evangeline League pitcher-manager, and Tony York, who played 23 years, all of them in the minors, except for 28 games with the Chicago Cubs in 1944. Powers had three years of managing experience and York one.

Chaillot had never managed before, but he had a vision for the Millers based on competing with and against blacks on the sandlots of Mobile and in the army. He was in the Dodgers organization during the time they were integrating Organized Baseball with the signings of Jackie Robinson, catcher Roy Campanella, and pitchers Don Newcombe and Dan Bankhead.

The Korean War was syphoning off young prospects in 1953, driving up salaries in the lower minors for veteran or so-called class players. It was becoming increasingly difficult for teams to be both competitive and financially stable.

"The good-looking 19-year-old rookie, once the goal of every club owner, has now been devalued," wrote *Washington Post* columnist Shirley Povich. "He's under the gun of the Selective Service."[8]

The situation prompted Jay Haney, manager of the Lamesa, Texas, Lobos, in the West Texas–New Mexico League, to sign black shortstop J. W. Wingate in 1951.

Haney made his case in an open letter published by the *Lamesa Daily Reporter*:

> Personally, I feel if we are able to obtain two very "above average" Negro men who can really play ball, it should be a credit to the league, as well as to our own town.
>
> Baseball is strictly a business just like any other business with employees. In any other business we choose the worker who can do the job best and at the most reasonable price. We are all aware of the fact that there is a definite shortage of ballplayers due to the drafting of our younger and most promising talent into the Armed Services.
>
> True, there are plenty of "class men" players available, but the league cannot possibly survive at their high salaries. . . .
>
> Since the American Negro works in our factories, helps harvest our crops, helps can our food, cooks our meals, takes care of our children, lives behind our homes, and, above all, fights overseas beside our own white boys, we feel baseball has every right to employ them if they can benefit by doing so.
>
> Bear in mind, we are not trying to rearrange the laws of the South. The Negro will be reminded of this and at all times must keep his place with his own race. The fact that he is a ballplayer will not give special privileges. He will be warned in advance of the abuse he must expect from opposing teams and fans. So if he wants to play ball under those conditions, we should be big enough to give him that opportunity.[9]

Wingate hit safely in his first six games, including three doubles.

"The crowd cheers lustily when he makes a play afield or gets a hit, and his appearance in the lineup has packed the Negro bleachers every night," one wire service reported after the Lobos' first homestand.[10]

After batting .250 in 27 games, Wingate was released because, as Haney put it, "Fans might be staying away from the games on account of his presence in the lineup."[11]

Haney elaborated, "We weren't drawing many fans. So we let him go. We still ain't drawing many fans."[12]

Attendance at Lamesa dropped 32 percent, to 59,283, even though the Lobos won 81 games and placed third, both franchise bests.

The Dallas Eagles fared better in 1952, with the signing of pitcher Dave Hoskins, the first black to play in the Texas League.

Hoskins won 11 of his first 15 decisions and was hailed as the "savior of the Texas League" for packing ballparks with black fans. Bus excursions were arranged from cities a hundred miles from Dallas so as many people as possible could see the "sensational Negro pitcher" in action. Hoskins finished with 24 victories, including two in the playoffs, and was credited with personally adding 92,850 to league attendance. [13]

A Louisiana state senator tried to stop Hoskins from playing in Shreveport by introducing legislation to prohibit whites and blacks from participating together in competitive sports where admissions are paid. The state already had a law barring blacks and whites from fighting one another in boxing matches.

"If Negroes are allowed to play with whites, it will break up the league," the senator insisted. [14]

The new bill was defeated by a single vote.

After the season, Hoskins revealed three death threats he received prior to a game in Shreveport. "First one said I'd be shot if I sat in the dugout. Second one said I'd be shot if I went on the field, and the third one said I'd be shot if I took the mound. I figured all three were from the same person. Probably someone just trying to scare me." [15]

Hoskins didn't tell anyone, pitched the game, and won easily.

Emile had the benefit of knowing the experiences of Hoskins and Wingate. He could only imagine what might happen if he tried to use black players in the lily-white Evangeline League. Would he succeed or find himself in the middle of a racial storm that threatened to break up the Cotton States League, a Class C circuit that "survived three wars, floods, pestilence, and a depression to keep going in 40 of its 52 years." [16]

The new owners of the Hot Springs Bathers announced in early April that they were going to use two black pitchers, Jim "Schoolboy" Tugerson and his brother, Leander.

The previous year, they played for the Indianapolis Clowns of the Negro American League. Schoolboy posted a 14–2 won–lost record and batted .325 while rooming with Aaron, a shortstop for the Clowns and a future Hall of Famer.

Schoolboy also starred for the Clowns in 1951, notching an 18–4 record and a miniscule 1.92 earned run average, and hitting .343.

Blacks had never played in the league. It was made up of Hot Springs, Pine Bluff, and El Dorado in Arkansas; Monroe in Louisiana; and Jackson, Greenville, Natchez, and Meridian in Mississippi. Segregation laws in Mississippi prohibited interracial teams from playing in the state.

Hot Springs promised to play the brothers only where home teams approved, but this didn't prevent the firestorm that followed.

"We are not convinced that a third-rate baseball league is any place to fight for equal rights because entertainment, and not need, is involved," the editors of the Greenville newspaper, the *Delta Democrat-Times*, commented in an editorial. "In other words, why can't we realize we're living in a world which is a lot more concerned about saving mankind's undeserving skin than in the color of baseball players?"[17]

Hot Springs was kicked out of the league, its president, Al Haraway, claiming the issue at stake was a "matter of survival of the league."[18]

The Tugerson brothers issued a joint statement that read in part,

> Are we fit to work in your homes and fields only? We can talk for you and help elect you when it's time for voting. When you were young, was it fair for a Negro maid to raise you? Now, we're the forgotten ones. . . . You haven't been fair to us in the South.
>
> We don't want to, as Negroes, stay with you or eat with you. All we want to do is play baseball for a living. This, too, is a job. We are still working for you.[19]

Schoolboy and Leander were promptly reinstated by the head of the minors, George Trautman, who ruled the agreement among the league's club directors not to use black players was illegal and "at war with the concept that the national pastime offers equal opportunity to all."[20]

A showdown was averted when Hot Springs optioned the brothers to Knoxville in the Class D Mountain States League. Schoolboy was recalled a month later to "lift attendance and boost the club from its seventh-place standing."[21]

On May 20, 1953, in Hot Springs, a crowd of 1,500, the largest of the season, turned out to see Schoolboy break the league's color barrier and perhaps teach segregationists a lesson in the process. The Bathers were scheduled to face the Jackson Senators, piloted by Marland "Duke" Doolittle.

Duke was one of two managers in the league who said his team would play against Schoolboy. He had played against blacks in Panama. "It didn't matter to me what color they were," he said. "We weren't playing a game with color; we were playing it with bats and balls."

As Schoolboy was warming up in the bullpen, Bathers coowner Lewis Goltz received a telegram from Haraway warning that if Tugerson played, the game would be forfeited to Jackson. League umpires had already been ordered to "forfeit every game to the opposing club when Tugerson's name appears on the roster."[22]

When Schoolboy was officially announced as the pitcher, Duke walked to home plate, so the umpires could tell him what they both already knew—the game was being forfeited to Jackson.

"The orders from the league president to all of the managers were that if Jim Tugerson's name was in the starting lineup and he was the pitcher that took the mound for the opening pitch, which was never made, then, we were not to play," Duke said. "That's exactly the way it happened."

Some 500 fans were still waiting to get into the ballpark when the game was called off. Schoolboy never made it to the mound. A wire service photo shows him standing shoulder to shoulder with four white teammates, a blank expression on his face as the forfeit was announced.

"I hope I land in the majors someday," Schoolboy said. "I want to be in a league where they will let me play ball."[23]

Schoolboy went back to Knoxville; won an amazing 33 games, including four in the playoffs; and filed a $50,000 civil rights suit against Haraway and other league officials. He eventually asked for it to be dismissed. In six minor-league seasons, Schoolboy compiled an 86–71 mark. He got to the top of the minors, the Triple-A American Association, but never made it to the majors.

That night in Hot Springs was the closest Duke came to seeing the 6-foot-4, 196-pound right-hander pitch. "I was halfway excited about the moment because I was ready to play the game. But I had nothing to say about it. I just happened to have a ballclub that was playing at Hot Springs that night, and I did as I was told."

The reason typically given for the Cotton States League's refusal to let Schoolboy play is that the league wasn't ready for integration. Ready or not, the league died in 1955.

In 1953, the military draft continued to be a dark cloud hanging over minor-league teams.

Branch Rickey, general manager of the Pittsburgh Pirates and the architect of baseball's farm club system, called the Korean conflict World War III, even though it was never declared.

"Some minor leagues have gone through the wringer," Rickey said. "Others will also go through."[24]

Emile wanted to avoid hard times by bringing in black players who would keep the Millers winning and atop the league in the standings and attendance. He pitched the idea to Miller directors.

"Emile was a baseball purist," said Harold Gonzales Jr., publisher of the *Crowley Post-Signal*, who played for American Legion teams Chaillot coached later on. "Emile is thinking about Ws and Ls. I'll guarantee you they were ballplayers. If he wanted to bring black players in, I guarantee you they were good."

The directors picked York to lead the team in 1953.

"Chaillot's contract was owned by a Florida club, and it is understood that his contract would cost the Millers 1,000 bucks," explained Dud Wilkins, sports editor of the *Crowley Daily Signal*. "A 1,000 bucks is a *thousand bucks*. While the directors did not express this view, we feel they were a bit leery of Powers's physical ability to take his regular turn on the mound."[25]

No mention was made of Emile's proposal to sign blacks. Years later, he told his son, Joe, and close friends about the plan.

York may well have been the best choice for the job.

The Millers needed a player-manager, and York, even at age 41, was a threat with the bat, hitting .315, with 14 home runs, the previous year at Texarkana in the Big State League. He also guided Texarkana to a third-place finish, just three games out of first.

York had the backing of Chicago White Sox manager Paul Richards, a cold, tough taskmaster he endured at Seattle in the Pacific Coast League (PCL). York once missed a bunt in a game, and in the clubhouse afterward, Richards ordered him back into his uniform and onto the field for bunting practice.

"You have given me everything you've got," Richards said later, adding, "and if you ever want to manage, I'll see what I can do to help you."[26]

Emile was ahead of his time in trying to play blacks in the Evangeline League.

Two months after he was passed over for the Millers job, the Dallas Eagles played an exhibition game in Crowley. The Eagles' power-packed lineup featured two former Negro League stars and big-leaguers, third baseman James "Buzz" Clarkson and outfielder Willard "Downtown" Brown.

"This marks the first appearance of Negro ballplayers in Miller Stadium for professional play," the *Daily Signal* reported without mentioning their names.[27]

The game story that followed didn't reference the players even though both had two hits.

Six nights later, it was impossible to ignore Lenny Hunt, a black outfielder for the Texarkana Bears, who singled, homered, and just missed a double in a game against the Millers.

"Somehow, we feel bound to comment on the fine manner in which the Negro ballplayers conducted themselves on the field," Wilkins wrote.

He described a line-drive smash by Hunt that was caught and, then, dropped by a Millers outfielder after crashing into the fence. Hunt was standing on second base when the umpire ruled him out.

"Hunt immediately trotted to the dugout without a word," Wilkins said, noting, "There are very few ballplayers that would not have put up a prolonged argument."

Wilkins went on to observe that blacks know "they are on the spot" with Southern fans and "seem to be trying their best to bring about the fans' acceptance of them."[28]

Acceptance for black players was mostly dependent on letting their athletic skills do their talking.

This is exactly what Aaron did in 1953, to integrate the South Atlantic League, along with Jacksonville teammates Felix Mantilla and Horace Garner, and Savannah's Fleming "Junior" Reedy and Elbert Isreal. The 19-year-old Aaron hit a league-high .362 and homered 22 times to pace Jacksonville to the pennant and more than double attendance to 142,721.

The Gulf Coast League (GCL) folded at the end of the 1953 season, and three of its teams, Texas City, Port Arthur, and Lake Charles, moved to the Evangeline League. The ban on blacks was not a rule, but an unspoken "gentleman's agreement" among Vangy clubs dating back to the circuit's formation in 1934. It was ratified by all eight teams at a meeting prior to the 1954 season.

This didn't stop Texas City Pilots manager Bones Sanders from playing three dark-skinned Cubans—shortstop Tony Taylor, third baseman Julio Bonilla, and pitcher Pedro Naranjo.

A wire service correspondent envisioned "more fireworks than the mix-up which caused some forfeitures in the Cotton States League" the year before.[29]

"Everybody waited with bated breath, expecting an explosion that would rival Hiroshima," wrote Truman Stacey, a sports columnist for the *Lake Charles American-Press*.

"What happened?" Stacey asked. "Nothing. Absolutely nothing."

At first the Cubans were limited to games at home and the former GCL cities of Port Arthur and Lake Charles, which previously had black players. They didn't play on the team's first swing through Baton Rouge and Alexandria.

Sanders used Taylor and Bonilla at Lafayette and New Iberia, "where everybody said it couldn't be done, and the only result was a bumper gate."

"Now," Stacey concluded, "about all the fans in New Iberia and Lafayette have said about the situation is, 'When are we going to get a Negro player?'"[30]

At Crowley, black fans showed up in large numbers to cheer Taylor and Bonilla. "You wouldn't have noticed anything different at all as far as the crowd was concerned unless you were looking for it," Millers manager Tony York said.[31]

When Taylor and Bonilla finally played in Baton Rouge, the largest crowd of the season showed up, black fans accounting for 40 percent of the total.

"The swing to the Negro players will be rapid as soon as some of the other clubs can find suitable talent," a Baton Rouge sports columnist predicted. "The success of the Texas City Pilots on the road with their trio of Negro players has led most of the owners to believe they too can cash in with a Negro player."[32]

It never happened.

Texas City fans, black and white, stayed home, forcing the Pilots to move to Thibodaux, Louisiana, in mid-June.

That's when the 18-year-old Taylor became homesick and would've returned to Cuba if he had had enough money. "The fare to Havana was $72. I looked in my pocket, I had only $62. So I stayed."

"I had no one to talk to," Taylor continued. "The only English word I knew was 'Okay,' and I would order meals by pointing at the food."[33]

Taylor batted .314, and tied for the league high in triples, with 12. He went on to play for the Cubs, Philadelphia Phillies, and Detroit Tigers in a stellar big-league career that spanned 19 years and three decades.

Chaillot followed George to Dublin in 1953, and left mid-year when the ex-Millers manager put the club up for sale. Both finished the season at New Iberia.

Emile quit baseball in 1954 to return to Crowley and work for his wife's uncle in his television sales and repair shop. He eventually took over, expanded into furniture, and ran the business for 35 years.

"Dad was one of the first in Crowley to hire and promote blacks," Joe said. "Blacks loved him. They gave him all their business, plus he had the business of whites because he was so popular as a player."

Emile lived in Crowley until he died in 2008, at the age of 82.

All he said publicly about interviewing for the Millers' managing job was, "I think the only reason why they wanted me to be the manager was because of the popularity from 1950."[34]

Heading into the 1953 season, the Millers were first in the standings, first in attendance, and well positioned to be the first pro sports team in the state of Louisiana to field black players. It was a missed opportunity that likely cost Crowley more firsts.

9

"THE COOPERSTOWN OF DIXIE"

Miller Stadium is on the south end of Crowley across from the rice mills that inspired the team's nickname and the town's slogan, "Rice Capital of America."

On game days before dawn, a man carrying a paint can and brush walked along the main thoroughfare, Parkerson Avenue, stopping at every corner to paint "Baseball Tonight" on the sidewalk.

At the crack of dawn, the bus station coffee shop was filled with folks talking baseball and savoring the buttery biscuits as fast as they came out of the oven.

A popular topic was Conklyn Meriwether and whether he would plaster another home run over the right-field fence.

"The Conker" was back to begin his third season in Crowley, the longest he lasted anywhere. He was eventually joined by outfielders Jimmy Moore and Art Edinger, but for a while, it looked like they were goners.

Red Mitchell of the *Crowley Daily Signal* related a conversation he had with Millers director Joe Dore Jr., who showed up at his office after the Minor League Baseball draft in early December with a "long chin, the kind of look a guy gets when he's found out somebody ran over his dog."

"I got news for you, and it ain't good," Joe said glumly.

"How's that?" Red asked.

"Well, Red, we led 'em in attendance, we led 'em in the flag fight and in the playoffs, and be damned if we didn't lead 'em in the draft."

"Oh, oh! How bad?"

"The Class B boys gobbled up our entire outfield," Joe moaned. [1]

Moore, Edinger, and Ray Stockton were plucked in the minor-league draft, as well as pitcher Hugh Blanton, who teamed with Willard Sterling to win 43 games, counting two each in sweeping the playoffs.

The military draft took three Millers: Sterling; third baseman Tony Mele; and Al Ogletree, a backup catcher to Johnny George, who flew the coop to manage his own team.

Dore was a rice miller and a member of the Millers' board of directors from the beginning. At the end of the '53 season, he would become the team's president, succeeding Monte Loving, another rice miller.

The Millers belonged to the fans themselves, not a major-league team or a wealthy family that viewed them as a plaything. Some 400 fans from Crowley and other towns in Acadia Parish held $40,000 worth of stock purchased at $25 per share. Rice farmers and millers, car dealers, and area merchants made up the board of directors, along with doctors and lawyers. They handled all team business, including player deals, with advice from the Millers' manager.

"They just love baseball," Loving said of Millers fans. [2]

The biggest cheerleader of Crowley baseball was Sam Tarleton, pitcher-turned-sports columnist for the *Beaumont Enterprise*.

In various stories, he called Crowley the "Best Little Baseball Town in the World," the "Hottest Baseball Town in the World," the "Greatest Little Town in Baseball," and the "Cooperstown of Dixie" after the birthplace of baseball in Cooperstown, New York.

"There's nothing wrong with baseball that towns like Crowley and teams like the Millers won't or can't cure," he gushed as early as 1951. "Crowley's fans, wherever they reside, are the answer to 'what's wrong with baseball.'" [3]

Crowley wasn't the first minor-league town to be put on a pedestal.

In 1950, Lamesa, Texas, of the Class C West Texas–New Mexico League drew 87,000 people during the season and 13,000 more in the playoffs—a total of 100,000. That was 10 times its population and more than Amarillo, Texas, and Albuquerque, New Mexico, the largest cities in the league. Area newspapers hailed Lamesa as the "Biggest Little Baseball City in the United States," a claim printed on the club's letterhead.

Even when Lamesa went on the road in the playoffs, nearly 1,500 fans showed up at the team's ballpark to sit in the grandstands and cars nearby

Some 400 fans owned stock in Crowley Baseball, Inc., led by a board of directors with varied backgrounds that handled all team business, including player deals. Monte Loving, a rice miller, headed the board in 1952, when this photo was taken. Seated, left to right, are H. E. "Buddy" Lyons, Crowley mayor; J. B. "Ike" Broussard, Crowley city clerk; Chester Faulk, camera store owner; Clyde Hodges, livestock dealer; Doug Kloor, newsstand owner; and Charlie Lewis, accountant. Standing, left to right, are R. E. Schlicher, rice miller; Philip Cagnina, truck line operator; Barton W. Freeland, banker; W. A. Breaux, insurance agent; Loving; Joe Dore Jr., rice miller; and Jerry Ashley, car dealer. Photo courtesy of the *Crowley Post-Signal*.

to listen to an announcer enliven telephone reports from the game sites with a colorful play-by-play account via loudspeakers.

"Regardless where a person might perambulate," sports editor "Irish" Matthews wrote in the *Lamesa Daily Reporter*, "we don't think they will find more baseball enthusiast(s), grandstand umpires, and managers or just plain old peanut-crunching baseball fans than right here in Lamesa."[4]

In 1947, Lamesa, Visalia of the California League, and Twin Falls, Idaho, of the Pioneer League touted their cities as the best in Class C baseball based on attendance, which was six to 10 times their respective population. El Centro, a town with 13,000 people, challenged the trio, pointing out that its club attracted 45,429 fans despite finishing last in the new Sunset League. Visalia tied for second, Lamesa placed fourth, and Twin Falls won the pennant.

In 1946, Greenville, Texas, population 14,000, boasted that it was the biggest little town in baseball because the hometown Majors, a fourth-place team, attracted 160,186 fans in the Class C East Texas League.

"The Greenville owners believe this year's attendance is a record for any city in baseball—almost 12 times the population of the city," the *Sporting News* reported. The 100,000-plus figure "topped by several thousand the attendance of several cities in the Class AA Texas League, whose smallest city is some half-dozen times the size of Greenville."[5]

The difference between Crowley and the others was the chest-thumping came from outsiders, not locals.

A crowd of 1,236, roughly one out of 10 people in Crowley, attended the Millers first exhibition game against Port Arthur, Texas, in 1953. A month later, 6,367 fans jammed Miller Stadium for the home opener.

"Everybody in Crowley starts talking baseball months before the season opens, and they keep on talking baseball months after the campaign ends," raved Dick Oliver, sports editor for the *Port Arthur News*. "I never have seen a hotter baseball town."[6]

Mel Stein didn't know anything about Crowley or Conk when he reported for spring training in 1953. He was with Bob Wuesthoff, a ballplayer buddy on his way to New Orleans. They were in the Millers clubhouse getting ready for the team's first workout when Conk asked Stein, "What position do you play?"

"First base," Stein answered.

It was obvious Stein didn't hear Conk's comment, so outside the club-house Wuesthoff inquired, "Did you hear what that guy told you about playing first base?"

"No," Stein admitted.

"He said, 'Not on this team you don't.'"

Stein was primarily a first baseman and didn't want to switch to the outfield. He pleaded his case with Tony York, the team's new player-manager.

"You really can't play first base on this team," York told him. "Conk is the local hero."

The next day Conk drove Stein to nearby Lafayette to buy a fielder's mitt so he could play right field.

A streamlined Conk was 25 pounds lighter and fully recovered from a leg injury that made him a mere mortal the last half of the '52 season. He served notice with a mighty clout in the Millers' first regular-season game. Mike Scivoletti also homered, his first and only four-bagger as a pro. Conk marked the occasion by wrapping a big arm around the diminutive shortstop and saying, "Mike, you and the Conker are now tied for the league lead in home runs."[7]

Conk belted three homers as the Millers scored 53 times in the first five games to crush opponents by an average margin of seven runs. This prompted the *Beaumont Enterprise* to report, "Crowley has shown every other baseball club in the country how to break records in the turnstile department, and now, the 1953 team may be the first [Evangeline League] club to win 100 games in one season."[8]

The league was down to six teams, Abbeville and Houma dropping out because of poor attendance. Teams were allowed to carry six veterans because of the scarcity of quality rookies.

Newcomers to the Millers pitching staff were rookie Gil Ross and Marv "Lefty" Holleman, a 16-game winner at Abbeville the year before. They joined Chuck Nelson, another southpaw, who was 8–8 for the Millers in '52.

Edinger and Moore were back in the outfield after their release from the Class B teams that drafted them over the winter. The addition of second baseman Juan Izaguirre, catcher Don Keeter, and York at third base had *Alexandria Town Talk* columnist Mack Owens calling them the "ideal murderers' row for a Class C circuit."[9]

Six weeks into the season, the Millers had a 30–11 won–lost record, and Owens predicted they would "waltz away with the flag," while Izaguirre won the batting title and Holleman and Ross combined to notch 50 victories.[10]

The columnist was spot-on, as the Millers won the pennant by 13 games, Izaguirre finished second in the batting race with a .339 average, and the Holleman–Ross combo totaled 46 wins—24 for Holleman and 22 for Ross. Nelson chipped in with 20 more wins and a 3.23 earned run average, best of the trio.

Besides Izaguirre, five Millers topped the .300 mark—York, .324; Keeter, .311; Edinger and Moore, .306; and Meriwether, .305. Even Scivoletti was a threat with the bat, hiking his average 52 points, from .217 to .269.

Six Millers had 10 or more home runs—Stein, 10; York, 11; Izaguirre, 13; Moore, 23; Edinger, 25; and Conk, 42, to tie the postwar league

Marv "Lefty" Holleman, far left, combined with Gil Ross, center, and Chuck Nelson to win 66 games for the Millers in 1953. Holleman was tops with a league-leading 24 victories, followed by Ross and Nelson, with 22 and 20, respectively. Holleman and Ross were one–two in complete games (30 and 29) and innings pitched (283 and 271). Nelson's 262 innings were third most in the circuit. Photo courtesy of Steve Holleman.

record. "That's a lot of home runs for a team in the minor leagues," Stein said.

"One of Conk's wrists was about the size of both of mine put together," marveled Stein, a 6-foot, 180-pounder. "He'd stand there with the bat straight out in front of him but perpendicular to the ground, and pitchers tried to throw the ball past him. He'd hit those balls a mile."

Daily Signal sports editor Dud Wilkins described a typical Conk home run this way: "The crash of bat against ball sending the horsehide skyrocketing to the pasture back of right field, a slow jog around the bases, a handshake by teammates at home plate, a wide grin, a wave of the cap to the fans seated near the Miller dugout."[11]

Conk also led the league in runs batted in (RBIs), with 134.

"Conk was the star of the team, and people loved him," Stein said.

He recalled the time Conk swung so hard that the bat flew out of his hands, landing between first and second base. "The first baseman picked up one end of the bat and the second baseman picked up the other end, and they walked the bat up to the batter's box and presented it to Conk. Everybody had a good laugh."

Fans showered the slugger with gifts on "Conk Meriwether Night," his teammates contributing a hatbox containing "a huge straw hat, a metal hat, and a pair of lady's panties." One could only imagine the story behind the items. [12]

Through the first 20 home games, the Millers were averaging 1,763 customers—on track to hitting the 130,000 mark.

"It is doubtful if any other 12,000 population town in baseball has done, is doing, or will do as well," Tarleton wrote. [13]

Crowley baseball was even the topic of conversation at a barber shop in Cheyenne, Wyoming. On hearing that the man he was about to shave was from Crowley, the barber said, "Say, you people in Crowley take your baseball seriously, don't you? I heard Dizzy Dean talking on the radio about Crowley the other day. It must be some town." [14]

The colorful Dean was a popular commentator on weekly radio and television broadcasts of Major League Baseball. People remembered what he said even if they didn't always understand his country twang.

The hot topic of conversation the last month of the season was whether Crowley could top the 100,000 mark for the third straight season.

The streak was endangered by Mother Nature, rain forcing 11 games to be canceled and made up as part of doubleheaders. A flood forced one game to be postponed.

"We got to the park for one game and all the dirt sections were mud, and there was standing water on many grassy sections of the field," Stein said. "They poured gasoline on the dirt areas, lit it, and when the dirt dried, we started the game before a pretty good-sized crowd."

With seven home games to play, attendance was at 88,276. This figure included three car giveaways that attracted 15,522 fans combined.

"Reaching the 100,000 mark would materially improve the club's financial condition, as well as give the Millers considerable nationwide publicity," Millers president Loving reminded stockholders. [15]

The Millers added two more car giveaways the final week of the regular season to finish at 100,239. The team lost money—$1,430.05 to be exact. Given there were nine more rainouts than the year before, this was generally viewed as a "good showing."[16]

At least one Millers player knew better.

"One of the board members stopped me on the street near the end of the season and suggested I cash the checks I had not cashed because I might not get the money," Stein said.

A month earlier, Stein had gotten a call from a friend in San Jose, California.

"Stein," he said, "when are you going to quit foolin' around with baseball? I've got a high school coaching job for you here."

Stein skipped the playoffs and headed to San Jose.

Crowley was eliminated in the opening round of the playoffs, losing four of six games to the Lafayette Bulls, a team that tied for fourth in the regular season, 15½ games behind the first-place Millers.

"I couldn't believe that they lost in the playoffs," Stein said. "There was a lot of firepower on that team."

The playoff collapse was the beginning of the end for baseball in Crowley. The Millers didn't win another championship or come close to drawing 100,000 fans again. To cut costs, they got rid of their biggest star and meal ticket—Conk. He was sold to Tallahassee, Florida, of the Florida International League.

Stein quit baseball the following summer after playing briefly for Victoria, British Columbia, of the Western International League. He was 27 years old.

"We all want to be in the majors, but not very many of us made it," he said, summing up his four years in the minors.

Stein returned to Crowley with his family in 1972.

"I'm going to show you the stadium that I played in," he announced proudly.

"I was told that I was only guy to ever hit a ball over the scoreboard in left field, and I wanted my kids to see it," he said. "I got $100 for the home run from a local undertaker."

There wasn't much to see, as Miller Stadium was falling down.

Stein drove to a gas station nearby.

"I played baseball here in Crowley in 1953," he said to the attendant.

"You did? What's your name?"

"Mel Stein."

The guy rattled off the names of players on the mighty '53 team.

"He must've named everybody on the club, but he couldn't remember me," Stein said. "I've got my three kids in the car and they're all young."

Stein was speechless. Finally, he said, "Well, guys, I *really* did play here."

10

THE WRITING WAS ON THE WALL

Joe Fazzio was a local legend.

At one time he was a pro boxer billed as Kid Fazzio from Pennsylvania, Philadelphia, not the other way around. Joe wound up quitting boxing because he thought it was rigged and run by cheats and double-crossers.

Joe became a candymaker, a master at concocting different kinds of brittles and fudges. He had a green thumb that was the envy of other gardeners in town, producing blue-ribbon flowers, fruits, and vegetables. He also was a champion short-order cook and waiter extraordinaire, except during the 1947 World Series, when his beloved New York Yankees beat the Brooklyn Dodgers in seven games.

"Joe was so intent on listening to the broadcast," the *Crowley Daily Signal* reported, "he picked up some dishes from the restaurant table during the last game and walked right out in the street instead of the kitchen."[1]

Joe loved his wine. He kept a bottle stashed under the house where he lived with his sister, Leona Pizzolatto, and her family. After a few swigs, he sounded like Plato. "It's nothing but a shadow on the wall," he said with the authority of the ancient philosopher, describing how things are not always what they appear.

Joe often took his bottle of wine on walks with his dog, Blue, a blue-gray terrier he counted on to tell him when it was safe to cross a street. Blue failed to do so one day in late 1953, and Joe was hit by a car, breaking a leg. He used the money he received from the motorist who hit him to buy a new television and antenna for the Pizzolatto home.

"You had to have an antenna as high as the seven-story bank building to get a good reception," recalled his nephew, Richard Pizzolatto.

By 1954, 26 million (55.7 percent) American households had TVs, and Minor League Baseball attendance was down to 19.7 million, the lowest since 1945, the final year of World War II, when only a dozen leagues operated.

George Trautman, president of the National Association of Professional Baseball Leagues (NAPBL), maintained the future was bright. "Minor League Baseball in 1954 will have stronger leagues, stronger teams, and will have greater community support than in any year since 1949."[2]

That was the year attendance peaked in the minors at 41.7 million—double what it was entering 1954.

The end of the fighting in Korea meant more good ballplayers for the minors, Trautman pointed out. "Hundreds of these players are coming back to the game."[3]

Instead of seeing the writing on the wall, Trautman saw the same shadow as Joe.

When Joe and Blue strolled around Crowley the previous summer, they saw about 100 TV antennas. By the start of the 1954 season, there were 700 to 800.

"For the first time the Millers this year face real competition from television," *Daily Signal* sports editor Dud Wilkins wrote in early May.[4]

A crowd of 5,312 turned out for the home opener, but the next 12 games averaged 788.

"Cold and rain have kept the fans away from the park, and the folks have just not yet got into the 'habit' of an almost nightly visit to the stadium," Wilkins explained. "Many of the proud possessors of TV sets are sports fans. We hope the coming of warm weather will drive these fans away from the living room and out to the ballpark."[5]

Even with towering antennas, TV reception in Crowley was poor at first. As it improved, the antennas got smaller and popped up throughout Crowley and nearby towns—Jennings, Gueydan, Lake Arthur, Kaplan, Eunice, Rayne, Church Point, and Iota.

"When the TV got clear, that's when people started clearing out of the ballpark," Pizzolatto said.

The Millers now had to compete with top-rated television programs featuring Lucille Ball in *I Love Lucy*; Jack Webb as Los Angeles detective Joe Friday in *Dragnet*; *Arthur Godfrey's Talent Scouts*; and variety shows hosted by comedians Jackie Gleason, Jack Benny, Milton Berle, and George Gobel.

The Millers weren't laughing. They no longer had their biggest gate attraction, slugger Conk Meriwether. They were also without Gil Ross and Chuck Nelson, 22- and 20-game winners, respectively; catcher Don Keeter; shortstop Mike Scivoletti; and right fielder Mel Stein.

The ever-reliable Art Edinger and Jimmy Moore were back, along with the versatile Juan Izaguirre and the tireless Marv "Lefty" Holleman, the workhorse of the 1953 pitching staff, pacing the league in innings pitched (283) and wins (24). Also returning was player-manager Tony York.

The addition of two Texas teams, Port Arthur and Texas City, made the Evangeline an eight-team league once again. Rosters were cut to 15 players, with an equal number of five veterans, limited-service players, and rookies. Teams could carry National Defense Service players, regardless of classification, over and above the 15-man cap.

Conk's replacement at first base, Gene Grigiski, was wounded in action during the Korean War.

"Gene is undoubtedly one of the finest glove men in Class C ball and has thrilled fans with his spectacular play around the first-base sack in the spring tilts," Wilkins observed in the *Daily Signal*.[6]

The $64,000 Question quiz show had yet to appear on TV, but it already was being asked about Grigiski's hitting ability.

Another military veteran was Jerry Simon, a right-handed pitcher who posted a 5–2 won–lost record for the Millers in 1951, before he was drafted.

"I grew up in the city of Philadelphia," Simon said. "I had never eaten shrimp. I didn't even know what a crawfish was."

Simon rented a room at a woman's house for $5 a week. One day she persuaded him to have dinner before going to the ballpark.

"She had all these things crawling around in the kitchen," he recalled. "I thought they were bugs. And they were crawfish. She'd pick them up and toss them into the hot water, and they went from brown to red and I thought, 'Oh, my God, I've got to eat this and I don't even know what it is.'"

Before and after TV, the one constant in Crowley was the attention showered on the players.

A favorite hangout of Crowley Millers players was Toler's newsstand in downtown Crowley, offering magazines and newspapers, shoeshines, cigars, snacks, and cold drinks. Here, several members of the 1954 Millers team posed for a photo. Sitting, left to right, are third baseman Nick Petti; Laura Siff and her husband-pitcher, Alan; Marv "Lefty" Holleman and his wife, Sue; outfielder Jimmy Moore; and pitcher-outfielder Juan Izaguirre. Standing, left to right, are pitcher Bradley Gandee; catcher Gifford Reynolds; pitcher Doug "Duke" Roberts; first baseman Jim Bello; manager-third baseman Tony York; outfielders Frank Brucato and Art Edinger; and second baseman Joe Giel. Photo courtesy of Steve Holleman.

"It was a special town at a special time," Simon said. "I was a young kid, and I felt like I was something special. They made you feel that way. The families. The high school kids. The druggist. Everybody. Wherever you went, it was fantastic."

Judge Edmund Reggie often hosted the players for dinner on Sundays. Another family treated Simon to fried chicken on a regular basis. "The people adopted us. They were absolutely amazing."

A standout pitching performance usually was rewarded with a handshake and a $20 bill from Jerry Ashley, a car dealer and Millers director. "Nice game, Simon, nice game," he said.

Ashley had a standing offer of a new Chevrolet for any Miller that hit a home run into a net attached to the flagpole in center field.

Jerry Simon logged 297 innings, while posting a 21–13 won–lost mark, for the Millers in 1954. He went on to coach baseball at Southwestern Louisiana Institute (now the University of Louisiana at Lafayette) and become a national softball star, inducted into the U.S. Senior Softball Hall of Fame in 2004. Photo courtesy of Richard Pizzolatto and the *Crowley Post-Signal*.

"When Conk came to bat, Jerry Ashley would quiver," said Bobby Barras, a Millers batboy at the time. "He could hit a line drive so hard 20 feet off the ground, and it just buzzed by that fence. But he never did hit one in the net."

Ashley was sitting in box seats behind home plate with banker Bart Freeland and other Millers directors when the 6-foot-4, 180-pound Moore, nicknamed Lanky, blasted a ball that shot straight toward the net. Moore dropped his bat, turned around, and yelled at Ashley, "Start that engine!"

"Bart got to his feet, took his hat off, and was fanning Jerry's face as the ball was heading for that net," said Ed Keim, the Millers' radio announcer.

The ball hit the flagpole, just missing the net.

Izaguirre and Grigiski came close to hitting the net in another game only to be upstaged by Moore's four circuit swats. His first homer went over a $10 sign in right field, and his third sailed over the scoreboard in left to earn him $100 from another sponsor. Afterward, he said if he could've batted one more time, he would've hit five.

Moore was the proverbial free spirit, a good ol' farm boy from Georgia that teammate Chuck Nelson called a showboat.

During a downpour at New Iberia, Moore entertained rain-soaked customers by stripping off his pants to expose his shorts and sliding pads, and shouting, "Watch me!" He raced toward puddles of water at first and second base, diving headfirst into the mud.

Out from Conk's shadow, Moore led the Millers in four offensive categories—batting average, at .342; hits, with 195; doubles, with 42; and runs batted in, with 113. His 21 homers were second to Edinger's 31.

Moore still took a backseat to Juan Izaguirre, selected by fans as the most valuable Miller. The Cuban outfielder-pitcher batted .322, with 16 circuit blasts and 104 RBIs, while posting a 14–5 won–lost record and 3.02 earned run average. He even played some at first base after Grigiski, batting only .239, with four homers, left the club suddenly in early June.

Simon and Holleman each notched 21 victories, the latter leading the league in shutouts (5), complete games (31), and innings pitched (314). Allen Siff added 14 wins.

The Millers' 1954 season was best symbolized by a bowl of gumbo Moore loaded up with homemade hot sauce late in the season.

Siff looked on in disbelief as beads of sweat popped up all over Moore's head. "These beads of sweat accumulated and began to travel down his nose and drop one after another into his gumbo. Jimmy never missed a beat."[7]

Moore kept on eating and perspiring, never noticing the sweat cascading from his nose and diluting the gumbo. "I sure do like my gumbo hot," he admitted.[8]

The New Iberia Pelicans were as peppery as the Tabasco sauce produced on nearby Avery Island and too hot for the Millers to handle. The Pelicans captured the regular-season and playoff titles, and topped the Evangeline League at the gate, attracting 87,350 fans.

Meanwhile, the Millers placed third, with a 77–63 mark, eight games behind the Pelicans, and lost to them in the playoff finals, four games to three. Despite two car giveaways, attendance plunged to 65,099.

The good news was the Millers did better financially, as the team's directors ran the club at minimum cost.

"The days of laying $1,500 to $2,000 on the line to add strength to the ballclub are gone," the *Daily Signal*'s Wilkins concluded.[9]

In the eighth inning of a game, the Millers were leading, 13–5. Siff gave up two runs on three singles and a walk.

"Stick a fork in him, York, he's done!" Edinger hollered at the Millers manager from his left-field position.[10]

York was done, too.

In November, the *Daily Signal* published a ballot for Millers fans to vote on whether to rehire York.

"Any deal that you feel is right is okay with me," the easygoing York said on renewing his contract the year before. "The Miller directors and fans have been very fair to me, and I'm sure they will continue to treat me the same way."[11]

Of the 66 fans that voted in the *Daily Signal* poll, 34 favored keeping York and 32 against. At a stockholders meeting that followed, a majority preferred a new manager to "add color to the club and increase attendance."[12]

That was wishful thinking, just like Joe Fazzio swearing he was going to find the treasure supposedly left behind by Jean Lafitte, the famed Gulf Coast pirate in the early nineteenth century.

One night, Joe told his nephew, Richard Pizzolatto, that he had found a treasure.

"You found the treasure?" Richard said, assuming it belonged to La-fitte.

"Yeah, your sock," Joe said, laughing.

"I used to hide my change in a sock," Richard said. "He dipped into my sock so he could get a bottle of wine for 35 cents."

The Evangeline League was back down to six teams in 1955, and seven weeks into the season half of them were looking for money wherever they could find it. Baton Rouge was "tottering dangerously" and Lake Charles "near collapse."[13]

The Baton Rouge Red Sticks launched a campaign to raise the $10,000 needed to operate the team the rest of the season.

The Evangeline League temporarily took over the Lake Charles Lak-ers, appointing Sam Tarleton, sports director of a Lake Charles radio–TV station at the time, to organize a citizens group that would buy and run the team. The Lakers were broke, with Tarleton revealing they had "about $20 in the bank and owe nearly $2,000 they borrowed to meet ex-penses."[14]

Subscribers to the *Crowley Daily Signal* opened the newspaper one day to find a stamped envelope with the words "Keep Baseball in Crow-ley" printed on it.[15]

"Through this medium," a front-page story explained, "the board of directors of Crowley Baseball, Inc., is seeking outright donations from baseball fans in the area to help get the club over a serious financial crisis which has the Millers with their backs to the wall."[16]

The directors were operating the Millers more efficiently than ever, the article continued, but "dwindling attendance" left the team at "the brink of financial ruin and the more than strong possibility that baseball in Crowley will be ended."[17]

A *Daily Signal* editorial asked, "Has Crowley, the most baseball-con-scious little city in the United States, lost that distinction?"

"The picture has changed," the editorial conceded. "Patrons no longer attend games by the thousands. They are counted now in the tens and hundreds."[18]

A *Daily Signal* columnist imagined a conversation between a father and son 15 years later.

"Hey, Dad," the boy said, "Didja ever see a baseball game? I mean a real baseball game, not in the movies or on TV."

"Sure," the father said. "Used to see 'em right here in Crowley when we had a team in the old Evangeline League."

"They were a lot of fun. It was kinda nice going out to the park on a summer night and sitting around with your friends, watching the game and talking to the guy in the next seat," he continued. "And, believe me, you got a gen-yu-wine charge out of hearing that bat crack loud when a big guy like Conk Meriwether or Jimmy Moore belted one over the wall."

"If it was so much fun, how come y'all quit, Pop?"

"We ran into a little financial snag that we didn't lick, and that was the bear in the buckwheat as far as Crowley baseball was concerned."[19]

The column concluded with a plea: "Keep Baseball in Crowley" and "Keep Crowley in Baseball."[20]

The Millers were next to last, with a 23–31 record, when the fund-raising drive started.

The season opener drew an overflow crowd of 3,892. There was cause for optimism, as new Millers manager Marv Holleman had the one–two punch of Moore and Izaguirre returning, as well as three members of the '52 club that won it all—third baseman Tony Mele, catcher Al Ogletree, and pitcher Willard Sterling, a 19-game winner. They were back from the army.

Sterling injured his throwing arm in early May, and the Millers lost 12 of 14 games the last half of the month.

One game brought back memories of the electrical storm that killed Millers center fielder Andy Strong four years earlier.

"Lightning was flashing around Miller Stadium like the Fourth of July," according to the *Daily Signal*. "Gusts of wind tore across the field, and the dust was soon mixed with rain drops."[21]

Mele couldn't see the ball at third base as the driving rain covered his glasses. Fans were running for cover, and the drenched Millers players wanted to do the same. None of them had been around to see the Strong tragedy, but they knew all about it.

Trailing the New Iberia Pelicans, 3–0, in the top of the fifth, the Millers began stalling to force the two umpires to stop the game before it went the required five innings.

"We'll play it out if it takes all night," the home plate ump told Holleman.[22]

Moore took about two minutes to tie his shoelaces and, then, ambled from deep center field to the mound for a chat with Holleman, who had already used long windups, pickoff attempts, and lengthy discussions with his infielders to slow the game to a crawl. Moore and Holleman were ejected, and the game was forfeited to the Pelicans.

"They aren't the best in the game," league president Edmund Deramee said of the umpires, "but they are no worse than some of the baseball I've seen in this league this year."

He suspended Holleman five days for the incident.

The beleaguered Holleman had nowhere to go for help. Millers directors quashed rumors he was going to be fired, but they didn't have the money to acquire power hitters that could carry the team on their backs like Conk and Edinger once did.

Every day during the weeklong "Keep Baseball in Crowley" campaign, the *Daily Signal* published the names of donors and the amount given. Contributions ranged from $1 to $250, producing a total of $1,712. Half of the money went toward paying various taxes the club owed.

At about the same time league directors decided to split the season in half to give the struggling Crowley and Lake Charles clubs, buried at the bottom of the standings, a fresh start on the field and at the gate.

The Millers responded by winning 16 of their first 20 games, including 10 straight. They were in first place going into August, with the speed and .331 batting average of Venezuelan first baseman Fernando "Freddy" Basante blazing the way.

Basante joined the Millers in early June on option from the Cincinnati Redlegs. He didn't speak English, so no one was sure if his name was spelled "Basanta," as in the letter introducing him, or "Basenta," as it was scribbled on the lineup card. The Spanish-speaking Izaguirre set the record straight—"Basante."[23]

The Millers arranged for Basante to stay at a boardinghouse where Mele and outfielder Joe "Duke" Voso were living.

"Look," Holleman told Mele, "Freddy can't speak English, so I figure he will feel at home with you Brooklyn guys because you can't speak English either."[24]

Basante's locker in the clubhouse was next to the door. Every day Holleman walked in; playfully messed up Freddy's hair; and said, "Hello, Freddy, how are you?"

Freddy always answered, "Fine, thank you."

Mele decided it would be fun to teach Freddy a couple of new words so he could greet Holleman differently.

"Hey, Freddy, how are you?" Holleman said several days later.

"Fine, f*** you!" Freddy replied.

Mele recalled the scene nearly a half-century later. "Holleman stopped cold in his tracks. He was astounded, bewildered, flabbergasted, didn't say a word, couldn't say a word."[25]

Holleman realized it was a joke when the entire clubhouse erupted in laughter.

The Millers were doing fine, thank you, until a rash of rainouts forced them to play a grueling 15 doubleheaders at the end of the season. During one 10-day stretch, they endured eight twin bills.

Twice Holleman pitched an entire doubleheader, lasting 21 innings in one of them. Izaguirre hurled a no-hitter. The Millers still lost 18 of their 30 games to tumble from first to fifth, the same place they finished in the first half. Basante ended up hitting .281. Attendance for the year dipped to 45,130, putting an exclamation mark on Crowley's reign as the "Best Little Baseball Town in the World."

"Crowley really had the spirit of that era," Jerry Simon said.

The era ended with a knockout punch worthy of boxer Kid Fazzio.

In the last game of the season at Lafayette, Louisiana, Moore and Holleman slugged it out.

The previous day, Moore was honored by Crowley fans as the most popular Miller in recognition of his 25 home runs, 101 RBIs, and league-leading .354 batting average. It was the fourth time he had topped the magic .300 mark. His 185 hits and 34 doubles made him the all-time leader for the Millers in both categories.

Moore batted in the top of the first inning and, in the bottom half, trotted past Holleman at shortstop. Moore had a cardboard sign on his back reading, "Evangeline League—.354."

Holleman took Moore out of the game and ordered him to leave the field.

Pitcher Don "Boo" LeBlanc was on the mound. "I could hear them behind me, talking back and forth," he said. "After a while, there was silence. I turned around and all of a sudden, Lefty reached up and hit Jimmy in the jaw."

Another eyewitness described the blow as a "smashing left hook to Moore's chin."[26]

Marv "Lefty" Holleman, left, and Jimmy Moore, far right, weren't clowning around the last day of the 1955 season when they got into a fight on the playing field, Moore getting the worst of it with a fractured jaw, broken tooth, and cut ear. Holleman won 15 games in '55, as the Millers' player-manager, while Moore was the Evangeline League batting champ, with a .354 average. Photo courtesy of Richard Pizzolatto and the *Crowley Post-Signal*.

Moore was taken to the hospital with a double fracture of his jaw, broken tooth, and cut ear. The smaller Holleman escaped with a bruise and a lump above one eye.

"I think there was some liquor involved," LeBlanc said.

Holleman never said anything about the fight except that, "Moore had apologized to him."[27]

Moore insisted otherwise: "That story that said that I apologized to Holleman was all wrong. *He* apologized to me."[28]

Millers directors continued the fight to keep baseball in Crowley by signing a working agreement with the Kansas City Athletics and selling Moore, Izaguirre, Sterling, and Mele, plus three other players, to Midland, Texas, in the newly formed Southwestern League.

The Millers got $3,000 in the deal, a feat of sorts according to Wilkins of the *Daily Signal*, because "veterans playing in Class C ball are pretty much a drag on the market today and are becoming increasingly hard to dispose of."[29]

The Athletics had no use for the veterans, as they were already stocking the roster with young talent from their farm system. They also replaced Holleman as manager.

"The players had been with the Millers a number of years, and it was about time to give the fans a look at some new faces," Wilkins wrote. "The men had all about 'served their time' in Crowley."[30]

The writing was on the wall for baseball in Crowley. Not even Joe Fazzio was calling it a shadow.

11

THE KID AND THE OLD PRO

Terry Fox and Billy Joe Barrett were sitting around the kitchen table at Fox's home in New Iberia, Louisiana, reminiscing about their time together with the New Iberia Pelicans in 1954–55, when they knocked the Crowley Millers off the top of the Evangeline League standings.

Terry was "The Kid," winning 13 games as an 18-year-old the first season and 21 the next. At age 26, Billy Joe was the "Old Pro," a speedy center fielder with three stolen base titles and two pennants in three Evangeline League seasons already on his resume. He swiped a league-leading 67 bases in 1954, and a second-best 27 in 1955.

When Billy got on base, he usually looked at his teammates in the first-base dugout. "I'm going to steal that base, me ya!" he would shout, adding a Cajun touch at the end.

"And he'd steal it!" Terry said.

"Mayhem on the basepaths" was how one sportswriter described Billy.[1]

He once was clocked at 3.8 seconds running from home plate to first. "He could outrun his shadow," Terry added.

Billy grew up in Paw Creek, North Carolina, a village of about 500 people on the outskirts of west Charlotte.

"They ought to check the air, the Paw Creek soil, the vittles the natives eat, the inhabitants' living habits," a *Charlotte News* pundit suggested in 1950, noting the textile mill town was "breeding baseball players . . . faster than a Detroit assembly line."[2]

"There were 16 guys from that little town that went into the major leagues and pro baseball," Billy said.

He rattled off the names of Whitey Lockman, an infielder-outfielder for 15 years in the majors, primarily with the New York Giants, and journeymen outfielders Ken Wood and Pete Whisenant, who bounced around with several big-league teams. "I can't remember all of them sons-of-a-gun," he admitted.

Both Billy and Terry, a native of Illinois, married Southwest Louisiana girls and made the area their home after leaving baseball.

Billy married Nita Jeoffroy of Lafayette in a wedding ceremony at home plate of the ballpark in Thibodaux, where he was playing at the time.

"There were 5,000 people, and they couldn't get them all in the stands," Billy recalled. "They had to put them in the outfield."

Fans covered a 100-foot-long table with gifts. "We counted at least 15 coffee pots."

Gifts continued to pour in afterward, "sacks of shrimp and crab meat, all kinds of seafood" delivered to the newlyweds' apartment.

"These are the finest people I've ever been around," Billy said. "They just took me under their belt. They looked after the players from out of state."

Terry married Shirley Dugas of Loreauville, a wide spot in the road seven miles from New Iberia.

"Yeah, I got stuck here," Terry chuckled. "I drank the water and married a local girl. It's hard to understand unless you come here and associate a little bit with the people.

"I'm from Chicago originally—South Side," he continued.

> We knew the people that lived across the street on the corner. We knew the people that lived one house over—on both sides. But, then, you didn't talk much. When I came to New Iberia and walked down the street to go eat or to a movie, I'd pass people and they'd say, "Hey!" I'd turn around and look and go, "I don't know them." There wasn't anybody that I met in New Iberia that wasn't friendly.

Terry pitched seven years in the majors, mostly for the Detroit Tigers in the early 1960s. He ranked consistently among the top relievers in the American League with a reputation for being tough to steal on.

An overflow crowd of 5,000 showed up at the Thibodaux, Louisiana, ballpark in 1951, to see Billy Joe Barrett and Nita Jeoffroy get married at home plate. They walked under an archway of baseball bats held by Billy Joe's Thibodaux Giants teammates to a 100-foot-long table filled with gifts. The couple was married 65 years at the time of Nita's death in 2016. Photo courtesy of Connie Barrett Stover.

Luis Aparicio, the American League's stolen base champ nine straight years (1956–64), warned another speedster, José Cardenal: "Watch out for him. When he has been working, I've been out stealing second nine straight times."

When José was asked if he had ever been nailed at second with Fox pitching, he replied, "No, he picked me off first."[3]

Billy never made it to first base in the big leagues. But in the eyes of one young fan, he was as big as any major-league star when he played first base for the Lafayette Bulls in 1950.

"I believed Billy Joe Barrett's name would be part of baseball for years," Andre Dubus wrote in his book of autobiographical essays, *Broken Vessels*.[4]

Dubus was 13 years old and a Bulls ballboy when Billy became his hero.

"I have never seen a first baseman whose grace thrilled me as Barrett's did," Dubus wrote 40 years later, "and one night in Lafayette he hit a baseball in a way that I have never seen again."[5]

The ball shot off Billy's bat like a bullet and barely cleared the glove of a leaping second baseman before climbing sharply. The right fielder stopped and "simply stood and watched while the ball rose higher and higher, and was still rising and tiny as it went over the lights in right field."[6]

The ball never came down as far as Dubus is concerned. It is still "rising white over the lights high above the right-field fence, a bright and vanishing sphere of human possibility soaring into the darkness beyond our vision."[7]

The sight so captivated Dubus he failed to mention that it was a grand slam or that afterward a guy went through the stands collecting money in his cowboy hat.

"The game was over," Billy said. "I'm taking a shower, and he walked in with the cowboy hat full of $5, $10, and $20 dollar bills. There was over $400 in that hat."

The story reminded Terry of the time he was given a dollar bill for winning a game. "I had that dollar bill for years until I needed to pay a toll some place in Chicago."

Billy moved from first base to the outfield and played four more seasons in the Evangeline League for Thibodaux and New Iberia before quitting baseball after the 1955 season, settling in Lafayette and getting into the oil business. In seven minor-league seasons, he hit a modest 63 home runs. But one of them made a lasting impression on a young boy who grew up to tell the world about it.

The closest Billy got to the majors was Atlanta, the Class AA farm club of the Milwaukee Braves in the Southern Association. He appeared in five games for Atlanta in 1953. "I never could get halfway to Milwaukee."

At a tryout with Milwaukee when he was 17, Terry was told to pitch batting practice.

"My knowledge of batting practice playing in high school was to let the players hit," he said.

The Braves admired Terry's control, but his fastball wasn't fast enough for them.

"You didn't say that you wanted me to try and throw the ball by them or not have them hit it," he pointed out to the folks running the tryout. "You said it was batting practice."

Terry also tried out with the Pittsburgh Pirates, Chicago White Sox, and Atlanta Crackers. The Pirates and White Sox offered a "Class D as in Dog contract" for $150 dollars a month, while Atlanta tendered a contract worth $250 monthly to play in the Class C Evangeline League.

In 1954, Class C teams could carry as many veterans and limited-service players as the required five rookies.

"You had a lot of age difference, which I thought would give me an opportunity to learn more," Terry said.

He was scheduled to join the Thibodaux Giants midway through the 1953 season, but with the future of the franchise uncertain, Atlanta delayed his pro debut until the following spring at New Iberia.

One of the first things Terry did in New Iberia was go to St. Peter's Catholic Church and pray. "I asked God to give me a chance. I said, 'I don't want to be famous. I don't want to be the star. I just want a chance to see if I can pitch in the big leagues.'"

New Iberia was a charter member of the Evangeline League, until it dropped out early in the 1956 season. Over the years the team had working agreements with the St. Louis Cardinals, Boston Red Sox, Pittsburgh, and Atlanta.

The Pelicans hooked up with Atlanta in 1954, after poor attendance forced Thibodaux to drop out of the league. Most of the Thibodaux players transferred to New Iberia along with business manager Art Kowalski and player-manager Billy Adams.

They guided Thibodaux to a second-place finish and playoff title in 1953, while New Iberia ended up in the cellar with a 52–84 record, 31 games behind first-place Crowley.

"We won't finish last," Kowalski promised Pelicans fans entering the '54 season.[8]

Kowalski revamped the roster, blending Fox and other young pitchers with such experienced position players as outfielder Mauro Iacovello, the '53 batting champ, with a .347 average; third baseman Adams, a .323 hitter the year before; and catcher Roy "Red" Smith, a crusty 11-year veteran. At 30-something, Adams and Smith were old-timers.

"They were past their prime, but, in turn, they could teach you how to play," Terry said.

One of the most valuable lessons Terry learned was from a grizzled veteran trying to make the team at spring training in 1954. "Walked by me as I was throwing on the sideline, and he says, 'If you brought your front leg up around you more, you'd hide the ball and have better control.' I started doing that, and it helped me continue in baseball."

Billy spent the '53 season at Atlanta and Hagerstown, Maryland, in the Class B Piedmont League. After riding the bench for nearly a month in Atlanta, he told Crackers manager Gene Mauch, "If you don't have anything for me to do here, I'm fixin' to go back to Louisiana."

The Crackers sent him to Hagerstown, and in his first game for the Braves, he had six hits in as many at-bats, including a homer and two doubles, and batted in seven runs.

"They thought Ted Williams came to town," Billy said, laughing.

The perfect game made headlines in the local newspaper.

"I ought to send this newspaper to Gene Mauch!" he joked with his wife, Nita.

In New Iberia, Adams gave Billy the green light to steal bases whenever he pleased.

"Man, I was running like crazy," Billy said.

"I don't remember him ever being thrown out," Terry added.

"I think I was thrown out one time in '54."

"Did you stumble, Billy?"

An already potent lineup was bolstered by the addition of Remy LeBlanc, a hometown hero and legend known by the nicknames "The Flying Frenchman" and "Eagle," because of the way he flew around the bases and made circus catches in center field with a "glove that looks like it belongs in a museum."[9]

One hitter consistently robbed of hits by Remy suggested letting him "play the outfield by himself."[10]

The outfield combo of Billy in left and Remy in center was the baseball equivalent of Death Valley.

"You talk about some speed in left field and center field?" Billy said. "That ball had to go out of the ballpark. If it didn't, one of us had it. Remember that?"

"Sure do," Terry said.

"And we missed each other by just a hair running after line drives," Billy said.

"It was very competitive for me coming out of high school," Terry said. "To be able to play my first year with experienced people that knew how to play, that's what helped me succeed."

Terry turned toward Billy sitting at the kitchen table. "I still owe Billy part of my major league pension," he said. "We try to take him out to eat every once in a while."

"I knew Terry would go up because he was a great pitcher." Billy said.

"Let me get my wallet," Terry cracked.

"Terry was great because Remy and I chased down his line drives," Billy needled.

Remy and Billy helped in other, smaller ways, like running the bases.

In a spring training drill, Terry circled the bags in 16 seconds, three seconds slower than Billy and Remy.

"I'm thinking, 'How the heck can they be that much faster?'" Terry said.

They pointed out he was taking too wide of a turn, joking, "If you quit shaking hands with the second baseman and shortstop, you save time."

Billy and Remy were one–two in the league in stolen bases in 1954, swiping 67 and 28, respectively.

Remy also was a power hitter, socking 80 home runs in a three-year stint with New Iberia from 1949 to 1951, including 42 the last season to tie the Evangeline League record.

One sportswriter wondered why "if Remy LeBlanc is such a good ballplayer, he didn't succeed in climbing the ladder of success."[11]

"He didn't want to leave New Iberia," Terry said.

Remy was born in New Iberia, graduating from high school and breaking into pro baseball there in 1942, when New Iberia was a Cardinals farm club. He spent the next three years in the U.S. Marines, returning in 1946 to marry his hometown sweetheart and begin working his way up the Cards' chain.

The Cards soon found out Remy was "as good at being stubborn as he is at playing ball." [12]

Remy was known in the baseball trade as a "jumper," four times leaving teams of his own volition to go home to New Iberia. The Cards were ready to leap off the Empire State Building after Remy jumped their Triple-A farm club in Rochester midway through the 1948 season.

Remy arrived in Rochester while the Red Wings were on the road. He was told to stay put until the team returned, but without telling anyone, he caught the first train to New Iberia.

"LeBlanc has ever been one man with a mind of his own," Jim Wynn of the *Daily Iberian* reported just before the start of the 1954 season. [13]

Remy belonged to the Dallas Eagles of the Class AA Texas League even though he hadn't played a game for them yet.

"The truth of the matter is, he doesn't want to play for Dallas," Wynn continued. "He wants to stay at home where both he and his wife are employed. He will play for the Pels, however, if and when Dallas makes up its mind to release him or sell him to the local club." [14]

"He didn't like it out there, so he came back to New Iberia," Billy said.

Remy matched the 42 home runs he slammed in 1951. He hit two more in the playoffs.

"For every home run, you got a steak dinner," Billy said. "Remy never did go eat one so at the end of the season they took a black Angus cow out on the field and gave it to him. People in the stands went crazy, man, when they saw that."

Remy was a loner and didn't say much.

"When Remy said something, it was a little slurred at times because of the Cajun dialect," Terry said. "He'd say, 'Yeah, I'm having trouble hitting.' He had only 24 or 27 different stances at home plate, a variety that he would switch to because he was having problems. He'd say, 'I'm going to use number 15 tonight' or whatever it might be."

In addition to Remy, four Pels hit 22 or more homers—Billy Adams, 27; Red Smith and infielder Jim Smith, 24; and rookie first baseman Billy Reynolds, 22.

Reynolds led the team in hitting with a .340 batting average, followed by Jim Smith at .324, Barrett at .322, and jack-of-all-trades Ben Dye at .312. LeBlanc batted in a team-high 129 runs; Reynolds, 124; Jim Smith, 115, and Marco Iacovella, 101.

Kid pitchers Jim Stuart, age 20, and Ted Del Rio, age 22, won 21 and 18 games, respectively.

"We had power, we had speed, we could catch the ball, steal bases, and pitch," Terry said. "We had a great, great team."

The Pelicans captured the pennant with an 85–55 record and, then, beat Crowley in the playoff finals, Terry outdueling Millers ace Marv Holleman, 3–2, in the decisive seventh game. Remy homered, doubled, and singled to drive in all of the New Iberia runs.

"That was the best baseball team I've ever seen in my life," Billy said. "There ain't no way Crowley could've beat us that year. We had a team."

New Iberia even topped Crowley at the gate, drawing a league-high 87,350.

At the end of the season, Atlanta Crackers owner Earl Mann purchased Remy's contract and tried persuading him to leave his beloved New Iberia.

"If we could ever get that Frenchman Remy LeBlanc out of Louisiana, we'd have a fine center fielder," Mann told *Atlanta Constitution* sports columnist Furman Bisher. "He hits everything they throw at him, got power, lots of it. But he loves home cooking, 28 years old, and still in Class C league because he hates to leave Louisiana. We'll import a tabasco factory and a few cases of shrimp, and see what we can do with him."[15]

There wasn't enough hot sauce and shrimp to entice Remy to leave New Iberia, so Mann sold him and Billy to the Mexico City Reds for $50,000.

"Can you believe that?" Billy asked. "Remy told me he wasn't going to Mexico. I didn't want to go either."

But Billy was tempted. "I said, 'Well, gawd-dang, thank goodness I'm getting out of the Braves chain. Maybe I can move a little bit.' The Washington Senators were interested in my contract."

Mann didn't have any better luck convincing the Pelicans' Adams to manage the Crackers in 1955.

"I'll tell you what I'll do," Adams told Mann. "If you let me bring this ballclub I've got here in New Iberia to Atlanta, I'll come and be your manager. If not, don't call me."

Adams didn't get another call and retired from baseball. So did Remy. Billy stayed in New Iberia to play one more season.

"Red Smith took over as manager, and we won the pennant again," Billy said.

The Evangeline League had a split-season schedule in 1955, New Iberia winning the first-half title and placing third in the second. Overall, the Pelicans had the best record, 77–62–1.

Billy batted .293 and pilfered 27 bases. Terry tied for most wins in the league, with 21, while completing 25 games and posting a spiffy 2.95 earned run average and 192 strikeouts. They were headed in different directions—Terry to the top of the baseball world and Billy out of it and into the oil business in 1956.

"I knew as long as I was in the Milwaukee chain, I'd never move up," Billy said. "I was trying to get up from way down in Class C ball. There's no way I could move."

From 1953 to 1960, fleet-footed Billy Bruton patrolled center field, as Milwaukee won two National League pennants and a World Series title, and placed second five times and third once. During the same period, Atlanta was Southern Association champ four times.

Besides, Billy didn't want to leave Louisiana to continue his baseball career. "I didn't really push it to go up. I just got hooked on this Cajun country with all these nice people."

The road to Milwaukee for Terry was clogged with bonus-baby pitchers getting a lot more attention and money than his monthly salary of $400.

At spring training in 1956, Atlanta manager Clyde King took two of the team's high-priced prospects to the pitcher's mound. "I don't want any other pitchers out here," he said. "Just these two."

Terry was curious so he watched closely from the foul line as King demonstrated the pickoff move he later used in the majors to stop the game's swiftest runners from stealing bases.

"It was the bent-knee motion that was eventually outlawed," Terry said. "It helped me to advance in the minors and stay in the big leagues.

Basically, you moved your front leg and not your back foot to go to first base. If you did it correctly, you had a chance to keep them close and throw some of them out."

Terry was a serious student of pitching, something King raved about to a reporter: "I'd like to think that someday I'd manage a team on which every player is like him . . . hustling all the time, interested in learning, already good, but working to get better."[16]

"I had a problem covering bunts," Terry said. "It was a big problem in New Iberia."

In 1957, at Austin, Texas, he practiced fielding bunts hit by a batboy for 15 to 20 minutes prior to every home game. "I learned how to cover bunts, and it helped me get to the big leagues."

Terry was a starting pitcher until 1959, when the Braves sent him to their Sacramento Solons farm team in the Class AAA Pacific Coast League (PCL). The Solons' manager was Bob Elliott, a major-league outfielder for 15 years. "He didn't know who I was or if I threw right or left. He said, 'We'll put you in the bullpen and try to work you in and see how you do.' I started off well, and I became a relief pitcher. That's how I got to the big leagues."

A right-hander, Terry appeared in 42 games, all in relief, compiling a 9–3 won–lost mark and 2.70 ERA. In 53 games as a reliever for the Solons in 1960, he was 12–9, with a 3.07 ERA, to earn a promotion to Milwaukee late in the season.

"If a manager likes you, you've got a chance to play," Terry said. "If they don't like you, you don't have a chance."

The Braves' manager in 1960 was Charlie Dressen, a supreme egotist who once tried to rally his team by saying, "You guys hold 'em; I'll think of somethin'."[17]

"In spring training that year, Charlie put me with the 'B' team most of the time," Terry noted.

Terry was throwing on the sidelines in Milwaukee when Dressen declared, "Look, in order for you to pitch here in the major leagues, you're going to have to learn to throw a screwball."

Dressen turned and walked away.

"He didn't say how to throw it," Terry said. "Just that's what you have to do."

Terry got into five games with the Braves, who were in second place and battling the Pirates for the National League pennant. He pitched well in eight innings but got bombed in part of another.

Milwaukee coach Bob Scheffing was so impressed that he grabbed Terry in the first trade he made after becoming manager of the Detroit Tigers. Scheffing even told a Detroit sportswriter the Braves "would have won the thing" if they had Terry the entire season. [18]

The Braves' bullpen was "pretty terrible," the ex-catcher acknowledged, "and he came up in September and did a pretty good job for us. He doesn't have that overpowering fastball or that big, sweeping curve. But all of his pitches are good." [19]

Terry had a manager who liked him, and he would excel despite a throwing arm he hurt polishing his car at Atlanta in 1956. "My arm was never the same until after I got out of baseball."

Terry pitched with a sore right elbow throughout his six years in the majors, five in Detroit and most of the sixth in Philadelphia with the Phillies. He wound up with a 29–19 won–lost record, with 59 saves and a 2.99 ERA. Most amazing were his miniscule ERAs the first two seasons in Detroit—1.42 in 1961, and 1.71 in 1962.

In 57.1 innings pitched in 1961, he gave up only nine earned runs, and two of them were on a home run the New York Yankees' Roger Maris hit off him in the 12th inning of a game at Tiger Stadium in mid-September. The moment is preserved on a YouTube video that has Yankees announcer Phil Rizzuto calling the shot: "There's a drive. That might carry all the way . . . and it's number 58 for Roger Maris." [20]

"I've only seen it one time on TV," Terry said.

Maris went on to hit 61 homers, breaking Babe Ruth's hallowed single-season record of 60.

"Just once," Terry said in early 1964, "I'd like to pitch a whole season without my arm hurting." [21]

He never did, making even more remarkable his big-league accomplishments.

Terry paused as he reflected on the defining moments of his baseball journey.

The only pitching tips he got were from the old-timer walking past the mound in New Iberia and eavesdropping from the sidelines in Atlanta as bonus-baby pitchers received special instructions on a pickoff move.

Terry Fox stands in front of Acadian Ballpark in New Iberia, Louisiana, where as a teenager he won a combined 34 games for the hometown Pelicans in 1954–55. Terry went on to become one of the greatest relief pitchers in Detroit Tigers history, notching 25 and 28 saves, respectively, in 1961–62, with super-stingy ERAs of 1.41 and 1.71. Terry married a local girl and made New Iberia his home. Inset photo courtesy of Terry Fox/main photo by the author.

"I can see all these different things through my career that we've talked about," Terry said. "Coming here to New Iberia was God's will. Meeting my wife and getting to play with Billy on the '54 team that made me a better pitcher. Going to Sacramento and becoming a relief pitcher. Why would it be that way?"

He answered his own question: "It was all part of His direction."

12

A LEFTY FOR THE AGES

George Stuart Brunet had one thing in common with another southpaw legend named George who passed through Crowley.

"Brunet's got a real strong arm," one manager said. "He hasn't dropped a beer in years."[1]

Another offered, "He's never had a sore arm. But he has callouses on his elbow."[2]

The other lefty was George Herman "Babe" Ruth, a renowned beer drinker who gave up pitching for the outfield and powered his way into the National Baseball Hall of Fame at Cooperstown, New York.

Brunet was a legend in his own right, pitching 32 consecutive years until he was 49 years old and revered in Mexico as "El Viejo"—"The Old Man." There's a bronze plaque at Mexico's Baseball Hall of Fame, Salón de La Fama, in Monterrey, honoring his 132 victories and record 55 shutouts in 13 Mexican League seasons.

While Babe was a national icon and a fixture at the original Yankee Stadium, widely known as the "House That Ruth Built," Brunet was a homeless pitcher who passed through more towns than a Greyhound bus.

By the time he got to Crowley in mid-May 1956, he had already pitched for five teams in five states. He would go on to play for 10 more minor-league clubs in the United States, one in Canada, and seven in Mexico.

Brunet pitched for 32 different teams, including nine in the majors, where he wound up with a 69–93 won–lost mark. In the minors, he won 244 games and lost 242, as he was striking out a record 3,175 batters.

Altogether, he appeared in 990 games and pitched 5,472 innings, prompting one writer to interview his tireless left arm.

"He never had a bad arm," said Rocky Bridges, one of his many managers. "Maybe a few bad other things, but never a bad arm."[3]

In the late 1950s and early 1960s, baseball had its own version of the Wild West's infamous Dalton Gang, and while Brunet was not officially a member, he often was mistaken for one.

Brunet was in an elevator at a Boston hotel when George Scott, a rookie for the Red Sox, got on. Earlier in the day, Scott had belted a game-winning home run off of Brunet, pitching for the California Angels at the time.

"He was drunk, and on the way up he pulled a gun and pointed it at me," Scott said. "I thought he was going to shoot me for sure. When that elevator stopped, I got off and ran to my room. I was never so scared in my life."[4]

Brunet was a hired gun for the Angels longer than any team in the Big Show, perhaps because the team's owner was Gene Autry, a singing cowboy in the movies. In four full seasons and parts of two others, George notched 54 victories in his belt. He took more than his share of bullets, losing eight games by the score of 1–0, and twice leading the American League in defeats (19 in 1967, and 17 in 1968).

With the Angels, Brunet went from wearing a black hat to a white one. The transformation lifted Jim Murray, the award-winning sports columnist for the *Los Angeles Times*, to lofty literary heights.

"He was the most unwanted player in the history of baseball," Murray wrote.

> General managers shopped him around like he was an unadoptable child with polka dots for skin. Every time a doorbell rang, there would be George Brunet in a basket on a front stoop.
>
> Every time there was a song to be sung, a beer to be opened, a card game to be turned over, or a town to be closed up or a fight to be started, George was your man. Have temper, will travel.[5]

Brunet traveled to Seattle when the Angels sang "Happy Trails" to him two-thirds of the way through the 1969 season. On hearing the news, Seattle Pilots pitcher Jim Bouton said, "He'll fit right in on this ballclub. He's crazy."[6]

George Brunet started the season opener for the California Angels in 1967, prompting a *Los Angeles Times* sportswriter to comment on his 15-year journey up to that point: "Name a town, name a bush, George has been there." In four full seasons and parts of two others, Brunet won 54 games for the Angels but twice topped the American League in losses—19 in 1967, and 17 in 1968. He ended up pitching 32 consecutive years and piling up a record 3,175 strikeouts in the minors. *Los Angeles Times* Photographic Archive, Library Special Collections, Charles E. Young Research Library, UCLA.

Not surprisingly, George was featured in *Ball Four*, the tell-all book by Bouton that was published the next year and instantly became a best seller.

"George, I got to know something," Bouton said as he watched him getting dressed in the locker room. "This is not a knock. I don't mind guys who do things differently. But I got to know. Did you forget to put on your undershorts?"

"No, I never wear undershorts," Brunet replied. "Hell, the only time you need them is if you get into a car wreck. Besides, this way I don't have to worry about losing them."[7]

Brunet's fastball could tie knots in the underwear of opposing hitters, but he had trouble getting it over the plate early in his career.

"George Brunet calmed down somewhere between Shelby, Alexandria, Hot Springs, Abilene, Crowley, Buffalo, Little Rock, Columbia, Vancouver, Hawaii—or winter ball," Murray wrote in 1965.[8]

When Brunet arrived in Crowley, three weeks shy of his 21st birthday, he was close to getting a one-way ticket home to Houghton in Michigan's

Upper Peninsula. All he had to show for three-plus seasons in baseball's bushes was a 21–28 record and 6.22 earned run average, and he had walked nearly as many batters as he whiffed—287 to 303.

George turned things around in Crowley with a 7–2 mark and 2.17 ERA. He tossed three straight shutouts while striking out 114 and walking only 44 in 87 innings.

"He's major leaguer!" Crowley Millers catcher-manager Vince Plumbo scribbled in a notebook after Brunet hurled a no-hitter.

On signing a two-year working agreement with the Millers, the Kansas City Athletics filled the roster with first- and second-year players, mostly age 23 and younger.

A native of St. Paul, Minnesota, and a graduate of St. John's University in Minnesota, the 32-year-old Plumbo had 12 years of catching experience in the minors. The previous season at Burlington, Vermont, in the Provincial League, he was named manager of the year and lauded by a local sportswriter as a "great teacher of young players and a marvel at handling pitchers."

He also had a reputation for being "plenty rough on the field and especially rough on the umpires," leading the league in getting kicked out of games.[9]

Plumbo kept a daily log that included the box score for each game, the Evangeline League standings for that particular day, and terse assessments of the game and performance of his players.

After Plumbo was booted from the first game of a doubleheader and the team's other catcher, Walt Laurie, thumbed out of the second, he vented, "The hell with umpires." The second game was played under protest, and the Millers won because of a league rule prohibiting all of a team's catchers from being ejected.

"What a laugh, those umps," Plumbo griped two days later.

"He had a bad temper," said Laurie, who left the Millers at the end of the season to become a policeman in New York City. "If any girls came out to look at us practice, he used to scream, 'I know who you are! You're with Laurie! You're with this guy! You're with that guy! Get out of here!' Oh, he was a wild man. He was wacko!"

Brunet appeared in 11 games for the Millers, and Plumbo's comments provide insight on his meteoric rise from Class C to the majors in 1956.

The Millers lost Brunet's first game, falling into seventh place with a 12–20 record, 12½ games out of first. In eight innings, he allowed five earned runs and 11 hits, and walked four and struck out three. "Brunet like the rest of my pitchers," Plumbo lamented. "Worked always behind hitter."

The day before Brunet's second game, Plumbo penned, "Pitching is in bad shape. No starter or no relief men in farm."

Brunet again lasted eight innings, giving up three runs on as many hits, walking eight, and striking out three. He did not get a decision. Plumbo called one of the hits a bleeder. "Brunet looks as though he may come around. He can really throw. Behind hitter constantly. Very wild . . . must practice follow-through and smooth delivery. OK if he does."

In his third outing, Brunet went the distance to beat his former team, the Alexandria Aces, 2–1, on a six-hitter. He whiffed 14 and walked only two. "Brunet saved game in ninth by backing up third base on throw from outfield," Plumbo wrote.

He gave Brunet's fastball, curve, and changeup number-one ratings, adding, "Following through with smooth delivery big reason for control and stuff."

Plumbo couldn't believe the Millers were in fifth place. "I don't know how," he wrote.

His comments on Brunet's next game, won by the Millers, were equally blunt. "Brunet wild as hell—walked three men in first. Wasn't following through. All mixed up in mind."

Three straight walks in the first led to two runs and two free passes in the second to another tally, and an early exit for Brunet. "Must learn to steady self . . . not get mad at self," Plumbo concluded.

The wilder Brunet got, the madder he became.

"I guarantee you he threw a hundred miles an hour," Laurie said. "But he was wild and a little flippy. He used to bang around the bats and jump up and down."

"Will you stop for Christ's sake?" Plumbo pleaded.

Laurie knew a little about being a human backstop for bullet-firing lefties still learning to shoot straight.

Walt's father, Milton, a longtime sandlot manager in Brooklyn, discovered the great Sandy Koufax and persuaded him to join his club, the Parkviews, in the Coney Island Sports League.

"We were high school kids playing married men with kids," said Walt, the team's catcher. "Everybody got pissed off because they couldn't beat us."

Koufax was unhittable.

"Matter of fact, the first game we played, only one guy hit the ball in the infield," Walt said. "They were afraid to get up against him because he was throwing the ball so hard. They didn't want any part of him."

At one point the home plate umpire said, "Walter, you better catch that gawd-damn ball or I'm going to the hospital."

Walt was Koufax's personal catcher at tryouts with big-league clubs. "Koufax had a ball that rose on you," he said. "He threw a lot of wild balls, and he was so fast, you couldn't get over and block them sometimes. But when he was on, it was easy. Nobody could hit him."

Brunet also had Walt scrambling behind the plate, trying to corral his errant pitches. "Brunet was fast and everything," Walt said, "but he wasn't anything like Koufax. You could get wood on the ball against Brunet."

This wasn't much consolation to Evangeline League hitters.

New Iberia withdrew from the league in late May, leaving scheduled game dates open for the seven remaining teams to practice. Plumbo used this time to work with Brunet on throwing strikes and improving such fundamentals as pickoff moves and fielding bunts and grounders hit back at him.

Sports Illustrated revealed in 1980 that Brunet didn't wear anything under his uniform pants, making him the "greatest pitcher in baseball history never to wear a jockstrap and cup."

Brunet said he "felt more comfortable that way" but acknowledged "getting out of the way of ground balls up the middle has cost me a few singles over the years."[10]

The best defense against a hot grounder up the middle is to strike out as many batters as possible. That's what Brunet did his second and last month with the Millers.

He struck out 11 batters in his fifth appearance for Crowley, giving up two runs and seven hits, and walking seven in 8⅓ innings. "Brunet in first walked first two men . . . got out of it," Plumbo noted. "Didn't have his stuff but still great."

Plumbo summed up Brunet's 12-stikeout, one-hit shutout against Baton Rouge by writing, "Brunet had a damn good game. One scratch hit.

Ahead of every hitter. Had a smooth delivery with great follow-through. Didn't hit a hard ball off of him ever. Should have been a no-hitter."

Brunet followed up with a three-hit shutout, whiffing 14 and walking two. "Brunet looks like he's on his way," Plumbo commented, praising Brunet's fastball, while criticizing his curveball. "Really humming hard. Curve has been off the last couple of games—no break and no control."

Plumbo found things for Brunet to improve even when he no-hit Alexandria for his third straight shutout. He fanned 15 and walked three, one runner reaching third on a failed pickoff attempt. "Was just great," Plumbo raved. "He's major leaguer!"

The manager also pointed out Brunet's "display of temper when he gets wild," adding, "Let's up to get it over—even after reminded not to."

The Millers nipped Lafayette, 4–3, to give Brunet his sixth consecutive victory, even though he "didn't have his usually good stuff." He struck out 12 but allowed all 3 runs, 13 hits, and 4 walks. According to Plumbo, "Brunet seemed to tire late in game. Curve was short but fairly fast. He's gotta learn not to let up when he gets panicky."

Brunet made it seven wins in a row with a five-hitter to beat Monroe, 4–2, striking out 12 and walking four. "Since no-hitter he has been getting worse. Not following through. Gets angry when he gets wild and also let's up to get it over."

Four days later Plumbo jotted in his notebook, "Jamison and I had battle."

M. L. Jamison, a Crowley attorney, was the team's president in 1956. The A's wanted to send Brunet to their Class A farm club in Columbia, South Carolina, in exchange for three players from their Class B affiliate in Abilene. Jamison wouldn't agree to the deal unless the trio was made available to the Millers immediately.

Plumbo won the battle, as Brunet made his final appearance for the Millers the following day. "Brunet Farewell," he wrote, underlining the words. "Struck out 17—all hits and runs came in seventh."

Brunet whiffed 15 of the first 20 batters, and, then, in the seventh inning, he allowed four runs on a walk, double, bunt single, and home run. He added two more strikeouts in the eighth before the game was suspended because of a curfew rule and completed at a later date. Brunet was charged with what a local columnist described as "one of the toughest losses a hurler could possibly take."[11]

Brunet left Crowley with a sparkling record on the field unsullied by anything he did at Ed's Lounge, a popular hangout for eating late-night snacks, drinking beer, and doing the polka. No one yelled, "He's one of the Dalton Boys. Hide the beer."[12]

That eventually happened in the big leagues. But first there was Columbia.

Brunet wasn't too shabby in his 10 games there, striking out 59 batters in 56 innings and posting a decent ERA of 3.86. Unfortunately, he issued 54 walks, nearly one per inning, and didn't win any of his six decisions.

"If you're in the second division, you may as well lose with kids," sighed Kansas City manager Lou Boudreau. "One day they will pay off for you."[13]

The A's were at the bottom of the American League standings when Brunet joined them for the last month of the season.

In his first game, against the Washington Senators, he faced four batters, walking one and getting the other three out.

Boudreau was impressed enough to call on Brunet to protect a two-run lead with the bases loaded and no one out in the eighth inning of a game against the Boston Red Sox. Up to the plate stepped Ted Williams, "The Splendid Splinter."

Williams took a called strike, then hit a sharp grounder to Vic Power near the second-base bag for what should've been a double play. Instead, he juggled the ball and got only one out, allowing a run to score.

The next hitter was Mickey Vernon, two-time American League batting champ. On the second pitch, Vernon popped out.

"The kid had thrown four pitched balls to two of the best hitters in baseball—Williams and Vernon, both old enough to be his father—and he should have been out of the inning," Roger Birtwell reported in the *Boston Globe*. "But, thanks to Power's juggle, the kid still had one out to go."[14]

Brunet didn't get that last out, leaving the game after Jackie Jensen ripped a score-tying single. The A's went on to win in the bottom of the ninth. "Well, you got to hand it to Georgie," Birtwell wrote. "He did all right."[15]

The next day, Williams told Brunet, "Kid, if you keep that fastball down, you've got a long career ahead of you."[16]

Williams was right, but he had no idea how long.

In the late 1950s, the A's filled their roster with young, unproven players, hoping they could make the future much brighter than their recent past—three last-place clubs, each with 100-plus losses since 1950. "It's the only way a club as bad as this one was—and still is—can operate," Boudreau admitted. [17]

Brunet was the most promising of the bunch, and that included promises to lose weight and stay out of trouble.

At Little Rock in 1957, he won 14 games and paced the Southern Association in strikeouts, with 235. He reported to spring training in 1958, weighing 194 pounds, 21 less than the 215 he bulked up to at Little Rock.

"I've been laying off stuff like beer and sweets," the 6-foot-1 Brunet said. "I want to make the club in the worst way this season, and I know I can pitch better if my weight is down around 200." [18]

Near the end of training camp, the A's shuffled the slimmed-down Brunet to Buffalo in the Class AAA International League. "His failure to make the Kansas City staff was a severe blow to the big youngster," Joe McGuff wrote in the *Kansas City Times*. [19]

A's pitching coach "Spud" Chandler, a two-time 20-game winner with the New York Yankees in the 1940s, pulled a despondent Brunet aside for a pep talk.

"I want you to go over there and give it your best," Chandler said.

"I will," Brunet replied.

"I want you to go over there and be a leader, not a follower," Chandler continued. "I know this is rough. I've gone through it."

Chandler sounded like Plumbo when he told Brunet not to "take something off the ball to get it over" the plate. "Reach back and throw your good fastball. Sure, you'll walk a few batters once in a while, but you'll strike out a few, too. You've got the good arm. Don't waste it."

He closed with some fatherly advice. "Take good care of yourself, and don't let anyone lead you into bad habits."

"I won't," Brunet said. "I'm going to be back in a couple of months." [20]

He returned the following spring but wasn't around long. After a night of carousing, he was found directing traffic around 3 o'clock in front of the team's hotel in West Palm Beach, Florida. Passengers inside one of the cars he stopped just so happened to be the A's general manager and field manager.

"Some people are secret drinkers," Jim Murray mused. "George was a secret teetotaler."[21]

From Kansas City, Brunet roamed through the majors, making stops in Milwaukee, Houston, Baltimore, Los Angeles/Anaheim, Seattle, Washington, DC, Pittsburgh, and St. Louis. Sprinkled into this mix were minor-league gigs in Portland, Louisville, Vancouver, Hawaii, Oklahoma City, Rochester, and Eugene.

"The longest he's ever been on the wagon is nine innings," one manager complained.[22]

Brunet was running out of places to pitch in the United States, so he headed to Poza Rica, Mexico, in 1973. It was a perfect match. Poza Rica was off the grid, and except for the nickname, Santa Claus, Brunet didn't have to put up with constant wisecracks about his eating and drinking habits.

He pitched five full seasons for Poza Rica, longer than anywhere else, and then went wherever his left arm took him in the Mexican League— Coatzacoalcos, Mexico City, Veracruz, Saltillo, and Monterrey.

Brunet's pro baseball career spanned seven U.S. presidencies—from President Dwight D. Eisenhower through the first term of President Ronald Reagan.

Babies born in 1953, Brunet's first year as a pro, were old enough to be U.S. senators by the time he retired.

There were 16 big-league teams when Brunet started his career and 26 when he stopped.

What's most amazing is that he was always a fireballing starter, not a knuckleballing relief pitcher.

Brunet didn't begin his pro career in Crowley, but his performance there catapulted him into the majors. He was the first Miller to get that far.

In the twentieth anniversary edition of *Ball Four*, published in 1990, Bouton listed the whereabouts of Brunet and others mentioned in his book. Unaware his Seattle teammate retired in 1984, Bouton wrote, "Best report is that he could still be pitching in the Mexican League at age 54."[23]

When Brunet died in 1991, of a heart attack, in his adopted hometown of Poza Rica, his left arm should've been preserved and put on display at either Cooperstown or Salón de La Fama in Monterrey. After all, he was a lefty for the ages.

13

ALMOST ARMAGEDDON

Mix politics and football, and you've got what the 1956 Sugar Bowl became—a political football.

The segregation laws that shadowed the annual college football classic also dogged the beginning of the 1956 Evangeline League season, eventually forcing five talented black players out of the circuit and leaving it bruised and shaken like a prizefighter about to go down for the 10 count.

Smack dab in the middle of the Sugar Bowl maelstrom was Bobby Grier of the University of Pittsburgh, a 6-foot-1, 200-pound second-string fullback and defensive back. Grier was different from his teammates and the entire Georgia Tech team Pitt was scheduled to play on January 2, 1956, at Tulane Stadium in New Orleans. He was black. No one with black skin had ever played in a Sugar Bowl game since it was established in 1935.

Georgia Tech was a member of the Southeastern Conference (SEC) at the time, and it would be another 11 years before Nate Northington of Kentucky would become the SEC's first black football player.

Sugar Bowl officials didn't intend to break any color barriers when they picked Pittsburgh. They were poised to invite the snow-white University of West Virginia Mountaineers, undefeated and rated sixth in the country, going into their annual "Backyard Brawl" against archrival Pitt, thrice beaten and ranked 17th. The Mountaineers were a three-point favorite.

One of the two Sugar Bowl representatives at the game asked the other early on, "By the way, which one of these teams did we come to scout? I'm beginning to think we're looking at the wrong team."[1]

With an injured Grier on the sidelines, Pittsburgh won in a rout, 26–7, and just before Thanksgiving weekend the team was tabbed to play in the Sugar Bowl. Georgia Tech was selected a few days later, triggering a telegram of protest to Tech coach Bobby Dodd from the States Rights Council Executive Committee, a staunch segregationist group made up of some of Georgia's most powerful business leaders.

Dodd was urged not to play Pitt, "preventing any breakdown of our laws, customs, and traditions of racial segregation."[2]

Marvin Griffin was elected governor of Georgia in 1954, the same year the U.S. Supreme Court ruled segregation of public schools was unconstitutional. He blasted the decision, vowing, "The races will not be mixed come hell or high water."[3]

Governor Griffin sent a telegram of his own to the chairman of the state's University Board of Regents, requesting that no Georgia school be permitted to play "other teams where races are mixed" or where spectators are not segregated.

"The South stands at Armageddon," Governor Griffin proclaimed.

> The battle is joined. We cannot make the slightest concession to the enemy in this dark and lamentable hour of struggle.
>
> There is no difference in compromising integrity of race on the playing field than in doing so in the classrooms. One break in the dike and the relentless seas will rush in and destroy us. We are in this fight 100 percent. Not 98 percent. Not 75 percent, not 64 percent—but a full 100 percent.[4]

Reaction was swift and angry.

A member of the Board of Regents labeled the governor's stand as "ridiculous and asinine."[5]

Approximately 2,000 Georgia Tech students gathered on campus to protest. They hung the governor in effigy four times before marching one mile to a major intersection in downtown Atlanta and hanging him again. The march continued to the state capitol, protestors breaking windows and uprooting parking meters on their way. They staged a sixth hanging. Finally, the students headed to the nearby governor's mansion, "guarded

Bobby Grier of the University of Pittsburgh was the center of attention before, during, and after he broke the color barrier at the 1956 Sugar Bowl. Georgia governor Marvin Griffin, a staunch segregationist, threatened to block Georgia Tech from playing in the game, provoking Tech students to hang and burn the governor in effigy, and Grier's Pitt teammates to give him a thumbs down. Gathered around Grier, left to right, are end Bob Kiesel, guard Nick Carr, and tackles Jim McCuskar and Don Agafon. Bettmann via Getty Images.

by a phalanx of police, state troopers, and Georgia Bureau of Investigation agents."[6]

As shouts of, "Turn him loose!" rang outside the mansion, the governor paced the floor inside, repeatedly telling his wife that a "man who believes in a principle doesn't change his position because of a demonstration."[7]

The protest ended around 3:30 in the morning, just in time for the governor to leave for a weekend of quail hunting. He remained defiant: "In Rome, do as the Romans do. If we played in the North, we would play under Northern rules. Although Louisiana is not Georgia, we should play under Southern rules."[8]

Governor Griffin's hard-line stand united opposition as diverse as students at the University of Georgia, Tech's hated archrival, to the *Augusta Chronicle*, a prosegregationist newspaper.

About 1,500 Georgia students rallied in downtown Athens, waving a huge banner reading, "One Time We Are for Tech."[9]

The *Chronicle* used an editorial to give the governor an old-time tongue-lashing that called it a "shame" he "has seen fit to strain at gnats . . . and bring ignominy upon the state." His action was "petty, picayunish" and "stultifying the reputation of our two great state universities whose football teams have brought fame, glory, and prestige to Georgia."[10]

The regents voted 13–1 to allow Georgia Tech to play in the Sugar Bowl, while passing a resolution praising Governor Griffin "for his courageous stand in upholding his oath as governor and for his inspiring leadership in protecting inviolate the sacred institutions of our people."[11]

A conversation between two of the regents exposed what they really thought.

"The Negroes are determined to break segregation in the fields of sports and entertainment first," one claimed.

"Don't you think the absurdity of this (Griffin's move) has hurt segregation?" he was asked.

"No," the regent replied, "it's the finest thing that ever happened to this state."[12]

The Sugar Bowl game had its own controversy, and, again, Grier was in the middle.

Playing defensive back, he was flagged on a questionable pass interference call in the first quarter that advanced the ball from the 32-yard line to the one, setting up Tech's only touchdown in a 7–0 victory.

Grier topped all rushers by gaining 51 yards on six carries, but afterward all of the attention was focused on the penalty, which he insisted "should have been called" on the intended receiver, Don Ellis. "He pushed me from behind," Grier said. "That's why I fell forward."[13]

There were no video replays, so the call was hotly debated.

"The majority of Pittsburghers present thought the official erred in dropping the handkerchief on this one," reported Al Abrams, sports editor of the *Pittsburgh Post-Gazette*. "Most of the neutral observers about me in the press box thought they saw definite interference. This one is for the movies to decide—if the films can."[14]

Observers at a private screening of the official game film in New Orleans a month later reviewed the disputed play "25 times in both slow motion and natural speed," and "it showed clearly that Grier did not make bodily contact with Ellis in the end zone," where the penalty was supposed to have occurred. The film also revealed the pass was too high for Ellis to catch inside the playing field. [15]

At the beginning of the Sugar Bowl fireworks, Furman Bisher, *Atlanta Constitution* sports editor, found it ironic that the telegram to Bobby Dodd, asking him not to play the game, was sent from Augusta on the same day Horace Garner, a black outfielder, was purchased by the city's baseball team in the South Atlantic (Sally) League. "And whatever became of Nat Peeples?" Bisher teased. [16]

A fan from Rochester, New York, asked the same question in a letter to the *Constitution* in May 1954, soon after the Atlanta Crackers' Peeples became the first and only black to play in the Southern Association. "I often wonder what happened to Nat Peeples? Has the Atlanta manager sold him, or why doesn't he ever appear in the Atlanta lineup lately?" [17]

In spring exhibition games, Peeples accounted for six of the club's 14 homers, knocked in 13 runs, and hit .348.

"I can't pass over a boy who has the kind of spring Nat has had," raved Crackers manager Whitlow Wyatt. "Right now he's been the best outfielder and has impressed me with his speed, arm, and power." [18]

Peeples batted only five times and, then, 10 days into the season, was relegated to Jacksonville in the Class A Sally League.

Bisher defended Mann against charges that he caved to pressure from other club owners.

"Mann refused some time ago to be swayed by opinion around the Southern," he wrote, maintaining Peeples "got a full trial" and "was sent out because he wasn't ready for Double A." [19]

That was far from the case.

Mann was warned by the league president that integration wasn't going to work in the Southern Association. "Ain't nobody tried it but you," Mann was told. "It ain't gonna work like that. There have to be two, three, or four teams to try this. No one else wants to try." [20]

In turn, Mann said to Peeples, "It ain't the right time. They're just not ready yet. . . . We'll have to wait awhile." [21]

The 29-year-old Peeples played four more years but never made it back to Atlanta.

"They didn't try to bring in any other black players after me," he said. "Those teams told Earl Mann not to bother."[22]

What happened to Peeples would be repeated two years later in the Evangeline, leaving the league on the brink of Armageddon.

No one saw it coming.

The league's color barrier was broken in 1954, by Texas City infielders Tony Taylor and Julio Bonilla, and pitcher Pete Naranjo. In two games each at New Iberia and Lafayette, Texas City attracted 8,639 fans, 3,000 of them black.

"No law against it . . . just 'unwritten law,'" the black-owned *Pittsburgh Courier* reported after the first contest. "Game drew capacity crowd. No incidents!"[23]

The same year, Crowley elected two black aldermen, the first Louisiana city to do so.

Five of the league's eight clubs had working agreements with major-league teams that stipulated they use black players assigned to them. Crowley was connected to the Kansas City Athletics, Lake Charles to the New York Giants, Lafayette to the Chicago Cubs, Monroe to the New York Yankees, and Thibodaux to the Washington Senators.

There was cause for optimism despite minor leagues folding like accordions across the country.

The boss of the minors, George Trautman, was encouraged by only a 2 percent drop in attendance, the smallest in five years. "Maybe we have turned the corner and will be on our way up soon," he said.[24]

"The minor leagues that can keep on going will be the salvation of baseball," predicted Harry Strohm, president of the Alexandria Aces. "The time will come when the majors will say: 'Forget the Blue Mountain League. The Evangeline League is solid. Send players there, and you won't have to worry about getting them back in mid-season because the league has folded.'"[25]

Truman Stacey, a sports columnist for the *Lake Charles American Press*, made another forecast: "The Evangeline League will be younger, faster, and more spirited than any other time during the postwar session. In fact, to some of the old-timers, it might even show some similarity to the Evangeline League of the late 1930s, that sent so many players to the majors."[26]

Stacey was right, as the '56 season produced a dozen big-leaguers, the most since 1939. Graduates included pitcher George Brunet and infielder

Chet Boak of Crowley; Jack Baldschun of Thibodaux, a star reliever for the Philadelphia Phillies in the early 1960s; and infielder Chuck Cottier of Baton Rouge, a defensive whiz primarily for the Washington Senators.

The best of them all was Lake Charles outfielder Felipe Alou, who went on to play 17 years in the majors, posting a career batting average of .286 and slugging 206 home runs.

Alou was one of five blacks to begin the '56 season in the league. The others were Lake Charles teammates Chuck Weatherspoon and Ralph Crosby, and Lafayette's Sammy Drake and Manuel Trabous.

The Cubs inked Ernie Banks's brother, Benjamin, to a contract in early 1956, and assigned him to Lafayette, but he never played for the Oilers.

Lafayette was the Cubs' minor-league training center.

Sam Brown, a black all-America tailback and baseball star at UCLA, was sent there by the Los Angeles Angels, a Cubs farm team in the Pacific Coast League (PCL). It was a culture shock for the Californian.

"You just had to watch what you were doing," he said of his two weeks in Lafayette. "As far as I was concerned, they weren't a friendly bunch of people at all."

Alou grew up in the Dominican Republic. He'd heard about racism in America's Deep South, but he had never experienced the black-and-white rules of segregation: sitting in the back of a bus and a designated section of the ballpark or using different water fountains and bathrooms than white folks.

In Lake Charles, the local newspaper Americanized Felipe to "Phil," and he came face-to-face with racism. [27]

"For the first time," Felipe wrote in his autobiography, "I started to hear words like 'monkey,' 'nigger,' and 'black son of a bitch,' all in that lilting Louisiana accent—a syrupy drawl, the sound and cadence of which have never left my ear." [28]

The Sugar Bowl left segregationists in a sour mood, hell-bent on keeping the races separate at future sporting events.

"We're going to use Negro players," a Lafayette Oilers spokesman promised on the eve of the season opener. "That is final. If we don't use them, we lose our working agreement. Our decision is final, and it won't change regardless of what happens." [29]

"There is no future for the Evangeline League or any other lower minor league without major-league backing," Stacey wrote in his

American Press column. "In the final analysis, the league may someday have to decide between accepting the Negro players or disappearing from baseball."[30]

A showdown loomed ahead at Baton Rouge's city-owned ballpark, which prohibited interracial games. The ban was adopted immediately after the Sugar Bowl, a city official announcing, "We want it known in advance so that no team will have a key Negro player and be hamstrung when he can't play here."[31]

The hometown Rebels had three choices: forfeit games against integrated teams, play the games elsewhere, or withdraw from the league.

"To attempt such a ban by subterfuge is attempting to hold back the clock, which has not been very profitable in the South since 1861," Stacey pointed out.[32]

By the time the new rule was tested, the Lake Charles Giants were missing Weatherspoon, diagnosed with a broken leg after cracking a three-run, pinch-hit homer to beat Crowley in the third game of the season.

The Giants' first game at Baton Rouge resulted in a stopgap compromise that eased tensions and satisfied the 919 fans in the stands. The Giants offered to sit Alou and Crosby in exchange for the Rebels benching their own center fielder and shortstop. The Rebels got the best of the deal, 7–4.

"They put us in the bleachers with the black fans," Alou recalled. "I'll never forget—the bleachers for blacks was in left field. We had to take our uniforms off and go outside the stadium and come in, like we were fans."[33]

Crosby, a 21-year-old from New York City's Harlem district, was in the lineup for the next game. Baton Rouge players remained in the dugout as the public address announcer informed some 600 jeering fans that the game was being called off. "Segregation 'Postpones' Reb–Giants Tilt," blared a banner headline in the *Morning Advocate.*[34]

Lake Charles was ruled the winner by forfeit.

The Rebels' next two games against the Oilers and their two blacks, Drake of Little Rock, Arkansas, and Trabous, a catcher from Puerto Rico, were moved from Baton Rouge to Lafayette. Rain postponed one game, and in the other, the speedy Drake put on a show, slashing three singles and a double in four at-bats, scoring three runs, batting in another, and turning in a nifty double play at second base. The Oilers romped, 12–3.

The *Morning Advocate* had seen enough to know the Rebels were fighting a losing battle.

"It is vain to expect that either the minor-league or major-league organizations will go along with a ban on Negro players," the prosegregation newspaper concluded in an editorial. "The best that could be hoped for in a showdown would be dissolution of the entire league."[35]

In a game against the Crowley Millers at Lafayette, four state troopers and a deputy sheriff were called to the ballpark to handle a ruckus on the field, but it had nothing to do with the racial controversy.

Crowley manager Vince Plumbo got into a heated argument with the umpires concerning a base-runner interference ruling that nullified three Millers runs. The rhubarb lasted 21 minutes before the officers arrived and escorted Plumbo to the dugout.

"Plate umpire beat us on so-called interference play," Plumbo jotted in his notebook. "Bases loaded . . . three runs scored . . . that's the truth."

The truth is that what everyone was seeking after a meeting of representatives from the league's eight teams to solve the problem in Baton Rouge turned into a Saturday night massacre.

All five black players were transferred to other leagues—Drake and Trabous to Burlington, Iowa, in the Class B Three-I League; Alou to Cocoa, Florida, in the Class D Florida State League; and Crosby and Weatherspoon to Missoula, Montana, in the Class C Pioneer League.

Evangeline League president Ray "Moon" Mullins called the solution a "matter of good luck" and insisted the "segregation problem had nothing to do with the shift in Negro player personnel."[36]

Drake and Trabous "received promotions," Mullins explained, while Alou, Crosby, and Weatherspoon were demoted because "they weren't good enough."[37]

Drake had 20 hits in 59 at-bats for a .339 average, and Trabous was 5-for-38 (.132). Weatherspoon was 1-for-3 (.333); Alou 2-for-9 (.222); and Crosby 3-for-19 (.158).

The general manager at Lake Charles was Sam Tarleton, the former sportswriter. He claimed the Giants were replacing the three blacks with better players. "Felipe Alou is a rookie and is not ready to play Class C baseball yet," he insisted. "There's no agreement between this club and the league to keep Negro players off the Lake Charles roster. If we ever get a Negro player who is good enough to make our regular lineup, he'll play."[38]

A New York Giants executive had a different explanation for why the players were dumped. A resolution that would allow the league to oust any club considered "undesirable" was passed by directors, Lake Charles and Lafayette the only dissenting votes. The teams were forced to get rid of their black players or face expulsion.[39]

No black players meant no black fans.

Attendance at Lake Charles games, which averaged about 400 before the departure of Alou and company, plunged to less than a dozen for one game.

"You may have these," one black fan said in returning his season tickets to the Giants. "I'll have no further use for them. . . . You let yourself down when you bowed to racial discrimination."[40]

Exactly two weeks after the league barred black players, the New Iberia club disbanded on what was supposed to be "Save Baseball" night, with free admission to the game. The team blamed a "mere trickling of fans averaging about 400 a game," noting, "it takes at least 1,000 to break even."[41]

The league was down to seven teams, and by July, the Baton Rouge Rebels were floundering financially and facing expulsion under the "undesirable" rule they ramrodded into the league constitution. The team cited the "loss of Negro fans" as one of the reasons they were drawing crowds of only 400 per game and losing money.[42]

Baton Rouge managed to hang on until the end of the season. So did Thibodaux despite a fire that destroyed a wooden grandstand and forced the Senators to play several home games nearly 80 miles away in New Iberia.

The ultimate test of fan interest in Crowley was "Car Night," when overflow crowds typically crammed Miller Stadium, hoping to drive home in a new Chevrolet, Dodge, or Buick.

In 1952, a throng of 7,381, more than half the population of Crowley, showed up for one of the several car giveaways. An estimated 1,900 fans attended "Car Night" late in the 1956 season, proving baseball in Crowley wasn't dead yet.

The Millers did better on the field than they did at the gate, placing third, with a 63–60 record. Attendance was down 17 percent from the year before, to 37,265, fifth in what was mostly a seven-team league. Two first-round playoff games at Crowley attracted a combined 699 fans.

The league's playoff finals were cancelled because of lack of interest. Both the teams and the league were losing money, and the last playoff game between Lafayette and Lake Charles, where the clubs were forced to unload their black players, drew 599 fans.

"I don't know how the league can survive," lamented Harry Romero, president of pennant-winning Lafayette. [43]

The outlook for national sports in Louisiana was bleak.

In July 1956, Governor Earl Long signed into law a bill outlawing racially mixed athletic competition in Louisiana.

"In signing it, I'm going along with a majority that I've heard from," Governor Long said, noting comments he got were about "four to one in favor of it." [44]

One Pittsburgh sportswriter observed, "Hooded heads prevailed." [45]

The racial ban prevented Major League Baseball clubs from playing exhibition games in the state, and the Sugar Bowl could no longer invite integrated teams to its annual football classic or college basketball tournament.

Notre Dame, St. Louis, and Dayton immediately withdrew from the next tourney, and Pittsburgh issued a statement reiterating its policy of only going to bowl games where its players can "travel together, eat together, and live together." [46]

Drake went on to play briefly in the majors for the Cubs and New York Mets.

Alou was the only member of the Lake Charles Giants to reach the big leagues, breaking in with the San Francisco Giants in 1958. His brother, Matty, joined him in 1960, and Jesús in 1963, and that year, on September 15, they became the first and only all-brother outfield in major-league history. In 14 seasons as a manager for the Montreal Expos and Giants, Felipe's teams won 1,033 games—12 more than they lost. Felipe's son, Moisés, continued the family tradition by playing 17 years in the majors and compiling a lifetime batting average of .303, with 332 home runs.

Exiled from the Evangeline League, Weatherspoon was embraced in Missoula, Montana, by Jack McKeon. If "Spoony," as he was called, had been a little younger or McKeon had started managing in the majors sooner, they might've been in the Big Show together.

"Every place I went, I took him because he was such an advantage of positives," McKeon said. "Of all the years I managed, of all the games I played, Spoony was right at the top of the list of my favorite guys."

That's saying a lot, because McKeon managed 15 years in the minors and 16 more in the big leagues.

"If we'd had the designated hitter (DH) in those days, he could've played in the big leagues," McKeon said.

The American League adopted the DH rule in 1973, the same year McKeon took the helm for the Kansas City Royals. Weatherspoon quit baseball in 1968, at the age of 38.

For eight years, 1956 to 1964, McKeon and Spoony had their own show. They shadowed one another from Missoula to Fox Cities, Wisconsin, to Wilson, North Carolina, to Vancouver, British Columbia, to Dallas–Fort Worth, to Atlanta. Spoony caught and played some at first base and third base, and in the outfield, wherever McKeon needed him.

McKeon called the shots and Spoony hit 'em. He knocked 35 out of the park at Missoula in 1958, to lead the Pioneer League, and 31 at Wilson in 1961, to top the Carolina League. Seven of his homers in '61 were grand slams and two of them in successive at-bats. Altogether, Spoony had 216 dingers in the minors, 151 of them for McKeon-guided clubs.

"Why do you think I carried him wherever I went?" McKeon joked. "He was beloved, and the big thing about him was guys could pull pranks on him. And I did, too."

The day before McKeon's Atlanta Crackers opened the 1964 season, they played an exhibition game at the federal penitentiary in Atlanta.

A 6-foot-2, 200-pounder with the chiseled look of a bodybuilder, Weatherspoon maintained he was two or three years younger than he was listed in souvenir game programs.

"We're at the prison in our uniforms," Jack recalled.

> The prisoners are in their cells, and they're hollering. I run over to one of the cells and said to the three guys in there, "Look, I got a guy coming in here from Pineland, Texas. His name is Chuck Weatherspoon. I'm going to call him over here, and you're going to tell him you went to school with him. And, then, I'm going to ask you guys how old he is."

"Spoony!" McKeon called out as soon as he appeared.

"Hey, Spoony!" the prisoners hollered.

"Come here, Spoony, you got some buddies over here," McKeon said. "These guys know you."

"I don't know them," Spoony replied.

"You guys went to school with him, right?" McKeon said.

"Yeah."

"How old is Spoony?"

Weatherspoon claimed he was 28.

"Let's see," one of the prisoners said, "he's got to be 31 or something."

Weatherspoon homered and doubled twice against the Feds.

On leaving the prison, McKeon was walking ahead of Weatherspoon as they approached security and the gate. They were still in their uniforms.

"When this guy comes in, grab his ass and throw him into one of these cells," McKeon said to a guard.

He looked on as the guard grabbed Weatherspoon and said, "Where did you get that uniform?"

"Skip!" Spoony yelled. "Skip!"

"I don't know him," McKeon said. "I don't know him."

McKeon laughed in telling the stories.

"How could you not win with a guy like that? He kept everybody loose. Everybody loved him, and he loved everybody."

That's the real shame of what happened in the Evangeline League in 1956. Fans barely got a glimpse of Spoony and the other black players. Maybe if they'd seen more of them, things would've turned out differently.

14

THE UNWANTED VISITOR NAMED AUDREY

The Evangeline League was a survivor.

Born during the Great Depression, the league regrouped after World War II forced a hiatus, survived a gambling scandal and racial ban, and stubbornly hung in there as television, air conditioning, and newly organized kids baseball leagues combined to keep people home or take them to watch their kids and grandkids play baseball instead of unknown professionals.

The drumbeat of doom continued in 1957, as the league was once again trying to find enough towns to field a team.

Crowley Daily Signal sports editor Dud Wilkins saw a ray of hope, writing, "They've managed it in the past, and they probably will again this year."[1]

Jim Wynn of the *Alexandria Town Talk* wasn't so sure, as the 1956 playoff finals had to be canceled because the players almost outnumbered the fans in the stands. "When the fans quit, it's usually time to throw in the sponge," Wynn concluded.[2]

New Iberia and Monroe were out of the picture, supporters in both Louisiana cities unable to stir up enough interest in a pro team.

Two other cities were on shaky ground. Thibodaux needed to rebuild the grandstand at its ballpark, which had burned up late in the '56 season, and Lake Charles was trying to rebound from the New York Giants ending their relationship because of the league's segregation policy.

Crowley, Lafayette, Alexandria, and Baton Rouge were good to go, as they had working agreements with clubs in the majors or higher minors. The Kansas City Athletics continued to send talent to Crowley, the Chicago Cubs to Lafayette, and the Cincinnati Reds and Atlanta Crackers to Baton Rouge. The New York Yankees replaced its previous partner, Monroe, with Alexandria.

Thirty-one days were sliced off the 1957 season schedule and the number of games reduced from 154 to 120. The season would end August 20, instead of early September, with the playoffs shortened by two games to a best-of-five series. The changes reflected the gloomy outlook for the minors shared by most baseball people.

George Trautman, president of the National Association of Professional Baseball Leagues, protested in a byline story for the wire service, United Press International: "It is high time that the people in baseball rerouted those storm clouds and begin to get a little sunshine into their thinking."[3]

He acknowledged many minor-league clubs had problems. "But we're scrappers. We're fighting back against the unfair competition of saturation radio broadcasting of major-league games into our territory," he declared. "We're battling to retrieve our 21-inch alumni, the living room fans who left our parks temporarily because of the lure of the ball games on the TV set."[4]

In 1957, the Evangeline League started with six teams and ended with four. What took place in between could only happen in a circuit called Pepper Pot.

An estimated 1,800 fans turned out for Crowley's home opener, leading the *Daily Signal* to observe that "while not the capacity crowd of past opening nights," it "showed that interest in Crowley Miller baseball is still high."[5]

After losing six of their first seven games, the Millers won seven straight. No one seemed to care, as attendance averaged around 500 fans per game.

"The present Crowley Miller club is without a doubt the best team fielded at this stage of the season for the past few years, and if the fire and hustle and just plain good baseball they display does not bring fans back to Miller Stadium, then baseball in Crowley is really dead," Wilkins observed in his *Daily Signal* column.[6]

Wilkins pointed out that the Millers were possibly the most talented of all Crowley teams, as they were young and well balanced, "without a 'weak sister' in the batting order."[7]

The best hitter on the team was Claude Horn, a 6-foot-2, 200-pound outfielder.

"Claude was the catfish," said Dan Pfister, the team's top pitcher. "He was a country 'Aw, shucks' kind of guy. He was strong, and man he could hit."

A line-drive hitter, Horn went on a .492 rampage (32 hits in 65 at-bats) in late May and wound up leading the league in hitting, with a .349 average.

Three other Millers ranked among the loop's top 10 hitters. Gordon Mackenzie, a 19-year-old third baseman, posted a .308 mark to place third, while outfielder Dave Gorrie and catcher Al Silvera were fifth and eighth, with averages of .289 and .286, respectively.

Three Millers pitchers won 13 games with earned run averages that were among the 10 lowest in the league—Leon Webrand, 13–6 and 3.70; Jack Fuller, 13–8 and 3.85; and Pfister, 13–6 and 4.04.

The Millers were in second place with a 32–23 record on June 20, when the league-leading Lafayette Oilers and Baton Rouge Rebels shut down operations, leaving the Evangeline with four teams.

Only 19 of the nearly 700 stockholders in the Lafayette Citizens Baseball Association showed up at the meeting to decide the team's fate. Directors voted 9–1 to quit. The parent Cubs refused to bail out the Oilers. The last game between the two dropouts was canceled.

"This is not the fault of the stockholders, or even the fans," one Oilers director said in a blunt assessment of the situation. "We are faced with a lack of public interest. We are not isolated. The same problem exists in Minor League Baseball all over the country. The public, of course, has no responsibility toward the game. It will exist if it is wanted or die where it is not wanted."[8]

The Evangeline League forged on with four teams.

Jerry Clifford arrived in Crowley the same day the new schedule was announced for the second half of the season.

The 22-year-old Clifford grew up in Northern California and was a standout catcher for San Jose State College, so he knew a lot more about earthquakes than hurricanes. He knew enough about lightning to do as he was told. "When I got to Crowley, the arm was not too good, so they decided to put me in left field. The first thing they did was give me a cap and said, 'Take the button out of the top.'"

That's how he heard about Crowley center fielder Andy Strong getting killed by lightning during a game at Alexandria in 1951. Combined with the metal spikes he was wearing, the button in Andy's cap made him a lightning rod.

Clifford experienced his first hurricane one week after joining the Millers.

"On the radio for days, they'd been talking about this hurricane that was out in the Gulf and headed our way," Clifford recalled. "Everybody said, 'Don't worry about it. Every year they turn and go towards Florida. Just don't worry about it.' So, we didn't worry about it."

"HURRICANE POISED OFF LOUISANA COAST," warned a banner headline on the front page of the *Daily Signal*.[9]

Named Audrey, the hurricane continued toward Crowley while the players boarded the team's old, red school bus to travel 80 miles north to Alexandria for a two-game series. Rain and high winds forced the second game to be canceled and hastened the Millers' return to Crowley.

"We had a few married guys on our team, so they wanted to get back to Crowley," Webrand explained.

"The experience of us getting home was incredible because we turned around and came back, and on the way back, the winds were blowing at tremendous speeds," Clifford said.

"We were right in the middle of the hurricane," Webrand added.

"I can remember seeing the wind blowing corrugated steel grain silos through the air like they were a frisbee," Clifford marveled. "The rain was really heavy."

The team took refuge at a restaurant/service station, the owner wisely keeping everyone away from the plate glass windows, which the wind smashed to bits and pieces.

"Everything that was on the shelves started flying," Horn said. "We got under the tables."

"We felt safer in the bus," Pfister said. "We said, 'Let's go!' and jumped in the bus and took off."

"There was a long line of cars following us because when we found a downed tree on the highway, we'd get out and move it," Webrand said.

The Crowley Millers and their red school bus weathered Hurricane Audrey in late June 1957, safely transporting the team back to Crowley from Alexandria, Louisiana, a distance of 81 miles. When the team encountered trees blocking the highway, players hopped out and moved them. Some trees wouldn't budge so the bus and the passenger vehicles following it had to turn around. "It took about three different tries to find the right road home," recalled pitcher Leon Webrand. Photo courtesy of Steve Holleman.

"Twenty guys jumped out, grabbed the tree, and pulled it off the road," Pfister noted. "All the people were honking horns and cheering. We'd go another few miles and find another tree, and we'd pull it off."

They eventually came to some trees that were too big to move.

"So we had to take a different highway and had a different group of people following us," Webrand said.

At one point the bus stopped so the players could help people get out of a car that was upside down in a water-filled ditch.

"The first guy out of the bus didn't know how to swim," Pfister said. "So the rest of us jumped in the water to pull out our teammate and the other people at the same time."

"We got back to Crowley and the bus stopped where there used to be a ballpark," Clifford continued.

"It took eight hours to go a hundred miles or whatever it was," Webrand said. "It was terrible."

Clifford walked home through water about four feet deep, up to his chest. "I remember worrying about the snakes," he recalled.

"It was scary," Webrand admitted.

Ed Keim, the Millers' longtime radio play-by-play announcer, was home when Hurricane Audrey hit Crowley.

"My wife and I lived in a rental house that wasn't too high off the ground," Keim began. "The water came over the front porch and into the house. And it was going on up. We decided to go to the courthouse. At least it will be dry. We got out of the house and into my Hudson to drive there. But the thing wouldn't start."

Eight inches of rain and winds as fast as 100 miles per hour forced hundreds of Crowley families out of their homes and into public buildings. Winds busted out the windows at one shelter, a gymnasium.

As the rain poured down, Keim led his wife and two children to the courthouse, about four blocks away. A doctor who lived in a house on a hill saw their plight and hollered for them to come inside. "They took us in and put us up," Keim said.

Hurricane Audrey ripped through the fishing village of Cameron, 64 miles from Crowley by air, pushing a 25-foot wall of water inland through the bayous and leaving a 100-mile trail of devastation and approximately 425 people dead, the majority in Cameron Parish.

Shortly thereafter, Keim visited the Cameron area. "The sight was something else," he remembered. "It was flattened. Aside from fishing boats being washed onto solid ground far inland, there were animals dangling out of what few trees were still left standing. They evidently had been washed up there by the waves."

Keim was reminded of the carnage he saw at the Battle of the Bulge during World War II. "Lives were lost. Lives would be changed. Recovering and rebuilding began."

Most leagues would've thrown in the towel, but the Evangeline wasn't like any other league.

"They don't quit no matter how hard their backs are pressed against the wall," columnist Wynn wrote of the team bosses in the league's four cities. [10]

The schedule was improvised so Crowley and Lake Charles played in Alexandria or Thibodaux while their heavily damaged ballparks were repaired. Night games were changed to day because of electric power shortages in the region.

At Miller Stadium, gaping holes in the left- and right-field fences had to be fixed, bleachers replaced, and debris cleared from the field. Alexandria manager Ken Silvestri refused to let his team play one game because of the danger to the outfielders from the fallen fence.

"The ballpark was pretty much gone," Clifford said. "They tried to fix up the field as best they could, but it was pretty sad playing there."

Daytime heat and humidity made conditions worse.

"We wore wool uniforms, and after a game, they would be soaking wet with sweat," Clifford said. "We'd hang them up to dry, and the next day they were just as wet as when we took them off."

It was particularly bad for pitchers.

"Every time you threw the ball, you had to grab the rosin bag before throwing the next one because your hands were wet," Webrand said. "It was awful."

Attendance figures for day games more resembled scores for a novice bowler: 75, 89, and 136. Only 27 fans showed up in Lake Charles for a game against the Millers.

"Attendance just dwindled from the aftershock of the hurricane and the heat," Keim said. "Air conditioning and TV were taking their toll."

The Millers finished the last half of the season in second place, with a 29–25 record, eight games behind Alexandria. Overall, they were 63–47.

They were third in attendance—17,779. The league attracted 132,822 fans, slightly more than the 119,933 who clicked the Miller Stadium turnstiles in 1952, to earn Crowley the nickname the "Best Little Baseball Town in the World."

"There were bright spots and hope on the horizon that 1957 would be a return to the good old days, but all that was to disappear June 27, 1957," Keim said. "Hurricane Audrey destroyed the countryside. It destroyed the league. The end of an era had come."

True to league history, the ending in Crowley was quirky.

Smoke from a huge warehouse fire two blocks from the ballpark forced the final game to be halted in the fifth inning, with the Millers ahead, 16–5. A crowd of 558, one of the largest of the season, saw the Millers score 10 runs in their last at-bats, Horn walloping two home runs to clinch the league batting title.

"We knew that it was the end of the season," Horn said, "and didn't know what was going to happen after that."

Horn and Mackenzie finished the 1957 season at Little Rock, Arkansas, in the Class AA Southern Association; Pfister at Columbia, South Carolina, in the Class A South Atlantic League; and Webrand at Pocatello, Idaho, in the Class C Pioneer League.

Pfister was the only pitcher on the '57 Millers team to reach the majors, compiling a 6–19 won–lost record for the Athletics in parts of four seasons (1961–64).

Mackenzie was the lone position player to graduate to the big leagues, playing in 11 games for the Athletics late in the '61 season.

Silvera was a 19-year-old outfielder at the University of Southern California in June 1955, when he signed a bonus contract to play for the Cincinnati Reds. "He's one of the finest prospects I've ever seen," Reds scout Bobby Mattick wrote in his report on Silvera.[11]

Two months later, a Cincinnati columnist wondered whether Mattick "needs glasses."[12]

Silvera was a so-called bonus baby, and the Reds had to keep him on the roster the rest of the season. He appeared in 13 games, getting one hit in seven at-bats for a .143 average.

Silvera lacked three things, according to his Reds teammates: "1. He couldn't hit; 2. He couldn't run; 3. He couldn't throw."[13]

Explained *Cincinnati Post* sportswriter Pat Harmon,

> Those are harsh statements, and they are made on a comparative basis. His teammates meant that he couldn't do those things as well as an average major leaguer can.
>
> Certainly, he can hit, run, and throw better than the average U.S. ballplayer. But the Reds gave him a 1955 bonus, said to be $20,000, with the idea he was a ready-made big-leaguer.[14]

The Reds released Silvera after converting him into a catcher. He never returned to the majors.

Horn didn't make it higher than the Southern Association, where he played for his hometown of Mobile, Alabama, in 1961.

The year before at Lancaster, Pennsylvania, a Cubs farm club in the Class A Eastern League, Horn was taking batting practice prior to a night game. "I was hitting the ball out of the ballpark on every swing," he recalled.

Horn went hitless in the game.

Looking on was the Cubs' batting instructor, Rogers Hornsby, a Hall of Famer considered by many to be the greatest right-handed hitter in history.

Hornsby walked into the Lancaster clubhouse after the game. "I wanna see Horn," he said.

He spotted Horn's name on his locker and said, "I just wanna tell you something."

"What's that?" Claude asked.

"You're the best six o'clock hitter I've ever seen!" Hornsby declared, referring to batting practice.

"I thought that if there was one player that should've made the big leagues, he was it," Clifford said of Horn. "I don't know why he didn't."

Clifford was a catcher at San Jose State College, but the Millers already had Silvera and shifted him to the outfield, where he played the rest of his four-year career, finishing with a respectable .281 average and 53 homers. "I had some good years in the minors but not good enough to be in the big leagues," he said, "and that's what it is all about."

At about the same time the Evangeline League became history, minor-league czar George Trautman hung out a "help wanted" sign in another wire service story.

"The difficulty in many of our leagues is not getting more fans in the stands," he wrote. "The big difference is in supplying a sufficient number of skilled players."

"Perhaps we haven't driven our message of opportunity home hard enough," he added. "Perhaps too many young DiMaggios are passing up the field of baseball for commerce or industry because they haven't realized that they had the potential to become professional stars."[15]

Webrand became president of a major division for a large U.S. defense contractor.

After a bum elbow on his right throwing arm ended his baseball career, Pfister was a firefighter for 30 years in Dania, Florida.

Clifford returned to California to teach and coach baseball for 34 years at Sequoia High School in Redwood City.

Gorrie coached college baseball for 28 years, guiding Pepperdine to a third-place finish in the 1979 College World Series.

Horn and Mackenzie stayed in pro baseball, Horn as a longtime scout for the Athletics and Mackenzie as a minor-league coach and scout for the Houston Astros.

Keim headed west, winding up in Coos Bay, Oregon, in 1960, working in real estate 18 years before starting his own mortgage brokerage business. Over the years, he broadcast high school football, baseball, basketball, boxing, wrestling, swimming, and bowling in Texas, Louisiana, California, Idaho, and Oregon.

When Keim died in 2018, at the age of 95, the *Crowley Post-Signal* referred to his nickname, "Oh, Happy Day," and recalled 2,011 fans attending a game at Miller Stadium in 1951, to honor him on "Ed Keim Night."

On May 14, 1958, the last rites for Crowley Baseball, Inc., were held in a Crowley courtroom. Overseeing the proceedings for the group that brought pro baseball to town was the president of the corporation who was conveniently co-owner of a local funeral home.

A story in the sports section of the *Daily Signal* doubled as a tongue-in-cheek obituary, tracing pro baseball's eight years in Crowley.

"In spite of rallies and citizens' drives, baseball on a minor level couldn't stave off the assault of television, air conditioning, and a suddenly lackadaisical public," the newspaper reported. "It was almost counted among the victims of Hurricane Audrey toward the tail end of the 1957 season but managed to totter through to the final out."[16]

The death of Crowley Baseball, Inc., was "only a matter of time" once its "mother," the Kansas City Athletics, stopped providing support after the '57 season ended.[17]

"The remains," the story concluded, "will be buried in the dusty basepaths of Miller Stadium following the courtroom services."[18]

It was a fitting farewell because pro baseball in Crowley had produced plenty of laughs, cheers, and joy.

"They were good days," Horn said.

They were happy days, no matter what happened at the end.

15

THE SHOWDOWN BEFORE THE STORM

It was the showdown before the storm.

As Hurricane Audrey roared into Southwest Louisiana, the only unbeaten pitchers in the Evangeline League squared off in Alexandria. Crowley's Dan Pfister had a 6–0 won–lost record entering the game, and Alexandria's Bob Riesener was 9–0.

The showdown was the defining moment in a season that was the springboard to the majors for Pfister and the high point of Riesener's brief but historic pitching career.

The right-handers were born in New Jersey towns 11 miles apart, Pfister in Plainfield and Riesener in Linden.

Pfister grew up in Hollywood, Florida, and was working there as a land surveyor in 1957, when he tried out with the Buffalo Bisons at their spring training camp in nearby Pompano Beach.

A member of the Class AAA International League, Buffalo was the top farm club for the Kansas City Athletics. The Bisons roster was filled with former major leaguers and piloted by Phil Cavarretta, a Chicago Cubs first baseman for two decades before he managed the team for 2½ years.

"Hey, kid, you're throwing batting practice," Cavarretta shouted at Pfister.

Unsigned out of high school, Pfister thought to himself, "Screw batting practice. I'm in a game. This is my first chance to smoke their ass out there. I'm going to make a name for myself."

The first hitter took a few swings and, then, left the batting cage without saying a word.

Pfister could hear the excited chatter of onlookers.

"This kid looks pretty good," someone said. "Who the hell is he?"

"Where did he come from?" another person asked.

Only Bisons pitcher Karl Drews could answer those questions.

A veteran of eight big-league seasons, Drews lived in Hollywood and played first base on the same fast-pitch softball team as Pfister. He knew all about Pfister's pitching exploits in softball and a local amateur baseball league.

The 37-year-old Drews arranged the tryout and offered Pfister some advice: "If they ask you how old you are, lie a year. You'll be 20 instead of 21. They like it when you're younger."

Luke Easter, the oldest and most intimidating Bison hitter, stepped to the plate. He knew a little bit about the age thing, shaving off 10 years.

In 1956, at his real age of 40, Big Luke slammed a league-leading 35 home runs for Buffalo. "I hit 'em and forget 'em," he often said of his tape-measure shots, which few people forgot.

Pfister vividly remembered an Easter blast in an exhibition game at the same baseball field he played on in high school. The ball soared over the right-field fence and the Dixie Highway behind it, landing on the railroad tracks. "It was a monster," Pfister recalled.

At 6-foot-4 and 240 pounds, Easter resembled one of the game's greatest sluggers. "Picture a black Johnny Mize," Pfister said.

Mize slugged his way into baseball's Hall of Fame with four National League home run titles and 359 four-baggers overall. Easter amassed 362 homers in the majors and minors combined, all of them coming after age 34.

Big Luke watched as Pfister whizzed three fastballs past him. "He dropped the bat, looked at me, and just walked away. He didn't even swing."

"Hey, kid, this is batting practice," a Bisons coach yelled. "You're supposed to let 'em hit it."

"I was throwing into the wind, and the ball was taking off good that day," Pfister said. "The curveball was really breaking good."

Buffalo signed Pfister on the spot for $375 a month—double what he was making as a surveyor. Married 10 days earlier, he went home and told his wife, Susan, what happened and that he was leaving the next morning for Houston, Texas, to finish spring training and report to the Crowley Millers, a team he didn't know existed.

"The big leagues weren't even in my sights," Pfister admitted.

This wasn't the case with Riesener, a pitcher for the Alexandria Aces, a New York Yankees affiliate.

Riesener's hometown of Linden is about an hour by train from Yankee Stadium. He knew the names of all the Yankees and had wanted to be one of them ever since his grandfather took him to see a game at the famed ballpark.

"I'd just started playing the game—sandlot stuff," Riesener said. "I walked into Yankee Stadium, looked out at the field, and thought, 'This is heaven.'"

In high school, the 6-foot-2, 190-pound Riesener was all-everything in basketball and baseball, attracting scholarship offers from West Point and the Naval Academy. All 16 big-league teams courted him. "I'm going to play in Yankee Stadium," he announced.

He wasn't too sure about that after a shaky start with the St. Petersburg Saints in the Class D Florida State League. "I went down there as a high school hero and got clobbered first two times out. All I was doing was throwing fastballs and curveballs, and they were nailing me."

"What am I doing here?" Riesener asked himself. "I don't belong."

Saints manager Ken Silvestri, a big-league catcher for parts of eight seasons, thought otherwise and pulled him aside.

"Riesener, you about ready to learn how to pitch?"

The 19-year-old was desperate. "Whatever you can do to help me," he responded.

"You ever hear of a changeup?" Silvestri asked.

"No," he replied, "I don't know even how to throw one."

He learned to use the changeup effectively and won six of his next 10 decisions to finish with a 6–6 mark and impressive 3.12 earned run average.

Silvestri continued to mentor Riesener at Alexandria in 1957. He called his players "scrubeenies"—a kinder, gentler variation of scrubs. "You can't make chicken salad out of chicken shit," he told them.

A manager in the lower minors might identify a problem, but players were primarily responsible for their own development and progress.

Riesener tracked his performance with a handwritten game-by-game self-assessment that ended up 11 pages long and featured blunt, sometimes critical remarks.

"You're coaching yourself," he said. "It keeps you on your toes."

He didn't know it at the time, but he was preparing for a coaching career that would produce 1,045 wins at Livingston University and the University of Montevallo in Alabama, the most in the state at the four-year college level, when he retired in 2003.

Riesener lasted only four innings in his first start, allowing 2 runs, 5 hits, and 3 walks. "Gave up one run and just stopped thinking because of arm," he wrote. "Future depends upon arm coming around. Who knows what?"

His first win came in his second start, a three-hit, no-walk shutout. "Arm behaved very good," he jotted down. "Still some stiffness in it. More bounce needed off the mound on fielding bunts. Must follow through more to get in better fielding position. Rock batters a little more than what am now doing."

Riesener won again despite walking eight batters. "Very wild," he lamented. "Still not following through enough. Change speeds a lot more. Keep cooler head when going gets a bit tough."

"If I walked four guys in a game, that was way too much," he said.

In winning his third straight, 9–3, Riesener walked two, while surrendering 11 hits.

"That's a lot and still win," he said later. "Somebody was looking over my shoulder the whole season."

He commented in his journal on the "tendency to ease up a lot when I get ahead and giving up too many hits, which I shouldn't when I have my stuff."

Details of his next six victories varied but not the reviews.

"It's repetitive," Riesener said. "That's what baseball is."

He blanked Crowley on two hits, observing, "Good control but got behind the batters more than was good. Must try to get very good control of curve so as to be able to use it in the pinch."

A month into the season he was 6–0, matching the number of wins he had the year before. "Something is going on here," he said to himself.

As the wins piled up, the going got tougher. So did Riesener. He pitched extra innings in four of five games, winding up with no decision in two of them.

His seventh win prompted him to write, "When batters move up, knock them down or loosen them up."

After going 11 innings to notch his eighth victory, he penned, "Dust off good hitters when they hit consistently."

He needed 10 innings to win his ninth straight, reminding himself to "change speeds more" and "keep hustling every minute on the field."

"I'm winning all these games, and I'm in Wonderland," Riesener recalled. "This isn't real."

None of these feelings appear in his journal. It was "just the facts ma'am," the catchphrase used by Joe Friday, the fictional police sergeant in *Dragnet*, a popular television series in the 1950s.

Riesener was on a roll and didn't want anything to jinx it.

"I'm going to keep doing what I'm doing," he decided.

This meant wearing the same undershirt when he pitched and eating at the same time and place in Alexandria on game days.

"I can't remember the name of the restaurant, but I can tell you the name of the waitress," he joked.

Next was the showdown with Pfister, billed by the *Alexandria Town Talk* as "Crowley's answer to Riesener."[1]

Pfister had to wait two weeks before Crowley manager Everett Robinson let him start a game.

"He didn't like my pitching style," Pfister said.

Pfister threw across his body, taking a little hop-step at the end of his delivery to recover his balance.

"You're never going any place throwing like that," Robinson said.

"They signed me to a contract watching me throw like that," Pfister countered.

Robinson wouldn't start Pfister until he changed. The former first baseman put his glove on the ground and had Pfister practice stepping to the left of it, so he didn't fall off balance.

"I chewed that glove up to pieces by the time he was finally done," Pfister chuckled.

Pfister won his second start and, then, beat Alexandria, 3–1, tossing a four-hitter. "As soon as I got a chance to start, I went right back to doing it my own way," Pfister related. "He [Robinson] left me alone."

Pfister was 4–0 and Riesener 7–0 when they faced one another in mid-June. Neither pitcher was around at the end of the 17-inning game won by

Alexandria, Pfister leaving in the seventh with the score tied 2–2 and Riesener after the 11th.

On the day of their rematch, Hurricane Audrey was front-page news in Alexandria, while Riesener's quest for number 10 was the top sports story. The night before the Aces got into a free-for-all with the visiting Lake Charles Giants. The police had to stop the fight.

"You could not sit on the bench during a donnybrook or your ass was grass," Riesener said. "You had to get in the pile."

Riesener was about to join the melee when he was suddenly grabbed from behind and carried off the field by Lake Charles player-manager Whitey McDowell. "You've got a future in this game," he told Riesener. "You don't want any part of that."

Only 99 people showed up for the Riesener–Pfister showdown.

The Millers scored twice in the third to give Pfister a 2–0 lead, but the Aces bounced back with five unanswered runs that Riesener made stand up for a 5–4 win. Both pitchers allowed seven hits, Riesener scribbling in his journal that "two of hits were bunt singles" and half of the four runs unearned.

Riesener spent the next two days with his teammates at a local movie theater waiting for the remnants of Hurricane Audrey to pass through town. "Go to the movies and stay there because it's safe," they were instructed by team officials.

Pfister already was itching for another shot at his archrival. "Every time he came to town, I went to the manager and said, 'I want him. I owe him.'"

He got his wish a month later in Crowley. Riesener was still undefeated—14–0. Pfister was 9–2.

The Millers got to Riesener for seven runs and eight hits, including two homers that he dismissed as "easy flies in home park." He departed in the eighth inning with the Aces ahead, 12–7, noting in his journal, "Should have left with the score 12–2."

Pfister was knocked out in the fifth, as the Aces tagged him for six runs and eight hits, and his third loss, on their way to an 18–13 decision. "The son of a bitch beat me again," Pfister said.

Riesener never mentioned the streak in his log. "That's superstition," he said. "You don't talk about no-hitters, and you don't talk about that streak."

He had an unspoken understanding with the rest of the team. "Don't wake me until it's over."

"To look at Riesener on the hill, you don't get the impression that he feels any strain," *Town Talk* columnist Jim Wynn observed, adding, "The biggest displays of pique are confined to grabbing at the dirt or kicking at the mound."[2]

Thibodaux manager Hank Robinson was in awe after Riesener shut out his team to tie the Organized Baseball record of 18 straight wins, saying, "I've never heard of anyone winning that many games without losing."[3]

The mark of 18–0 was set by Tony Napoles in 1946, at Peekskill, New York, in the Class D North Atlantic League. Napoles added four wins in the playoffs to finish 22–0 overall.

Riesener was an artist on the mound.

"He moves the ball around real good," Silvestri said of his prized pupil. "He'll pitch high and tight, and then come in low and outside, then the curve, then the fastball, all on the nose in the strike zone. He keeps a batter rocking."[4]

With Pfister looking on from the sidelines, Riesener stopped Crowley on one run and five hits to shatter the mark and make headlines nationally.

"Riesener's record reads like something an aspiring sandlotter might have dreamed," the Associated Press reported. The wire service hailed him as the possible answer to the Yankees search for "another mound great in the mold of Allie Reynolds or Vic Raschi."[5]

There also were comparisons with Mickey Mantle, who jumped from Class C to the Yankees in a single season, and Hal Newhouser and Virgil Trucks, pitching stars at Alexandria before making it big in the majors.

"I always expected to win," Riesener said.

He wasn't alone.

The *Sporting News* dubbed him "Automatic Bob" after his 19th win.[6]

He finished a perfect 20–0, beating Lake Charles on a four-hitter.

For the first time, Riesener showed some excitement in his journal: "Biggest goal of my short career has been achieved thanks mostly to God for letting me pitch with a sound arm, thanks to a wonderful manager, and thanks to a great team." The last sentence reads, "Don't forget all that has been learned this year and never be satisfied."

Bob Riesener didn't get to the majors, but he made it into Ripley's Believe It or
Not nationally syndicated column for his unprecedented 20–0 won–lost record at
Alexandria in 1957, and six halls of fame for his accomplishments as a college
baseball coach. The baseball stadium at the University of Montevallo in Alabama
also is named after him. Courtesy Bob Riesener.

The Yankees made sure Riesener didn't have time to get satisfied with his remarkable record, which included a league-leading 2.16 ERA, 4 shutouts, 18 complete games, and 204 innings pitched. They immediately sent him to the New Orleans Pelicans of the Southern Association. "I was tired and worn out," he acknowledged.

In the two games he started and lost for the cellar-dwelling Pelicans, Riesener was roughed up for 12 earned runs and 14 hits.

"I deserved to get beat," he said after the first shellacking. "If I had pitched like that in the Evangeline, they would have knocked my ears off."[7]

Despite the nightmarish ending in New Orleans, the '57 season was a dream come true for Riesener. "It's got a history to it. It's never happened and probably won't happen again. I was put in Ripley's Believe It or Not. The wake-up call came after I got hurt. That's when it hit me. I may not be in this game much longer. I want to be a part of this game. I want this game to be my life."

At spring training in 1958, Riesener posed for an Associated Press photo with the Yankees' Don Larsen, the only pitcher to throw a perfect game in a World Series. He warmed up in the bullpen next to Ryne Duren, a flame-throwing reliever. "I'm giving it everything I've got: puff, puff, puff. And he's going POW! POW! POW!"

Riesener returned to New Orleans determined to prove he was good enough to pitch there. This time he won his first two games and was close to winning a fourth when he heard a pop in the shoulder of his throwing arm. "I didn't say anything because I wanted a W," he admitted.

Riesener pitched the five innings required for the win before revealing his arm was hurting. "I played catch the next day and couldn't throw the ball 15 feet. I couldn't raise my arm over my head."

He was placed on the injured list to rest the arm. Eventually the Yankees flew him to New York to see their team physician, Dr. Sidney Gaynor.

"All a pitcher has is his arm," Yankees pitcher Jim Bouton writes in his book, *Ball Four*. "Pitching is a precise skill that requires a coordinated effort among many parts of the body. One small hurt and it's all gone. Like a tiddly-winks champion with a hangnail."[8]

Bouton described a visit to Dr. Gaynor, concluding, "There were a lot of guys who chose not to go to him with injuries because they didn't want to take his guff."[9]

True to form, Dr. Gaynor informed Riesener, "There's nothing wrong with your arm. You're a hypochondriac."

"If I'm a hypochondriac," he protested, "why is it when I pitch, I can't wipe my ass for the next three days?"

The doctor prescribed push-ups to strengthen the ailing arm. "Hell, I pushed-up, pushed-up, and pushed-up," Riesener recalled.

He spent the rest of '58 and all of '59 trying to rehabilitate the arm at Greensboro, North Carolina, in the Class B Carolina League. "Their idea of rehab was putting you in the bullpen," Riesener said. "You could get up and throw five or six times and never get in the game. The arm didn't get much better."

Riesener used the time in Greensboro to learn the intricacies of playing every defensive position so he could continue in baseball as a coach. "I was too young to get out of baseball."

He quit pro ball in 1960, with a 41–23 won–lost record, going on to get bachelor's and master's degrees in physical education and coach 45 years, including 30 at the University of Montevallo, where the baseball stadium is named after him.

Pfister's 13–6 record at Crowley put him on a rocky road to Kansas City that passed through Columbia, South Carolina; Albany, New York; Rochester and Winona, Minnesota; Pocatello, Idaho; and Shreveport, Louisiana.

Midway through the 1958 season, he had a chance airport encounter with another baseball player.

"Where you going?" the player asked.

"They're sending me down to Pocatello in Class C ball," Pfister said. "I started out last year 6-and-0 and now I'm 0-and-6. I'm getting killed."

He was really 0–8, losing twice at Albany in the Class A Eastern League before dropping all six decisions at Rochester and Winona in the Class B Three-I League.

"What are you doing differently?" the player inquired.

"Damn if I know. Last year everything worked—fastball, curveball, changeup."

"You ever throw a slider?"

"I know how to throw one, but I never have."

"What have you got to lose?"

The slider would both make and break Pfister's pitching career. "Started blowing guys away with it. Turned out to be something I could really throw accurately. It really broke sharp and fast. I went from two to three strikeouts a game to 10 to 12."

He had a 5–4 record at Pocatello, whiffing 66 batters in 58 innings, 16 in his last game, before serving a two-year stint in the U.S. Army.

The slider helped Pfister win a combined 23 games at Shreveport in 1960–61, and, the following spring, get the attention of the A's new pitching coach, Ed Lopat.

"I was like his baby," Pfister explained. "He latched onto me and pitched my ass off."

Lopat starred on five Yankees championship teams from 1949–53, earning the nickname "The Junk Man," because he never threw anything hard or good enough to hit. He wanted Pfister to mix in some junk with his other pitches so he had all the right stuff.

"You have a chance to be one of the greatest pitchers ever," Lopat told his protégé.

The previous year at Shreveport, Pfister had been called the "unluckiest flinger in the Southern Association" because he lost four times to the best pitcher in the league. [10]

The "unlucky" label would stick with him for the rest of his career.

He tossed a three-hitter in his big-league debut in 1962, and still lost, 1–0.

"A'S DON'T HELP PFISTER," the *Kansas City Times* declared in big, bold type, describing him as "unlucky" in a subheadline. [11]

One sportswriter summed up the loss this way: "Poise . . . confidence . . . a crackling curve . . . a tantalizing slider . . . three hits . . . defeat . . . heartbreak." [12]

Pfister had a one-hitter going into the eighth inning when he lost the shutout and the game on a run-scoring ground ball that deflected off the third baseman's glove. "Everybody's going, 'Tough luck, kid, you pitched a great game!' I kind of looked sad, but I wasn't sad. I went out and had myself a helluva time."

Through seven innings of his third start for the A's, Pfister had another one-hitter and Kansas City fans "reveling in every pitch he made," with a club-record 11 strikeouts. [13]

"I went out the next inning: BAM! BAM! BAM!" Pfister said of the 5–1 lead that became a 6–5 loss. "That was it."

Lopat commiserated with Pfister. "It isn't easy to take, but there are many heartbreaks in baseball," he said. [14]

The heartbreaks continued.

"I was 0–6 when I won my first game," Pfister said.

He had a five-hitter and was up, 4–1, on the Boston Red Sox when they pulled even in the ninth inning on a three-run homer belted off the pitcher who replaced him.

He had the Yankees down, 2–0, in the fifth inning when Mickey Mantle launched a game-tying missile over a 407-foot sign and halfway up the right-field bleachers at Yankee Stadium. Mantle angrily smashed his bat on the ground before realizing it was a homer. "I thought it was a pop up," he said. "I hit under the ball and didn't think it was going anywhere."

As Mantle circled the bases, one A's infielder wanted to know why he was mad. "Did you want to hit it over the scoreboard?" he asked.[15]

Pfister lost to the Yankees again despite holding them to two earned runs and seven hits.

"Having to pitch for this team can make a fellow look worse than he is," mused Joe Trimble of the *New York Daily News*, adding that Pfister "isn't that bad. His teammates looked as though they should have taken No-Doz tablets before the game to keep awake."[16]

Pfister finished with a 4–14 record and 4.55 ERA, while the A's ended up ninth in the American League standings for the second straight year.

"We were terrible," Pfister said. "But you know what? I was never upset about anything."

At spring training in 1963, syndicated columnist Red Smith wrote, "The demigods of the prairie may not be great this year, but they'll be gorgeous."[17]

He was referring to the A's new Tulane gold and Kelly-green uniforms made out of a polyester fabric called Dacron®—gold pants with green piping, a gold sleeveless vest with "Athletics" spelled out in green, a solid green cap, and sweatshirt sleeves.

"If you've got a club that has run sixth, eighth, seventh, seventh, seventh, eighth, ninth, and ninth in that order, the chances are your nine is not overburdened with color," Smith said. "So you buy it by the yard."[18]

Pfister was in the Kansas City clubhouse when the colorful attire was unveiled.

"I don't think it's so bad," he said. "I like it."[19]

A's coach Jimmy Dykes took one glance and yelped, "Whoops! We're home free. Everywhere we go, we'll start with a kiss."[20]

There weren't enough kisses to make Pfister's throwing arm feel better.

The slider that had gotten him to the big leagues messed up his elbow.

"The slider is very, very tough on your elbow," Pfister explained. "You approach the release zone with your arm going as fast as you can, and at the very last you snap the elbow. That little pop is what ruins your elbow."

He was limited to two relief appearances and one start in 1963, a win over last-place Washington, before he underwent exploratory surgery and doctors found bone grinding on bone.

"Your elbow is shot," Pfister was told. "The cartilage is gone, and there's no replacement. It'll be fine if you're going to be a surveyor, plumber, or carpenter, but you can't be a major-league pitcher anymore."

Pfister proved the doctors wrong for part of the 1964 season.

He appeared in 19 games for the A's, and one evening at Yankee Stadium he flashed the greatness Lopat envisioned. All the mighty Yankees could muster off Pfister in four scoreless innings was a single. The game was tied at three when Mantle stepped to the plate with one out in the bottom of the 15th inning.

The year before, Mantle had ended an 11-inning game against the A's by crushing a home run that hit the façade of the right-field roof at old Yankee Stadium, 117 feet up and 500 feet away from home plate, according to the Associated Press. The ball was still climbing and came close to becoming the first homer to leave the ballpark. "The hardest ball I ever hit," Mantle said.[21]

"I watched that ball and go, 'Holy shit!'" Pfister said. "I didn't think there was a human alive that could hit the ball that far. He had something inside of him that nobody else had."

Mantle proved that again by rifling a Pfister pitch into deep left field for a triple and, then, scoring the winning run.

"Never has any Kansas City club battled more gallantly," *Kansas City Times* sports editor Ernest Mehl reported.[22]

It was another heartbreak for Pfister. His elbow problems never went away, and after one last comeback attempt in the minors in 1965, he retired with a 6–19 big-league record that can be traced mostly to luck as bad as the A's teams that played behind him.

"I loved every second of baseball," he said. "After that I was a firefighter for 30 years."

And I loved every second of that. It was the same format. You went to work and fooled around with 10 or 12 other brother firefighters or baseball players. All of a sudden the umpire says, "Play ball!" or the bell rings and goes, "Dong! Dong! Dong!" Then you put your serious clothes on, and you haul ass and act like a responsible firefighter or baseball player for two or three hours. I loved every second of it.

Riesener feels the same way about the game.

"You know what it is I love about baseball?" he asked. "It's a book—a mystery. Somebody is a hero; somebody is a goat. You get another chance every day. Each season is a new chapter."

The perfect season at Alexandria taught Riesener to work hard and be honest with himself. "I took it into coaching. I required my players to work hard and be honest every day. When you go home, look in the mirror, and ask yourself, 'Did I give a 100 percent today?' that's working hard. Can you do that? I've done it."

Riesener is proudest of his coaching achievements. His teams won eight conference titles and seven National Association of Intercollegiate Athletics (NAIA) district crowns, and placed third in the 1970 NAIA World Series. Of the players who finished their eligibility, more than 90 percent graduated. He coached 36 All-Americans and 25 pros, notably Rusty Greer, who batted .305 in nine seasons with the Texas Rangers.

"I'm in six halls of fame," he said incredulously. "Six of them. The first one was the biggest thing to happen to me since the 20-and-0 season."

He was inducted into the NAIA Baseball Hall of Fame in 1990, the same year the University of Montevallo honored him. "I've lived a lifelong dream of being in the game."

Riesener remembers Hurricane Audrey but not the showdowns with Pfister. Except for what's written in his journal, he can't recall much about his 20th win. He was never told what was wrong with his throwing arm, so he wryly says, "I was a hypochondriac, remember?"

Riesener has the glove he wore at Alexandria. It's bronzed and mounted on a base as a reminder of his amazing season. "Every now and then I'll think about it and say, 'Gosh darn, nobody did it before, and nobody has done it since.' It was fantastic—a great experience."

Pfister returned to Crowley's Miller Stadium in 2000.

One of the home movies he took in 1957 shows him following through on a pitch, looking to see that the ball is going between the center fielder

The glove Bob Riesener wore at Alexandria in 1957 is now bronzed and mounted on a stand as a memento of his perfect 20–0 mark. "Every now and then I'll think about it and say, 'Gosh darn, nobody did it before and nobody has done it since,'" Riesener said in 2019. "It was fantastic—a great experience." Photo by the author.

In this 2017 photograph, Dan Pfister displays the stick he swung around with the
legendary Ted Williams as they discussed the art of hitting at a Florida Keys bar in
the early '80s. "It didn't matter that he was the greatest and I was a nobody,"
Pfister said. They played tennis the following day. 2017/Michael Laughlin/*South
Florida Sun-Sentinel*/TCA.

and right fielder for a "tweener" and possible double, and, then, running
to back up third base. He handed a camcorder to his wife and said, "I'm
going out there and see if I can recreate that same scene."

He repeated it in street clothes and without a ball. "It looked just like a
replay of what I did 43 years earlier," he said.

One evening in the early 1980s, Pfister was leaving the parking lot of
the popular Lorelei Cabana Bar in the Florida Keys town of Islamorada,
down the street from the waterfront home of Ted Williams, the Boston
Red Sox great. He looked in his rearview mirror and saw "The Splendid
Splinter" himself walking toward him.

Williams noticed the name of a baseball school on the side of Pfister's
van and asked, "You got that guy Charlie Lau working for you?"

Lau was a highly respected hitting coach at the time.

"No, we don't teach that," Pfister said.

"Good, he's horseshit!" Williams said. "What do you teach?"

That led to a lengthy conversation about hitting.

"We couldn't find a bat so we went into the parking lot and chopped a limb off a tree to make a stick that we could swing," Pfister said.

> It didn't matter that he was the greatest and I was a nobody. Ballplayers like somebody to talk with who played ball so you can use terms like "tweeners" and "kitchen," and the other guy knows what you're talking about. He was calling me Dickhead; I was calling him a big donkey. Had the greatest time of my life.

Pfister still has the stick and a photo of him and Williams with it.

"Everything about baseball was exciting," Riesener said. "If I had it to do over again, I would do it the same way."

Pfister would make at least one change. He'd turn back the clock to 1957 for another crack at beating Riesener.

16

THE MANAGER WAS A CROOK

During his three years in Crowley, Johnny George went from a nobody to somebody, obscurity to Cajun country celebrity. There was still a mystique about him that defied description and understanding.

Johnny guided the Millers to a pair of pennants in three years and going into the 1953 season had a championship team heavily favored to repeat. He quit so he could have a team of his own in Dublin, Georgia, a member of the Class C Georgia State League.

Ten days after the season opener Johnny announced the team had sold less than half of the 300 season tickets he was promised and threatened to move to another city if the goal wasn't met. "I can't continue under the circumstances," he said.[1]

Johnny hung on another two months before leaving Dublin to play briefly for New Iberia, Louisiana, and, then, work as a scout for a team in Tyler, Texas.

By the end of 1953, Johnny was wearing the hats of president, manager, and player for the Lake Charles Lakers, making its debut in the Evangeline League.

One of the first things he did was acquire Emile "Smut" Chaillot, his boyhood buddy from Mobile, who was a teammate at Andalusia, Crowley, Dublin, and New Iberia.

Emile was called "Smut" because of his dark-colored skin.

"Dad said many times people asked Johnny if he and Smut were cousins or brothers because they were the darkest members on the team," explained Emile's oldest son, Joe.

Johnny and Smut were alike in other ways.

"They were both street-smart city guys who always had one scheme or another," Joe said. "They were always working a con whether it was a short con or a long con."

A 6-foot-3 beanpole, Johnny was a smooth, fast-moving operator.

"Dad thought Johnny's appearance disarmed those around him into underestimating him," Joe said. "Johnny would use that to his advantage by playing the hokey guy or sincere but dumb guy and outswindle others."

Johnny got the short end of the deal in Lake Charles, as Lakers owner Claude Barker canned him shortly after ringing in the new year of 1954. Barker claimed Johnny was paying too much for the quality of players he was getting, pointing out the team acquired six players for $7,000 and, then, couldn't sell three of them back for $300 each. "That doesn't add up to me," Barker said.[2]

A week later, David Duke, chairman of a baseball boosters group in Tallahassee, Florida, got a telephone call from a man who had read a newspaper story about the city trying to get back into pro baseball after a two-year absence. Tallahassee had its eye on two Class D leagues it belonged to previously, the Georgia–Florida and Alabama–Florida circuits, plus the Florida International League, a high-falutin Class B loop with teams in Miami, Miami Beach, Tampa, St. Petersburg, and West Palm Beach.

The man said he was a former baseball player from Mobile with access to the talent needed to compete in any of the leagues and would operate the club with no financial strings attached. He asked to remain anonymous for a while.

The caller turned out to be Johnny, and the "mystery man" he represented was identified as "Emile Schillet."

"He, too, is a baseball player who obtained his release from a professional team in Louisiana to go into the operating end of the game on his own," the *Tallahassee Democrat* revealed. "Reports indicate that Schillet is in a position to obtain the proper financial backing."[3]

Johnny touted his pennant-winning teams at Crowley, which attracted more than 100,000 fans in two of the three years he was manager. He boasted of financial support from a second source and partial affiliation with a Class AA team he wouldn't name at the time.

"Directors of the local group and city officials questioned George at length looking for a 'joker' somewhere," the *Democrat* reported, noting "all agreed none could be found."[4]

"He's got a good deal," one baseball expert said after reviewing Johnny's plan.[5]

Fan reaction to Johnny's proposal was "unbelievable." "But what can we lose," they said. They considered the "jump from no baseball at all to Class B ball [an] ambitious venture, but with George assuming all the responsibility there's no risk involved for the local group."[6]

The deal was approved by league directors.

"It's an initial tribute to Johnny George that he so quickly was able to get Tallahassee people on his side," commented *Democrat* sports columnist Bill McGrotha. "The man's likeable. He gives an impression of assurance."[7]

Johnny and Smut were at the top of their game in the mystery-man scheme.

"They loved hoodwinking the high and mighty," Joe Chaillot said.

But the real mystery man was Johnny, not Smut.

Johnny's success in Crowley blotted out his numerous failures.

"The man is convinced that the formula that has made tiny Crowley one of the crowd-drawing phenomenons of the minor leagues can be applied successfully elsewhere," McGrotha wrote.[8]

Johnny immediately set out to replicate that formula by purchasing one of the key ingredients from Crowley—Conklyn "Conk" Meriwether.

"He's no spring chicken, mind you," Johnny said. "But he can give that ball a ride."[9]

Conk blasted 33 dingers for Crowley in 1952, and 42 in 1953. "He was injured part of '52," Johnny said. "Otherwise, he would have hit more than 33 homers."[10]

Johnny got excited just thinking about Conk. "He's got color. Kind of a ballplayer fans come out to watch take batting practice."[11]

He recalled giving Conk permission to hit as long as he wanted during one practice session if he knocked the ball over the fence every time. "Well, he poked nine in a row out of there," Johnny said. "The 10th one missed by inches, and he hollered when I told him that almost didn't count."[12]

Johnny was asked why Crowley let Conk go.

"Well, I told you he wasn't any spring chicken," Johnny replied. "He says he's 35, but that's sort of like me saying I'm 30. That's our baseball ages."

Johnny was 33 at the time, and Conk was actually 35.

"His power is tremendous," Johnny continued, describing how teams overshifted their defenses to the right side of the field on Conk, similar to another left-handed power hitter, Ted Williams. He recounted a game when Conk came up with runners on second and third.

"They sprung that shift, and I walk up to the plate and tell Conk to choke up on his bat and punch a short one into left. He says okay. Well, he grabs that bat up close around the trademark. He punches, and the ball sails over the left-field wall 360 feet away. The homer tied the game for us. He rounded third base, where I was coaching, and says, 'How's that for punching, Johnny?'"[13]

Johnny signed his pal, Smut, and Charlie Tuttle, a third baseman-outfielder who clubbed 54 home runs the previous two seasons. "I'm trying to line up the kind of colorful ballclub that will attract fans and revive baseball here," he said.[14]

There were season tickets to sell so Johnny hyped his new players. Most of them were familiar faces that played for him elsewhere.

Smut was billed as a ".300 hitter" known for the "long ball" even though he topped .300 and 20 homers only once in six seasons.[15]

Allen Siff, a pitcher with a 6–8 record for Class D and C teams the year before, and catcher Bob Bettin, a .305 hitter under Johnny at Dublin, were hailed as "definite major league prospects."[16]

Johnny conceded that except for Conk, he couldn't find players to fit the 378-foot right-field stone wall at Tallahassee's Centennial Field, prompting him to "fix things so we could get the fence to fit the ballplayers."[17]

A temporary barrier was placed about 50 feet in front of the existing fence and the space in between dubbed "Meriwether Gardens."

Johnny was building a Class B team out of lower classification players.

"Don't you worry none about us," Conk told a sportswriter. "You write them stories. We'll give you something to write about."[18]

The most interesting and intriguing player of the bunch was Walter "Monk" Stevens, a left-handed pitcher Johnny didn't bother to puff up.

"He ain't no 20-game winner," Johnny told McGrotha, the *Democrat* columnist who documented almost every word he uttered.

McGrotha interviewed Stevens when he went to the newspaper to have his picture taken.

"My name's Stevens," he said, introducing himself. "First name's Monk. Real name? Walter. But don't call me that."

Monk had been in Tallahassee four months, working for a trucking company. He started pitching in the Class D Eastern Shore League in 1948. "Got a sore arm right away—bursitis," he lamented. "Been sore ever since, on and off."

"What is your stock in trade?" Monk was asked. "Curveball? Fastball?"

"Prayers."

He elaborated, "Never had a good record anywhere. Liked to play around too much. You know, go swimming, play tennis. That's why they shipped me away from New Iberia in 1951 when I was doing my best pitching. Had a 6–5 record when they sent me to Americus. Couldn't win at all."

Actually, Monk won two games at Americus, including a shutout. "Used a blooper pitch in the game one time . . . this guy pops to short. The fans holler for more."

Monk threw another blooper. "It sails way over the catcher's head. No more bloopers for me. Never know where one's going. I'll stick to prayers."

McGrotha inquired about the nickname Monk. "Long story, and you can't print it," he replied. "It was short for monkey—and something else."

Monk ended the conversation by saying, "Better not build me up too much. Can't ever tell. I might not make the grade."[19]

Monk's parting shot reflected the uncertainty of the future of the team, its players, and pro baseball in Tallahassee.

Johnny tabbed Monk to pitch the home opener for the Rebels, a nickname picked by many of the 1,723 fans that filled the new grandstands at Centennial Field.

The day of the game a picture on the front page of the *Democrat* showed Conk hanging in the air over a scroll of "Take Me Out to the Ball Game" sheet music. Instructed by the photographer to jump as high as he could, Conk leaped like the acrobat he used to be and yelled, "Why don't you shoot one like this?"

It was the winning shot, "Meriwether looking for all the world like a ballet queen soaring 20 feet above Mother Earth."[20]

On the eve of the home opener, Johnny was apprehensive. "You can be reasonably sure that the club will get off to a slow start," he said. "I don't know just what it is, but every club I have ever had started slowly."[21]

Conk went hitless, but Monk tossed a seven-hitter to give the Rebels their first victory of the season.

They lost the next 15 games, Conk clouting two homers and driving in five runs to end the streak and inspire the following headline in the *Democrat*: "It CAN Happen Here—Rebels Win!" The accompanying photo of a mock burial featured Johnny, two Rebels players, and the clubhouse boy kneeling behind a tombstone reading, "Here Lies Rebels' Losing Streak . . . Gone but NOT Forgotten."[22]

It wasn't forgotten because four days later the Rebels were in the midst of a seven-game losing streak with a 2–21 won–lost record. Johnny had been relieved of his duties as president two weeks earlier by a group of local businessmen who organized Tallahassee Sports, Inc., to operate the team. The new bosses had seen enough and announced that Johnny resigned as manager.

"I never quit," Johnny protested. "I was released."[23]

Conk filled the position until Marland "Duke" Doolittle took over a week later.

Conk's finest moment at the helm was off the field when he stood up for Ernie Cretien, the lone black player on the team.

"We stop at this pizza joint to eat," Conk said. "While the other boys are ordering, I go in the back and see this guy who runs the place and ask him if Ernie can eat here in the kitchen. The guy says no, no, no, no."

Conk stormed out of the kitchen.

"'Come on, boys, let's go,' I tell 'em."

> And we go, too. Forty dollars' worth of orders we must have give by then. We load up on that bus and haul it.
>
> And this guy back at this joint, he comes out yelling as we drive off, "Come back, come back, come back."[24]

That was a lot of pizza dough—nearly $375 in today's dollars.

As sad a commentary as the story was of the segregated times, it was good for a much-needed laugh.

"I know this situation is bad here," Duke Doolittle said on arriving in Tallahassee. "But I knew of a ballclub once that won only two of its first 21. What are we now? Three-and-24? This ballclub, even as it is, is not that bad."[25]

Duke played eight seasons for the Little Rock Travelers in the Southern Association. He recalled a 21-game losing streak by the Travelers in 1950. "We went into the bottom half of the ninth not once, not twice, not three times, but four times with a five-run lead and couldn't win. It didn't matter who was pitching, who was playing, or what, we managed to lose those ballgames."

Travelers manager Otto "Jack" Saltzgaver figured a curfew wouldn't stop the players from staying out late at night so he handed out meal money every morning at nine o'clock. "I may not know when you get in at night, but I'm going to know when you get up in the morning," he said.

"It didn't get anybody in any sooner," Duke added. "I don't know where they went, but they were out until two or three o'clock in the morning. Not too many of them left their day's meal money on the table either."

As Duke soon discovered, the Rebels were far worse than any team he'd been around in his 10 years as a player and manager.

"I found a terrible situation," Duke said.

> There had been seven different businessmen that had put up money. It had been mishandled. Johnny George had talked his way into managing the ballclub and brought in a bunch of old buddies. They couldn't win in C ball let alone the Florida International League. We had a couple of fellows that couldn't catch the ball, and those that caught it couldn't throw it.

After watching the Rebels make seven errors in a game, the *Democrat*'s McGrotha lamented, "What it was, was *not* baseball. . . . I believe I will have another big orange."[26]

The day Duke got to Tallahassee, the Rebels jumped from sixth to fourth place. It had nothing to do with their performance on the field. Two of the league's six teams dropped out.

The Rebels finished the first half with a 12–50 mark. Team statistics even included a line with the totals for the players released. They accounted for almost half of the club's at-bats, runs scored, and hits. The "released" pitchers were a combined 4–28.

Duke bailed out at the end of June to rejoin Memphis, the Southern Association team he left to manage the Rebels.

"I was miserable," Duke recalled years later.

> The fellows running the team had put up so much money to start the season that they didn't have any left. Every check they wrote was bouncing. I'd take a check for meal money and go on the road with it. When I got to the hotel, they didn't want to cash the check. They said, "We've got your check from the last time." It got that way all around the league. I pitied whoever took over the ballclub.

Gene Harvey followed Duke and lasted three weeks. He was replaced by Charley Cuellar, the club's fourth and last pilot.

Cuellar took charge the same day the Rebels said goodbye to Conk.

Conk was hitting .287, with a team-high 14 homers and 75 runs batted in—numbers too low for the team-high salary he was making, roughly $400 a month. The Rebels tried to sell Conk but found no takers.

The entire league collapsed a week later.

"The Rebels is dead," the *Democrat* declared.

The team already owed $13,000 in debts and needed $4,000 to pay for an upcoming nine-day road trip. Directors dipped into their own pockets but came up $2,000 short. One of the directors apologized, saying they "had put about every cent they could into the club."[27]

As the fate of the Rebels was being decided, one of the players asked Cuellar if he had time to eat.

"Got more time than money," the manager replied.

"The Rebels had run out of money before, and something had always happened," McGrotha pointed out. "This time nothing did."[28]

The Rebels finished with an overall record of 22–76. Attendance was a paltry 12,151.

McGrotha concluded, "The Rebels, with few exceptions, were a miserable lot of players—good boys, mind you, but a pretty pathetic team for the most part. But even worse than the players on the field was the business operation off the field. Business bobbles were staggering."[29]

Johnny was blamed for most of the problems.

"George represented himself as a man with extensive financial backing," McGrotha wrote.

He had none at all. What he sunk into the club here was what he raised through the sale of advance tickets, concession rights, etc.

It later came out that there was enough in George's background to make Tallahassee shy away from him in the first place, but none of this was forthcoming from the National Association of Professional Baseball Leagues, which is supposed to know about such things.[30]

On hearing of George's Tallahassee troubles, New Iberia sportswriter Jim Wynn recounted the manager's slick dealings with pitcher Alan Siff and second baseman Nick Stanziani.

The players followed him from Dublin to New Iberia in 1953, and Tallahassee in 1954. In between, George sold them to and bought them back from Port Arthur during his brief tenure at Lake Charles. When fired by the Lakers, he took the pair to Tallahassee and, then, peddled them again, this time to Crowley.

"It now develops that the Tallahassee club (from which George was also ousted) has never paid Lake Charles for either player," Wynn reported. "But it's a near-certainty Crowley had to deliver cash before they picked up either Siff or Stanziani. George has manipulated those two players like a master operator of an army shell game. And I'll bet his pockets have jingled a bit merrier after every transaction."[31]

At Tallahassee, almost everything Johnny did or said turned out to be wrong.

Opposing teams hit more home runs into Meriwether Gardens than Conk.

The two players he labeled as major-league prospects were busts, Siff with a 0–4 record and Bettin batting .214.

Monk ("All I got is a prayer") Stevens, the pitcher George didn't think much of, led the Rebels in wins, with six. He was one of only three players to last the entire season.

Conk wound up at Valdosta, Georgia, in the Class D Georgia–Florida League.

Smut didn't appear in a single game for the Rebels. He quit baseball and went back to Crowley to work in the TV repair and furniture business.

Johnny drifted into semipro baseball, first in Minnesota and, then, Mississippi.

On December 5, 1956, Johnny George, age 36, collapsed and died of a heart attack in a Birmingham, Alabama, jail shortly after telling cell

At 6-foot-3, 190 pounds, hard-throwing Alan Siff was considered a genuine big-league prospect by manager Johnny George. Siff played for George at Dublin, Georgia, to begin the 1953 season, and followed him to New Iberia and, then, Tallahassee in 1954, where he lost all four decisions before landing in Crowley and compiling a 12–11 record. Photo courtesy of Richard Pizzolatto.

THE MANAGER WAS A CROOK

mates he was a former baseball player and wanted to exercise to "keep in condition."[32]

Johnny was awaiting trial on charges he embezzled a car from a Birmingham dealer where he was employed as a salesman.

The mystery was finally over.

The manager was a crook.

17

THE CONKER GOES BONKERS

Marland "Duke" Doolittle and Conk Meriwether were as different as fire and ice, but they shared a common bond. They blew a chance to play in the big leagues.

"Liquor was Conk's downfall early in his career," Duke said.

> Conk was a great hitter—a sure shot at Houston to go to the big leagues. The day that the St. Louis Cardinals called him up, he was too drunk to get on the train. He missed it. And the Cardinals forgot about him. They didn't want a ballplayer like that. We both threw away golden opportunities. I did it with the knife and fork.

Duke weighed 172 pounds in 1943, when he batted .324 in 33 games for the Little Rock Travelers. After serving two years in the U.S. Marine Corps during World War II, he rejoined the Travelers, tipping the scales at 246.

"When you left me, you were a big-league prospect," Travelers owner Ray Winder told Duke. "I'd already been offered $125,000 for you and wouldn't sell."

The moment Duke walked into the team's office afterward, Winder said, "I saw all that money floatin' away."

"He was heartbroken about it," Duke recalled. "He knew I'd never lose the weight."

Opposing players needled, "What time does the balloon go up?"

"If I heard that once, I heard it 50 million times," Duke said.

He was called Humphrey, after Humphrey Pennyworth, the fat boy who rode around on a bicycle pulling an outhouse in the Joe Palooka comic strip. The nickname and insults didn't bother Duke enough to stop eating. "I had a head like a coconut—a hard outer shell and not too much inside. I never did buckle down."

Doolittle was named after E. W. Marland, the 10th governor of the state of Oklahoma, where his mother was born. He was one of 10 children. Two older brothers were nicknamed "Doots" and "Dim," so he wound up being called "Duke."

He never made it to the big leagues, spending eight of his 13 years in pro ball with the Travelers, a team in the Double-A Southern Association. He left the Travelers in 1953 to manage the Jackson, Mississippi, Generals in the Class C Cotton States League and was a backup catcher at Memphis in 1954, when he got what amounted to a 911 call from Tallahassee.

Nothing could've prepared Duke for what happened in Tallahassee and to Conk the following year. That's saying something because Duke had been around some of the meanest, nastiest, most eccentric characters to ever play the game.

At Little Rock in 1949, he caught Ralph "Blackie" Schwamb, a pitcher-turned-killer.

The 6-foot-5, 195-pound Blackie had a reputation as nasty as the fastball and sinker that had earned him a shot with the St. Louis Browns in 1948. "Most of his weight was hair," Duke said.

He appeared in three games for the Travelers, winning his only two decisions. "He had better stuff than pitchers in the big leagues—as good as anybody I ever caught," Duke said. "He had no business being in Little Rock. The only reason he was there was he was a problem to somebody."

Blackie's problem was alcoholism, made worse by dealings with Los Angeles mobster Mickey Cohen. "Blackie didn't care about nuthin'," Duke said. "He didn't care that he wasn't in the big leagues anymore. It didn't bother him."

On October 12, 1949, Blackie and an accomplice robbed a Long Beach, California, doctor of $53 and beat him to death. "We were both pretty drunk, and we got the idea of robbing him," Blackie admitted. [1]

They avoided the gas chamber but were sentenced to life imprisonment. Blackie continued to pitch during the 10 years he served behind bars to become known as the greatest prison player of all time.

In his brief stint as player-manager of the Tallahassee Rebels in 1954, Marland "Duke" Doolittle and his son, Sandy, didn't get to enjoy moments like this one the year before when Duke managed at Jackson, Mississippi. Duke inherited a Tallahassee team that not only was bad and broke, but also its best player, Conk Meriwether, was deeply troubled by personal problems. Photo courtesy of Sandy Doolittle.

In 1943, at Little Rock, Duke caught Ed "Bear Tracks" Greer, a menacing-looking pitcher with two satchel feet who won 284 games in the minors but never went higher because, as one opposing hitter put it, "he might strangle a teammate, or throw somebody off a building, or go to a bar and get stabbed by a woman, or get himself beaten to death by a mob."[2]

"Bear's crazy," one teammate said. "He's not like other people. He's from the hills. He doesn't abide by normal rules of combat."[3]

In 1955, Bear Tracks, also called "Caveman," was employed by the city of Pueblo, Colorado, when he died of a heart attack following a fight with a member of a city jail work gang. He was 54.

Little Rock outfielder Ben Howard "Rosie" Cantrell was a good guy, but between innings he had a bad habit of taking a swig or two of bourbon from a bottle he stashed inside the ballpark's hand-operated scoreboard in center field. "If he wasn't going to hit during that inning, he didn't come in," Duke said.

Rosie was a fan favorite in Arkansas, playing five seasons for the Travelers and another four in nearby Pine Bluff. He never batted lower than .301.

"He was well liked because he could hit the ball," Duke said. "I don't know if people knew he had a drinking problem. They couldn't tell the difference whether he was half-loaded when he was playing or completely sober because he hit the same."

Every spring Rosie pledged not to drink any more. "He didn't drink anymore, but he didn't drink any less either," Duke added.

Rosie liked women as much as his booze, and he wasn't all that finicky about their looks. When a teammate pointed this out, Rosie replied, "Well, people are all alike. They all need love. I'm taking care of my share."

The main character in the baseball novel and movie *Long Gone* is Cecil "Stud" Cantrell, player-manager of the Graceville, Florida, Oilers in the Class D Alabama–Florida League.

There really is a Graceville, Florida, and the town once had a team named the Oilers in the Alabama–Florida League. But author Paul Hemphill notes at the beginning of the book, "That is where the facts in this story begin and end."[4]

This hasn't prevented speculation that Stud and Rosie shared more than a last name.

"He's not very big but well put together," Rosie was described by a *Los Angeles Times* columnist in 1945.[5]

"He was a good-looking man," Duke said. "I wish that I looked as good as he did."

Rosie broke into pro baseball in 1937, the year before Stan "The Man" Musial, one of the all-time great hitters.

Conk was compared with Musial after he blasted a homer and two doubles in an intrasquad game during spring training with the St. Louis Cardinals in 1946. A wire service correspondent wrote, "Sounds like Stan Musial, who also broke in as a pitcher."[6]

When Duke took over as Tallahassee manager a month into the 1954 season, Conk was batting .371, and tied for the league lead in home runs, with four. But he wasn't pleased with his performance.

"Why, I don't weigh nothing like I should," he said, blaming the removal of all his teeth during the offseason. "I've lost 40 pounds since last season. I ought to weigh 225, and right now I'm at about 190."[7]

"Meriwether might have no homers here, save for the new fence," observed *Tallahassee Democrat* columnist Bill McGrotha, referring to "Meriwether Gardens," the temporary wall that was 50 feet closer to home plate than the one it replaced. "All his round-trippers have been well hit, but no one yet has hit one over the high outer right-field barrier."[8]

"Conk was the best player that I had," Duke said. "There was no doubt about his ability. His power had diminished somewhat and he didn't hit as many home runs, but he could shake people up in the stands when he got a hold of one. Tallahassee wasn't an easy ballpark to hit home runs in."

In the short time they were together, Conk shared things with Duke that he shielded from others. "He confided in me to the extent of the problem he had that worried him constantly," Duke said. "I know it affected his baseball performance."

He told Duke what happened with the Cardinals, relating, "I had my chance, but when that happened, I lost it all."

The Cardinals assigned him to the Houston Buffs in the Texas League to improve his defense at first base. The *Houston Post* welcomed the news by reporting Conk had a "whale of a chance to show Texas League fans a thing or two when it comes to pounding a baseball."[9]

Conk had three hits in three of the seven games he played for the Buffs when it was revealed that he had "been ill most of the spring and decided to take a two-week vacation from the game."[10]

No details about the illness were provided. He returned to Houston a week later, appeared in six more games, and, then, suddenly exiled to Lufkin, Texas, a city in the East Texas League. He was hitting .343 (14-for-48) at the time.

Within a span of 2½ months, Conk tumbled from a spot on a big-league roster to a last-place team in a Class C circuit.

"All of his wrong moments in baseball came when he was with Houston," Duke said. "He was a prospect. He was going to the big leagues. The Cardinals had called him up, and by his own admission, he was too drunk to get on the train. From that time on, everything was downhill with Conk."

The *Allentown Morning Call* reported Conk had a nervous breakdown "brought on no doubt by his wartime naval experiences, when two ships on which he had been serving were sunk and many of his shipmates died each time."[11]

Conk played for the Allentown Redbirds in 1944 and 1945.

The team's business manager recalled Conk saying he "never felt right after an emergency abdominal operation while in the Coast Guard." He blamed spinal injections that caused "'funny spells' thereafter."[12]

Joe McCarron, a columnist for the *Morning Call*, described Conk as a "moody fellow" in Allentown who "wouldn't speak to his teammates for days at a time."

McCarron related how Conk went into a rage one night in the Texas League and "lined his teammates up against their dressing room wall and with a loaded revolver terrorized them for 30 minutes before he was persuaded to call it off."[13]

None of this can be corroborated by other news accounts.

McCarron claimed Conk was out of baseball for a while, but that wasn't the case. He was playing for Lufkin three days after the *Houston Post* reported that the Buffs had a deal they were "cooking up for him."[14]

Conk didn't mention any of this to Duke. Instead, he talked about the "golden opportunity" he squandered and the financial problems he was having because of his situation at home.

While playing for Greenville, Texas, Conk married Ruth Mills in April 1948. Three months earlier, in Bowling Green, Florida, Ruth had been crowned queen of the Hardee County Strawberry Festival.

A story in the *Tampa Tribune* called Ruth "comely," adding, "Her mass of waving brown hair, parted in the middle, frames a strongly featured, almost Hepburn-like face. Her eyebrows slide upward in exotic slant."[15]

The eldest of nine children, the 20-year-old Ruth worked as a nurse's aide in a local hospital to help her father, an electrician, support the large family. Ruth's mother was bedfast, her left side paralyzed by a tumor on her spinal cord. Eventually, Ruth's parents and a brother moved into the same house with her, Conk, and their three children.

"He got aggravated—really, really aggravated," recalled Mike Scivoletti, a shortstop for the Millers in 1952–53. "He decided to give them the house and move to Florida."

Donald Keeter, a catcher at Crowley in 1953, even heard Conk tell his 5-year-old son, nicknamed "Little Conk" by the players, "I'm going out and kill your Grandma."

"Oh, Daddy," the boy replied, "you're kidding."

Conk complained nonstop about his mother-in-law.

"You couldn't talk to him over two minutes without that problem coming up," Duke said.

> It was always the same thing: "I don't know what I'm going to do. It's driving me crazy." I don't know what kind of money they were paying him, but from what they paid me to manage the ballclub, they couldn't have been paying him too much. He didn't have money to do anything for a mother-in-law that desperately needed health help. And he couldn't get anybody to help him.

Conk was released by Tallahassee three weeks after Duke left town.

"Yes, we'd like to talk to Meriwether," said Miami manager Pepper Martin. "We couldn't pay him the kind of salary he was making there, but we might work something out. Be nice to have a guy like that sitting on the bench, just coming up and hitting one every now and then."[16]

"If Meriwether regains his weight and good health, he may have another year or two of good slugging ahead of him," columnist McGrotha wrote.[17]

The Valdosta Tigers figured Conk had enough left in the tank to power them into the Georgia–Florida League playoffs. They didn't make it, as Conk batted an anemic .222, mustering only six homers in 38 games.

It was the end of the line for a slugger who had a chance to be famous in baseball but instead became infamous for a senseless act committed the year after he quit baseball and became a carpenter.

Duke was with his mother-in-law in the kitchen of her house in Little Rock when she asked, "Did you have a ballplayer at Tallahassee by the name of Meriwether?"

"Yes," Duke replied.

"Well, he went crazy and killed his mother-in-law."

Newspapers throughout the country carried this United Press story:

> TAVERNIER, Fla., Nov. 20—A crazed 37-year-old carpenter chopped a bloody path of destruction through a small bungalow in this Florida Keys town today, killing his paralyzed mother-in-law and critically injuring her husband and son. [18]

On a Sunday, four days before Thanksgiving Day, Conk was eating lunch when he suddenly got up from the table and walked outside to his car. He returned with a hatchet in his hand and asked Little Conk, "Would you like to see me kill everyone in the family?" [19]

He went into the living room where Ruth's parents, Ellen and Charles Mills, and 16-year-old brother, Paul, were relaxing.

Without saying a word, Conk walked up to his mother-in-law and hacked her in the throat several times. Then he turned on Charles and Paul.

Ruth heard screaming and rushed from the kitchen to the living room, where her mother was slumped over in her wheelchair and Conk was slashing at her father.

"Now to get my wife and children," Conk shouted as Ruth fled with their three children to the nearby home of Reverend Damon S. Scott, pastor of the Tavernier Methodist Church and a close friend of Ruth and her mother. [20]

After the attack, Conk walked outside, tossed the hatchet into some bushes, and calmly waited for police to arrive.

He told a next-door neighbor, "I know I was wrong, I know what I did—don't shoot me." [21]

At the inquest, Reverend Scott testified that Conk had called on him two months earlier to request an affidavit that Ruth was a "religious fanatic and incapable of taking care of their children." He wanted a divorce because Ruth "is too big a fool about the Lord and the church." [22]

Reverend Scott refused, suggesting Conk pray for an answer to his problems.

"Mrs. Mills and her daughter were deeply religious," Reverend Scott explained. "Meriwether seemed to resent God and his wife's interest in the church. He brooded often, but usually he would go away and cool off by himself."[23]

Conk was prone to "sudden fits of rage," Ruth said, and on several occasions, he threatened her and the children.[24]

Two weeks earlier, Conk was wandering the streets of Key West when he was picked up by police and taken to jail for protection because he couldn't remember his name or where he left his car. They suspected amnesia. He finally came around and was given $2 to buy gas for the 90-mile trip home to Tavernier.

Sixteen days after the death of his wife, Charles Mills died of multiple skull fractures.

Conk never stood trial for the two murders.

A three-man commission ruled Conk was insane and ordered him confined to a state mental hospital at Chattahoochee.

"It is our medical opinion that Meriwether was, in all likelihood, incompetent at the time of the commission of the crime," the panel concluded. "It is our impression that although he might have known right from wrong, he was incapable of adhering to the right at that time."[25]

Court records also included a sworn statement from a Plantation Key psychiatrist who met with Conk and his wife prior to the killings:

Mrs. Meriwether made at least two calls to my office with emotional problems regarding her husband. She had apparently become quite religious and was disturbed that her husband was not quite as enthusiastic.

I then had Mr. Meriwether visit me, and he was quite disturbed and upset with the relationship between his wife, the church, and himself.

I do remember visiting the family and strongly suggesting that they seek mental health care for Mr. Meriwether as I felt he was mentally disturbed. . . . There was probably about a two-week interval between the first visits and the final episode of the deaths of Mr. and Mrs. Mills in Tavernier.

It was my medical opinion that Mr. Meriwether was mentally un-balanced and in need of care during the time of the office visit and the deaths of Mr. and Mrs. Mills. By care, I mean psychiatric care.[26]

On being admitted to the state hospital, Conk was examined and found to be psychotic with "schizoaffective symptoms."[27]

A team of five psychiatrists and two other medical doctors combined to file a report that summed up everything in a sentence: "He apparently was mentally ill at the time of the alleged murder."[28]

Emile Chaillot went to see Conk once during the nearly 16 years he was at Chattahoochee. "Hey, how you doing?" Emile said, greeting his former teammate, who was fishing at a creek on hospital grounds.

"What are you in for?" Conk asked.

"I'm not in for nothing," Emile said. "I come to visit you."

Conk didn't testify at the inquest and never commented publicly on the murders. At a subsequent hearing in Key West he cried and yelled hysterically before he was taken out of the courtroom and back to his jail cell.

He told Emile he went home for lunch one day and his wife said, "There's no room at the table." So he decided to make room.

Conk talked about the carpentry work he did at the hospital. "They don't bother me, and I get time off to go fishing," he explained. "Every once in a while, I gotta go off again because I don't want to leave."

By May 1971, Conk was considered sane and capable of standing trial for the double slaying. A psychiatrist testified that Conk's "schizophrenic fantasies" were "submerged by prescribed medication."[29]

The trial never took place, as some of the witnesses were dead and others scattered throughout the country.

Conk spent six months in a Key West jail, and in January 1972, he pleaded guilty to manslaughter, paid a $1 fine, and was placed on five years' probation in the custody of a sister living in central Florida. "You have a wonderful opportunity to redeem yourself—to undo the terrible thing," the judge told him.[30]

"I feel like I'm coming from another planet to earth again," Conk said. "I know the world outside is beautiful—I've seen it."[31]

He wanted to see his wife and children, but the top priority was "to go fishing . . . and then I'll play it (life) by ear."[32]

Two years later, Conk was arrested and pleaded guilty to assault with the intent to commit rape. He was sentenced to three years in prison and released on probation again. He died in 1996.

Ruth Meriwether, a devout Christian, became a nurse in a mountain mission in Kentucky and later at a hospital in North Carolina. She died in 2003.

"I knew something dreadful was going to happen to him," Duke said. "I didn't know that he would go insane and commit murder like he did. He was just driven out of his mind by not knowing what to do. He didn't have baseball to rely on anymore, and he just lost it completely. Mentally he flew off the radar."

Duke was still bothered by the memory of the Tavernier tragedy up to his death in 2016, at the age of 92.

"It grieved me when I heard about it," he said. "And it struck me that if somebody had helped him or gotten this problem off his mind, this might never have happened."

Duke sighed.

"There are times you'd like to help people, but you can't do it and you're forever saddened by that fact. I had nothing in my power to help him."

Unfortunately, no one with power did anything.

18

RESTORE IT AND THEY WILL RETURN

Everyone in Crowley calls Richard Pizzolatto "Coach Pizz."

He's a Crowley institution, his round, smiling face almost as familiar as the historic St. Michael's Catholic Church around the corner from the house where he was born in 1936, and lived most of his life.

Pizzolatto was a household name in Crowley from the time Louis Sr. and his wife, Leona, opened a candy kitchen downtown. They went on to operate a meat market and raise six children: Lena, Charlie, Angelo, Mamie, Louis Jr., and Richard.

Lena became a captain in the U.S. Army and received a Bronze Star Medal for her courageous work during World War II as a nurse on the front lines in North Africa, Italy, France, and eventually Germany, where she treated survivors of the Nazi concentration camp at Dachau.

Charlie was best known for the pizza pie served at his downtown café, Charlie's Place.

Angelo was a clutch-hitting center fielder for the semipro team that played at Miller Stadium before the pros arrived in 1950.

Richard was at every Millers home game until he started college. "That was our pastime," he said. "Everybody went to the ballpark. The rich, the poor, the blacks, everybody was there."

He sold peanuts in the stands and outscrambled other Knothole Gang members for baseballs Crowley manager Johnny George tossed into the outfield after each game.

Later on, he hid in the woods behind the right-field fence and waited for such left-handers as John Gregg and Gary Tuggle of the visiting

Lafayette Bulls to knock a ball out of the park. "They'd hit 'em and we'd get 'em and run," Richard recalled.

"Mr. George," Richard asked, "why don't you buy Gregg and Tuggle?"

"Son," George replied, "they may hit two home runs each, but when they go out in the field, they're going to let in nine."

Richard taught swimming for 37 years. His first job was as a lifeguard at the community pool. "Daddy, I'm working," he proudly announced.

"Sitting on your ass in the sun, you call that work?" his father scoffed.

Born in Italy, Louis Sr. moved to Crowley in 1910 and started a truck line hauling rice and anything else that needed moving.

"He had about a fourth-grade education, but he could speak three languages fluently," Coach Pizz said. "He was smarter than any of us that went to college."

The youngest Pizzolatto graduated from the University of Louisiana at Lafayette in 1958, and for the next 35 years was a highly accomplished coach described by the *Crowley Daily Signal* as the "man who gets things done."[1]

One of the things he did at Crowley High School in 1975 was resurrect the baseball program, which died shortly after the Millers folded in 1957.

When Coach Pizz took over as Crowley's recreation director in 1995, Miller Stadium was falling down and barely recognizable.

The outfield fences were a stone's throw from home plate, turning pop fly balls into home runs. The playing field was in terrible condition, the dugouts infested with termites, the stands unsafe to sit in, and the dilapidated tin clubhouse better suited for ghosts than players.

"It broke my heart to see Miller Stadium deteriorating," Coach Pizz said. "I grew up at that park. I played American Legion, high school, and semipro ball there."

Miller Stadium was a shrine, the cornerstone of the community in its heyday, a treasure trove of tales from the '50s.

"The Millers were like the Yankees and Red Sox to us," Coach Pizz explained.

Harold Gonzales Jr., publisher of the *Crowley Post-Signal*, felt the same way. "The true baseball players were the Crowley Millers, the Rayne Rice Birds, the Evangeline League. The New York Yankees? That was a fantasy. That was in never-never land."

The Millers and the Rice Birds, a member of the Evangeline League from 1935 to 1941, were real to Gonzales even though he was too young to see them in action. "I've always been fascinated by the Millers," he said.

The story goes that after a Millers loss, George would often storm into the clubhouse and head straight toward the back wall so he could bang on it and yell at the umpires in the adjoining dressing room: "Ya'll blind Toms. Ya'll cost me another."

The Millers' number-one fan, Gus Lafosse, sat near home plate with his young daughter, Lola. When the Millers bunched together several hits, he would holler at the opposing team's manager, "Warm up a pitcha'!" If an umpire made a call he didn't like, he would shout, "Warm up an umpire!" The umps had the last word. "He has to go!" they bellowed on one occasion, just before Gus and Lola were ushered out of the ballpark.

After a rainstorm, the grounds crew, headed by Abbie Baronet, the team's trainer and jack-of-all-trades, dried out the infield by saturating it with diesel fuel and burning it off. On one occasion Abbie got caught in the middle of the fire and had to be taken to the hospital for treatment of minor burns.

Smoke coming from Miller Stadium was a welcome sign to both locals and strangers.

One afternoon a young girl living in Egan, 10 miles north of Crowley, saw a cloud of smoke and ran up to her father and said, "Daddy, they're going to play tonight. It's not rained out. I see smoke."

On joining the Millers in 1952, catcher Al Ogletree pulled into a gas station to ask for directions.

"You see the smoke over there?" the attendant asked. "It rained, and they're working on the field, drying it."

Ogletree followed the smoke to the ballpark.

Miller Stadium is located near railroad tracks used by the rice mills that earned Crowley the nickname "Rice Capital of America." Sometimes fans parked along the track, and in the middle of a game the public address announcer would call out the license numbers of cars that had to be moved for a train to pass through.

The tracks were full on car-giveaway nights.

A seven-year-old girl won one car drawing that attracted 2,200 fans.

The mother of them all was a record crowd of 7,381, which filled the grandstands and bleachers two hours before game time and, then, jammed a roped-off standing room area 20 feet from the outfield walls.

"I couldn't believe it," marveled Billy Joe Barrett, center fielder for the visiting Thibodaux Giants. "Hell, the population is only 12,500, and they got 7,000 people in the ballpark. Where are they coming from?"

Everyone went home happy, as the Millers won, Conk Meriwether socked two homers, and a Crowley housewife drove off in a new Chevrolet.

"Oh, happy day!" Millers play-by-play announcer Ed Keim repeated time and again, to the delight of his radio listeners.

"Miller Stadium was our life and culture," Coach Pizz said. "It's part of our heritage."

It also was the future.

Restoring the ballpark would preserve a landmark and boost tourism by making it a highly desirable venue for state, regional, and national youth tournaments.

"When we bring all those players and their coaches and families here, they have to stay in our hotels, eat in our restaurants, buy gas, and shop," Coach Pizz said, adding, "We want people to come here and see our little town with our beautiful stadium and the biggest, I believe, historic district in the state."[2]

"Coach had the vision for Miller Stadium," said Isabella de la Houssaye, the mayor of Crowley at the time. "I immediately bought into the vision. It was a no-brainer."

Recreation for young people was at the top of her agenda. "If we don't do it for the youth, who do we do it for?" she questioned.

The community rallied around the theme: "Remember: It's for the children."

In addition to giving Miller Stadium a facelift, the goal was to spruce up a half-dozen baseball and softball fields for kids. "It's not for me, it's not for you, but it's for the children," Coach Pizz reminded everyone. "Recreation is for the children."

With Mayor de la Houssaye and the city council making the half-million-dollar project possible, area businesses, volunteers, and even prison inmates teamed up to refurbish the ballpark in just six months.

Everything was new, from the seating, to the lighting, to the dugouts, scoreboard, press box, umpire's room, restrooms, concession stand, and front entrance. A new metal outfield fence expanded the size of the playing field to 325 feet down the foul lines, 375 feet in the power alleys, and 416 feet to deepest center field. An underground sprinkling system was added.

"We took it out of the ashes and brought it back for generations and generations to enjoy like I did as a kid," Coach Pizz said.

He was at the ballpark one day in 1998, when a man asked in a heavy Brooklyn accent, "Is this Miller Stadium?"

"Yes," Coach Pizz replied in a thick Southern drawl. "It's great to have you back Mr. Scivoletti."

A shortstop for the Millers in their glory years of 1952–53, Mike Scivoletti was shocked. "How do you know who I am?" he asked.

"You were my hero when you played here," Coach Pizz said.

Standing next to Scivoletti was another Brooklynite, Tony Mele, the Millers' third baseman in 1952 and 1955.

Coach Pizz called Oscar Johnson, a former Millers pitcher who he replaced as the city's recreation director. He also phoned four other ex-Millers who lived in town—Emile Chaillot, Art Edinger, Ray Hensgens, and Harry Jukes. They met that night at a local restaurant for a crawfish boil. "Some great memories were rehashed," Coach Pizz said.

The impromptu gathering inspired him to organize a reunion in 2000, to mark the 50th anniversary of Crowley's entry into pro ball.

"Many people thought I was nuts," Coach Pizz said.

Jim Bello, a first baseman for the Millers in 1954, didn't beat around the bush. "I hate to bust your bubble, Pizz, but no one will come."

Some of the players were already at the great ballpark in the sky, and others were knocking on the door.

The idea wasn't as far-fetched as it sounded.

As part of a history project, Nicholls State University in Thibodaux hosted eight Evangeline League reunions. Attendance was dropping, so why not go cross-state to Crowley and make it a weekend event, Saturday devoted to the Millers and Sunday to other Evangeline Leaguers.

The plan worked, as 75 players and their families showed up in Crowley. "We're not stopping now," Coach Pizz declared.

He expanded the program from two to five days, adding an old-timer's game, tours of various historical sites, and lots of spicy Cajun food. One year, they visited Mama Redell, who demonstrated how to make chicken, sausage, and tasso jambalaya, as well as roux chicken and sausage gumbo. They sampled cracklins and baudoin, and capped off the day with a crawfish étouffée dinner. Mayor de la Houssaye entertained the visitors at her home, giving them a key to the city, which they referred to as the "Nice Capital of America."

The players kept coming back. Altogether, there were nine reunions, the last in 2010. They traveled from as far away as Hawaii.

Mele came from New York and Scivoletti from New Jersey.

Jimmy "Lanky" Moore arrived from Georgia with a bunch of watermelons for his many Crowley friends.

Pitchers Jerry Simon, Chuck Nelson, and Alan Siff journeyed from California, North Carolina, and Virginia, respectively.

Another pitcher, Roy Niccolai, came from Chicago with his daughters, Mary Ida and Eileen. "It was truly great for all of us to go together because we had a chance to see a part of his life that made him so happy," Mary Ida said. "The players embraced us. We couldn't wait for the next reunion."

It was a family affair.

Mele was accompanied by his wife Mary, daughter Annie, and Annie's husband and kids.

Knuckleball-throwing brothers Cletus and Nate Younger attended, Cletus from Kansas and Nate from Colorado.

Ogletree and his wife, JoAnn, drove from McAllen, Texas. "There are very few of the old parks left that were so important to our culture in the '50s," Ogletree said. [3]

Miller Stadium was once a field of dreams for Ogletree and his teammates. Those dreams were long gone. All they had left was their memories.

Ogletree recalled a conversation with manager Johnny George on reporting to the Millers in 1952, with a duffel bag containing three gloves, one for catching, one for first base, and one for the outfield.

"Have you ever played shortstop?" George asked.

"Yeah, one year in high school," Ogletree replied.

"Take infield at shortstop," George instructed.

It was common for new players to be viewed suspiciously by others who feared being replaced. Scivoletti played shortstop and Mele third base.

"You could see the daggers coming out of their eyes," Ogletree laughed. "When they found out I was a catcher, everything was okay."

In Ogletree's second stint with the Millers in 1955, he and Moore took turns on road trips driving the team's old school bus.

"One would drive up and the other drive back," Ogletree said. "There was a big bump in the road between Alexandria and Crowley, and we tried to go as fast as we could and hit that bump. We wanted to see how far the bat bag bounced up on the door in the back of the bus."

Ogletree reluctantly agreed to let Niccolai use his bat during a game. "Don't break it!" he pleaded.

Niccolai walked on four straight pitches, never taking the bat off his shoulder. "Boy, that's a great bat!" he told Ogletree.

Siff and infielder Nick Stanziani were teammates in 1953, at Dublin, Georgia, and New Iberia, and again in 1954, at Crowley.

"Nick Stanziani was as superstitious a ballplayer as I ever knew, more so than a lot of pitchers, and that's saying something," Siff said.[4]

Mired in a batting slump early in the '54 season, Siff told Nick that every bat has a certain number of hits in it, and he had likely used up most of them. The pitcher suggested Nick borrow his bat, noting there were plenty of hits left in it. "Nick looked at me with a little disbelief, continued to use his old bat, and that night went hitless."[5]

Nick decided to use Siff's bat the next game and got a hit with runners on base.

"He said the bat not only had hits left in it, but the bat knew where the holes were because it had radar in it," Siff said. "For the rest of the season whenever Nick came up in a tight situation and we needed a hit, he would ask me to find the radar bat."[6]

Stanziani wound up hitting a career-high .301.

Simon had a 5–2 record with the Millers in 1951, one of the wins earning him a free haircut at Comeaux's barbershop.

"I went all over town looking for Como's barbershop," Simon said. "I found out it was Comeaux. Everything ends with an E-A-U-X."

Simon got married at the end of his second season with the Millers in 1954.

Abbie Baronet, a fatherly figure to the team's younger players, pulled Simon aside and said, "Listen, here's what I want you to do. Every time you have an experience with your wife, you put a marble in this big case. The first year that thing will be full. The second year you won't be able to count how many times you do it."

It was a lesson Simon never forgot. "Abbie was always there for everybody. He was the nicest guy in the whole world. I loved him. All the guys did."

The reunions also gave fans a chance to reflect and reminisce.

"See that tall feller in the brown shirt?" a grandfather was overheard saying to his grandson as they watched the ex-Millers take batting practice. "That's old Jimmy Moore. Why, he used to be one of the most feared batters in the Evangeline League. I was here one night when he hit four home runs in one game, and afterwards, he said if he could have had one more at-bat, he would have hit five."[7]

The grandson was questioning this after Moore grabbed a bat and awkwardly swung at and missed several pitches.

"I saw him do some remarkable things with that bat," the grandfather insisted. "The fans loved him. He was not only an outstanding hitter, but he could play center field as well as anybody in the league."[8]

An umpire once said to Millers pitcher Hugh Blanton after Moore reached over the fence to make a spectacular catch, "The octopus got another one."

The grandfather spotted Siff in the outfield. "He was the Millers' pitcher the night Jimmy Moore hit those four home runs. He needed every one of those to win the game."[9]

It was hard to convince anyone that the old guy on the field was the Evangeline League's batting champ in 1955, with a .354 average.

"It's too bad we didn't have video cameras back then so I could show you just how good he was 46 years ago," the grandfather lamented.[10]

Everything the grandfather said was true.

In four seasons at Crowley, Moore batted .330 and averaged 22 home runs and 113 runs batted in. In 1956–57, at Ballinger, Texas, in the Class B Southwestern League, he hit .336 and .301, respectively.

"He was a legend in his own mind," Mele needled.[11]

The Yankees had their "M&M Boys," Mickey Mantle and Roger Maris, and the Millers had Mele and Moore. They were close friends and poked fun at one another every chance they got.

"He (Mele) should look up to me," Moore explained, "and say, 'Yes, sir!' and 'No, sir!' because I played two years of Class B ball."[12]

Moore pointed out, "Mele hit five homers in a season, and I hit four in one night."

When a boy would climb up on the fence during batting practice and holler for a ball, Moore would ask if he had a sister. If the boy did, he would toss him a ball.

"They learned fast and would hop up on the fence and say, 'Jimmy Moore, my sister told me to tell you, 'Hello,'" Moore said, adding, "Mele never learned this trick, and I tell him that's the reason I was voted the most popular player."[13]

The all-time favorite of Millers fans was Emile Chaillot, the most valuable player on the 1950 team, who regularly threw balls to black fans sitting in the right-field bleachers. He wound up living 54 years in Crowley and becoming a pillar of the community.

"It was amazing the things he did and the people he helped," Coach Pizz said. "He counselled alcoholics and took in troubled youngsters and homeless people."

Emile was a recovering alcoholic who stood up for others trying to do the same.

"Alcoholism is no more a disease than gambling . . . or chasing women . . . or getting hooked up on drugs," a *Crowley Post-Signal* editorial opined in 1986.[14]

Emile protested in a letter to the editor:

> Ask all the families who are suffering difficulties with their marriages, financial problems, trouble with the law, health problems and tell them it's not a disease.
>
> I, myself, have the disease of alcoholism. I am not ashamed of it no more than someone with high blood pressure, sugar diabetes, overweight, or heart trouble. It is not contagious, however, when I put the cork on the bottle all the other problems left, too. There is no cure for it. The only thing we have to offer is complete abstinence. . . .
>
> I haven't had any alcohol or mind-altering drug in five years, and it wasn't hard because it was done one day at a time.[15]

Emile stayed sober the rest of his life, running a highly successful TV repair and furniture business after leaving baseball.

He was well known for the advertising he did for the truckloads of mattresses he sold at cost plus 10 to 15 percent.

"How is your mattress?" he asked in a radio commercial. "Is your partner sliding over on top of you? It's time you get a new mattress."

A photograph in one newspaper ad showed Emile and his oldest son, Joe, in bed, the text reading, "No matter who you find yourself in bed with, come get a good mattress at Chaillot's TV and Furniture."

"Dad wanted to be the bride at every wedding and the corpse at every funeral," Joe said. "He loved telling stories, making jokes, and being the center of attention."

Emile was center stage at the reunions.

"The week of the reunions was his favorite week of the year," Coach Pizz said.

"Dad grew up hearing lots of stories from his father, his uncles and aunts in New Orleans every time he'd visit," explained Joe, a professional storyteller known as Joe Paris. "He took stories from real life that he could embroider around."

There was the game Emile was brought in to pitch in the top of the ninth inning with Crowley down by a run, two outs, and a runner on first base. "He picked the guy off first and then the Millers scored twice to win the game," Joe said.

Emile was the winning pitcher, and he didn't throw one pitch to home plate.

"It's true," Joe said. "It was written up in the Crowley paper and a trivia question on the radio."

When Emile thought Joe was making something up, he let him know by saying, "That was an interesting story you just told, Joe. It could be true."

Another story that could be true was the time Emile slid into second base in a cloud of dust, popped up, and noticed no one had the ball. He took off for third base and kept going until he got to the dugout. As his teammates gave him congratulatory slaps on the backside, he reached into the hip pocket of his baggy wool pants and pulled out the ball.

"The ball skipped into my father's back pocket," Joe said. "Of course, it wouldn't have been unusual for Dad to have slid into second, rolled onto the ball, grabbed it, and put it into his back pocket. But he never admitted to that."

One player who never made it to a reunion was Juan Izaguirre, a Cuban infielder-pitcher who put up some impressive numbers his three seasons with the Millers—1953–55.

He batted .339, .322, and .307, respectively, while averaging 13 home runs and 88 RBIs per year. On the mound, he posted won–lost records of

Cuban-born Juan Izaguirre was a fan favorite and the most versatile Millers player, pitching the first no-hitter in the team's history, playing wherever he was needed in the infield or outfield, and ranking among the league's top hitters the three years he played in Crowley—1953–55. Juan returned to Cuba to play and coach for the Marianao Tigers in 1957–58. Photo Courtesy of Ralph Maya.

14–5 in 1954, and 10–8 in 1955, one of the wins a no-hitter, the first in Millers history.

"He was something else," Ogletree said. "He threw a forkball, the first I ever caught. He could play any position on the field."

Ogletree went on to coach more than 1,200 college players in 41 years, 29 of them at Pan American University, where he guided teams to

13 NCAA regional appearances and a fourth-place finish in the 1971 College World Series.

"If he played today, I'd like to have him on my team," Ogletree said of Izaguirre. "He could do a lot of things and be a good influence on others."

The most amazing of Izaguirre's accomplishments with the Millers is that in 1,810 plate appearances, he struck out only 36 times, or once every 50 at-bats.

"He was a hitter," Ogletree continued. "He'd step in that batter's box, get set, and he wouldn't move a muscle until the pitch came. He was ready to swing."

Prior to playing in the United States, Izaguirre led the Cuban national team to the 1950 Amateur World Series title and a gold medal in the Pan American Games. He was the most valuable player of the World Series, with 4 homers, 16 runs scored, and a record 21 RBIs. "He was a national hero in Cuba," Ogletree said.

In 1957–58, Izaguirre was a player-coach for the Marianao Tigers, a Cuban team that captured back-to-back Caribbean Series titles.

The story making the rounds at the first reunion was that Fidel Castro seized a trucking company owned by Juan's father-in-law when his revolutionary army took over the Cuban government in 1959.

"He and Castro played ball together when they were growing up," Ogletree noted.

Juan sought Castro's help in getting the business back.

"Instead, Castro had Juan put in front of a firing squad and shot," Ogletree said.

The story appeared in the newspaper. It sounded like it could be true, but it wasn't—not by a long shot.

Izaguirre went on to manage in Guatemala and coach in Cuba, mentoring such pitchers as Rene Arocha, the first Cuban defector to play in the majors, and Orlando "El Duque" Hernandez, who sparked the Yankees to three straight World Series championships (1998–2000). Juan died in Miami, Florida, in April 2017, outliving Castro by five months.

"Al Ogletree gave me that story," Coach Pizz said of the highly respected coach, who died in 2019. "I thought anything that Al said was gospel."

Izaguirre outlasted most of his Millers teammates. Jimmy Moore died in 2004, Roy Niccolai in 2005, Alan Siff in 2007, Emile Chaillot in 2008,

Art Edinger and Oscar Johnson in 2011, Ray Hensgens in 2013, Tony Mele in 2016, and Mike Scivoletti in 2017.

Coach Pizz learned of Emile's death from three of his many black friends. "They stopped me and said, with tears in their eyes, 'Our buddy died.'"

The last Millers reunion was held in 2010. All that's left now is Miller Stadium.

At the front entrance is a bronze plaque describing the historical highlights of the Millers and the ballpark. Nearby, a large sign recognizing the accomplishments of Coach Pizz hangs over a concession stand covered with oversized signatures of all the Millers players.

"I got baseballs—things with their signatures—and we put 'em in pencil and traced them," Coach Pizz said.

"Look, there's Johnny George . . . Ray Smerek . . . Rusty Walters . . . Al Ogletree . . . Willard Sterling . . . Jimmy Moore . . . Ray Stockton . . . Chick Morgan . . . Johnny Patrick . . . Roy Niccolai . . . Gifford Reynolds . . . Andy Strong."

Seeing Strong's name stirs memories of the night he was killed by a bolt of lightning standing in center field at Bringhurst Field in Alexandria.

Walt Lamey was in left field at the time.

"There was an awful flash, and I put my hands over my eyes," Lamey said. "I'd been blinded if I had looked at it."[16]

John Pfeiffer was at shortstop and Smerek at second base.

"There was that flash, and I felt heat," Pfeiffer said.

> It jarred me and twisted my cap, and I couldn't hear for a while. It deafened me. I looked for Smerek and couldn't find him right away, and then I saw Andy laying there. I picked up his hat, and then somebody told us to take our shoes and belts and hats off. I could see Andy wasn't breathing.[17]

Lincoln Fowler, a pitcher, saw the flash from the dugout.

"It looked like it hammered right on top of him . . . it seemed to be about four seconds long," Fowler said. "We just put our hands up over our eyes in the dugout."[18]

It was a defining moment for Crowley, bonding the town and team, while opening the door for the legendary Conk.

Conk's name is on the concession stand, along with Art Pacanowski, the kid infielder from Chicago, and catcher Earl Herring, best remembered for marrying Joycelyn Aube, the queen of the 1948 International Rice Festival, in a wedding ceremony at home plate.

Jimmy Moore also married a local girl—Una Leger.

They met in front of a pool hall in Crowley. Una was walking home when she spotted Jimmy and asked for an autographed baseball to give to her 10-year-old nephew, Don Chaisson.

"I'll do better than that," Jimmy said.

He drove Una home and gave her a bat with his name on it. Wedding bells followed.

"I never played baseball with that bat," Don said. "I still have it."

One spring day, Coach Pizz was showing a visitor around Miller Stadium while the Crowley High Gents were warming up for a game. He pointed to a fishing net next to the flagpole in center field. "If you hit a ball into the net, Jerry Ashley gave you a brand new Chevrolet."

Moore came the closest to driving a Chevy home.

"Start that engine!" he hollered at Ashley as he watched a line-drive shot make a beeline toward the net. The ball missed by inches.

Coach Pizz motioned toward an old cemetery behind the scoreboard in left field. "I always said I wanted to be buried there so I could watch my park."

A headstone with his name and birth date already is in place. Etched on each side is the fleur-de-lis logo of his beloved New Orleans Saints. Underneath is a drawing of a baseball diamond and the slogan he used as recreation director: "Remember: It's for the children."

The headstone is part of his plan to safeguard Miller Stadium.

"I put the headstone there like I'm still living," he said with a wry smile. "I figure by not having the date of death on there, people will see it and say, 'I can't believe Coach Pizz is still here.'"

APPENDIX A

Crowley Millers through the Years

1950: Gulf Coast League (Class C)

Standings: Crowley, 90–56; Galveston, 80–68, 11 games behind; Jacksonville, 79–68, 11½; *Leesville, 75–70, 14½; Lake Charles, 59–88, 31½; Port Arthur, 58–91, 33½. (*Franchise transferred from Lufkin, Texas, to Leesville, Louisiana, July 15.)

Playoffs: Crowley defeated Leesville, four games to two; Jacksonville defeated Galveston, four games to one; Jacksonville defeated Crowley, four games to two.

Crowley Hitting and Pitching Leaders: Batting average: Bill Turk, .340; home runs: Emile Chaillot, 21; runs batted in: Ray Smerek, 90; wins: *Rusty Walters, 30; earned run average: Jack Balzli, 2.99. (*Led the league.)

Regular-Season Attendance: Galveston, 89,592; Crowley, 79,640; Lake Charles, 78,441; Port Arthur, 66,681; Jacksonville, 36,029; Leesville, 26,456. Total, 377,019. Playoffs, 22,354.

1951: Evangeline League (Class C)

Standings: Thibodaux, 75–61; New Iberia, 76–64, 1 game behind; Hammond, 73–64, 2½; Baton Rouge, 72–66, 4; Crowley, 70–70, 7; Alexandria, 68–71, 8½; Houma, 60–78, 16; Lafayette, 60–80, 17.

Playoffs: Baton Rouge defeated Thibodaux, four games to two; Hammond defeated New Iberia, four games to three; Hammond defeated Baton Rouge, four games to two.

Crowley Hitting and Pitching Leaders: Batting average: Walt Lamey, .342; home runs: Conklyn Meriwether, 19; runs batted in: Lamey, 98; wins: Parks Thomas, 13; earned run average: Thomas, 3.53.

Regular-Season Attendance: New Iberia, 105,077; Crowley, 100,595; Baton Rouge, 66,438; Thibodaux, 63,560; Alexandria, 60,621; Lafayette, 46,782; Houma, 32,716; Hammond, 28,230. Total, 504,019. Playoffs, 33,545.

1952: Evangeline League

Standings: Crowley, 81–59; Thibodaux, 75–63, 5 games behind; Baton Rouge, 76–64, 5; Lafayette, 74–65, 6½; New Iberia, 72–68, 9; Abbeville, 62–78, 19; Houma, 58–79, 21½; Alexandria, 59–81, 22.

Playoffs: Crowley defeated Lafayette, four games to none; Baton Rouge defeated Thibodaux, four games to three; Crowley defeated Baton Rouge, four games to none.

Crowley Hitting and Pitching Leaders: Batting average: Conklyn Meriwether, .335; home runs: *Meriwether, 33; runs batted in: Jimmy Moore, 128; wins: *Hugh Blanton, 21; earned run average: Willard Sterling, 3.10. (*Led the league.)

Regular-Season Attendance: Crowley, 110,814; Baton Rouge, 80,613; Lafayette, 78,706; New Iberia, 74,794; Alexandria, 66,196; Abbeville, 64,650; Thibodaux, 52,727; Houma, 25,821. Total, 554,321. Playoffs, 26,012.

1953: Evangeline League

Standings: Crowley, 84–54; Thibodaux, 71–67, 13 games behind; Baton Rouge, 69–69, 15; *Lafayette, 68–69–1, 15½; Alexandria, 68–69–1, 15½; New Iberia, 52–84, 31. (*Defeated Alexandria to decide fourth place and spot in playoffs.)

Playoffs: Lafayette defeated Crowley, four games to two; Thibodaux defeated Baton Rouge, four games to three; Thibodaux defeated Lafayette, four games to one.

Crowley Hitting and Pitching Leaders: Batting average: Juan Iza-guirre, .339; home runs: *Conklyn Meriwether, 42; runs batted in: *Meri-wether, 134; wins: *Marv Holleman, 24; earned run average: Chuck Nel-son, 3.23. (*Led the league.)

Regular-Season Attendance: Crowley, 100,239; Alexandria, 66,819; Lafayette, 62,525; Baton Rouge, 53,070; New Iberia, 53,407; Thibodaux, 31,745. Total, 368,405. Playoffs, 29,197.

1954: Evangeline League

Standings: New Iberia, 85–55; Port Arthur, 83–57, 2 games behind; Crowley, 77–63, 8; Lake Charles, 67–72, 17½; Baton Rouge, 66–74, 19; Alexandria, 65–74, 19½; *Thibodaux, 61–79, 24; Lafayette, 55–85, 30. (*Franchise shifted from Texas City to Thibodaux, June 17.)

Playoffs: New Iberia defeated Lake Charles, four games to two; Crowley defeated Port Arthur, four games to two; New Iberia defeated Crowley, four games to three.

Crowley Hitting and Pitching Leaders: Batting average: Jimmy Moore, .342; home runs: Art Edinger, 31; runs batted in: Moore, 113; wins: Marv Holleman and Jerry Simon, 21; earned run average: Juan Izaguirre, 3.02.

Regular-Season Attendance: New Iberia, 87,350; Lafayette, 74,882; Lake Charles, 71,555; Crowley, 65,099; Baton Rouge, 57,189; Alexan-dria, 51,793; Port Arthur, 46,512; Thibodaux, 19, 328; Texas City, 9,203. Total, 482,911. Playoffs, 32,727.

1955: Evangeline League

First-Half Standings: New Iberia, 42–28–1; Alexandria, 39–31–1, 3 games behind; Baton Rouge, 38–32, 4; Lafayette, 35–35, 7; Crowley, 31–39, 11; Lake Charles, 25–45, 17.

Second-Half Standings: Lafayette, 42–28; Alexandria, 35–34, 6½ games behind; Baton Rouge, 35–34, 6½; New Iberia, 35–34, 6½; Crow-ley, 34–36, 8; Lake Charles, 27–42, 14½.

Overall Standings: New Iberia, 77–62–1; Lafayette, 77–63, ½ game behind; Alexandria, 74–65, 3; Baton Rouge, 73–66, 4; Crowley, 65–75, 12½; Lake Charles, 52–87, 25.

Playoffs: Lafayette defeated New Iberia, four games to two; Alexandria defeated Baton Rouge, four games to one; Lafayette defeated Alexandria, four games to two.

Crowley Hitting and Pitching Leaders: Batting average: *Jimmy Moore, .354; home runs: Moore, 25; runs batted in: Moore, 101; wins: Marv Holleman, 15; earned run average: Bill Thompson, 2.83. (*Led the league.)

Regular-Season Attendance: Lafayette, 57,082; Baton Rouge, 56,603; Crowley, 45,130; New Iberia, 41,794; Alexandria, 37,977; Lake Charles, 33,881. Total, 272,467. Playoffs, 15,992.

1956: Evangeline League

Standings: Lafayette, 78–49; Thibodaux, 66–56, 9½ games behind; Crowley, 63–60, 13; Lake Charles, 62–62, 14½; Alexandria, 55–67, 20½; Monroe, 54–68, 21½; Baton Rouge, 53–70, 23; †New Iberia, 15–14. (†Withdrew from league on May 19.)

Playoffs: Lafayette defeated Lake Charles, four games to one; Thibodaux defeated Crowley, four games to one; final series cancelled because of lack of interest.

Crowley Hitting and Pitching Leaders: Batting average: Chet Boak, .308; home runs: Boak and Don DeGroote, 16; runs batted in: Boak, 71; wins: Bob Nonnenmacher, 15; earned run average: George Brunet, 2.17.

Regular-Season Attendance: Thibodaux, 61,000; Lake Charles, 48,482; Alexandria, 48,049; Baton Rouge, 42,000; Crowley, 37,265; Lafayette, 30,596; Monroe, 25,831; New Iberia, 11,252. Total, 304,475. Playoffs, 5,197.

1957: Evangeline League

First-Half Standings: *Lafayette, 36–21–1; Crowley, 34–22, 1½ games behind; Alexandria, 30–25–1, 5; Lake Charles, 24–24, 12½; *Baton Rouge, 24–25, 13; Thibodaux, 23–34, 13. (*Lafayette and Baton Rouge withdrew from league June 20, one day before close of first half.)

Second-Half Standings: Alexandria, 38–18–1; Crowley, 29–25, 8 games behind; Thibodaux, 22–32, 15; Lake Charles, 19–33–1, 17.

No Playoff: League did not name a formal champion.

Crowley Hitting and Pitching Leaders: Batting average: *Claude Horn, .349; home runs: Bill Balcom, 14; runs batted in: Balcom, 80; wins: Jack Fuller, Dan Pfister, Leon Webrand, 13; earned run average: Arlen Alderman, 3.26. (*Led the league.)

Regular-Season Attendance: Alexandria, 52,937; Thibodaux, 28,653; Crowley, 17,779; Lake Charles, 15,589; Lafayette, 9,567; Baton Rouge, 8,297. Total, 132,822. No playoff.

Source: Baseball Guide and Record Books published by Sporting News Publishing Company, St. Louis, Missouri.

APPENDIX B

Bus Station Biscuit Recipe

The biscuits at the Greyhound bus station coffee shop in Crowley were as popular as the Millers baseball team, people lining up for a slice of heaven every morning at seven o'clock.

Little Richard, the rock-and-roller, reportedly loved the biscuits and got his fill whenever he was in the area.

"They were top of the line," said Ray Hensgens, a pitcher for the Crowley Millers in 1951, who went on to establish a highly successful rice seed and fertilizer company in Crowley and champion the development of Hensgens Park, a complex of baseball fields built on land donated by him and his wife, Kitty.

Ray never made it past Class C in the minors, but as the *Crowley Post-Signal* observed on his death in 2013, "His legacy lives on with every child who takes the field with every at-bat, and with every young pitcher who takes the mound."[1]

Rice mill workers gathered at the coffee shop for "bull sessions" and devoured pan after pan of the buttermilk biscuits as quickly as owner-manager Lillian Bartell pulled them out of the oven. "She had a following," Ray said.

This recipe comes from Fred Reggie, nephew of Judge Edmund Reggie, a longtime Crowley city judge and political stalwart in Louisiana.

"Back in the days when the biscuits were baked in a rectangular cake pan and cut into squares, I remember I would always request the corners because of the two crispy edges," Fred wrote in a Facebook post. He claimed the recipe is the real deal and will make you feel like you're sitting in the Crowley bus station.

Ingredients:
2 cups flour
Pinch baking soda
¼ cup sugar
2 heaping tsp. baking powder (Clabber Girl)
1 tsp. salt
1 cup buttermilk
¾ cup Crisco, melted
½ stick butter or margarine

Directions: Mix all ingredients. Add half of the buttermilk, then Crisco (let cool slightly until almost thickened before adding), then rest of buttermilk. Mix well. Knead a few times on floured board (dough will be sticky—add a little flour but handle as little as possible). Spread gently in 8x8 or 9x9 pan. Bake at 450 degrees for 15–20 minutes or until brown. Melt butter and pour over hot biscuits.

BIBLIOGRAPHY

Adelson, Bruce. *Brushing Back Jim Crow*. Charlottesville and London: University Press of Virginia, 1999.

Alou, Felipe, with Peter Kerasotis. *My Baseball Journey*. Lincoln and London: University of Nebraska Press, 2018.

Bouton, Jim, with Leonard Shecter. *Ball Four*, twentieth anniversary edition. New York: Wylie 1990.

DiMaggio, Joe. *Baseball for Everyone*. New York: Signet, 1949.

Dubus, Andre. *Broken Vessels*. Boston: David R. Godine, 1991.

Erskine, Carl. *Tales from the Dodger Dugout*. Champaign, IL: Sports Publishing Inc., 2001.

Hemphill, Paul. *Long Gone*. Chicago: Ivan R. Dee, 2002.

Pietrusza, David. *Baseball's Canadian American League*. Jefferson, NC: McFarland, 2006.

Tygiel, Jules. *Baseball's Great Experiment: Jackie Robinson and His Legacy*. New York: Vintage, 1983.

Veeck, Bill, with Ed Linn. *Veeck—As in Wreck: The Autobiography of Bill Veeck*. Chicago: University of Chicago Press, 2001.

NOTES

PREFACE

1. *Crowley (LA) Daily Signal*, March 18, 1952, 3.
2. *Crowley Daily Signal*, March 20, 1952, 4.

INTRODUCTION

1. *Crowley Daily Signal*, June 8, 1953, 1.
2. *Crowley Daily Signal*, June 8, 1953, 1.
3. *Crowley Daily Signal*, June 8, 1953, 1.
4. *Los Angeles Times*, July 19, 1966, B1.
5. *Los Angeles Times*, June 21, 1965, B1
6. *Crowley Daily Signal*, May 12, 1957, 8.

I. ALL ROADS PASS THROUGH CROWLEY

1. *Crowley Signal*, October 31, 1908, 8.
2. *Crowley Signal*, November 14, 1908, 4.
3. *Crowley Signal*, April 17, 1915, 3.
4. *Crowley Signal*, November 19, 1915, 1.
5. *Crowley Signal*, March 14, 1921, 1.
6. *Crowley Signal*, March 17, 1921, 1.
7. *Crowley Signal*, March 17, 1921, 1.

8. *Crowley Signal*, March 17, 1921, 1.

9. *New York Daily News*, March 18, 1921, 46.

10. *New York Times*, March 18, 1921, 19.

11. *Crowley Signal*, March 17, 1921, 1.

12. *Sporting News*, August 27, 1952, 35.

13. *Crowley Post-Signal*, February 11, 1992, 1.

14. *Crowley Daily Signal*, May 15, 1948, 3.

15. *Crowley Daily Signal*, March 30, 1955, 7.

16. *Crowley Daily Signal*, October 17, 1959, 2.

17. *Crowley Daily Signal*, October 17, 1959, 1.

18. *Crowley Daily Signal*, October 17, 1959, 2.

19. *Crowley Post-Signal*, May 16, 2008, 1A.

20. *Crowley Post-Signal*, May 16, 2008, 1A.

21. *Crowley Daily Signal*, October 24, 1959, 4.

22. *Crowley Signal*, May 18, 1901, 1.

23. *Crowley Daily Signal*, March 17, 1921, 3.

2. BUILD IT AND THEY WILL COME

1. *Crowley Daily Signal*, October 20, 1945, 4.

2. *Baseball Digest*, September 1963, 55.

3. *Crowley Daily Signal*, October 13, 1945, 4.

4. *Hattiesburg (MS) American*, June 16, 1942, 6.

5. *Crowley Daily Signal*, October 11, 1945, 4.

6. *Crowley Daily Signal*, April 5, 1946, 1.

7. *Crowley Daily Signal*, April 5, 1946, 1.

8. *Crowley Daily Signal*, October 23, 1947, 4.

9. *Crowley Daily Signal*, October 23, 1947, 4.

10. *Crowley Daily Signal*, December 19, 1947, 5.

11. *Alexandria (LA) Town Talk*, December 5, 1951, 14.

12. *Weekly Acadian (Rayne, LA)*, September 16, 1948, 5.

13. *Opelousas (LA) Daily World*, September 21, 1948, 15.

14. *Crowley Post-Signal*, April 7, 1974, 4.

15. *Crowley Post-Signal*, April 7, 1974, 4.

16. *Crowley Post-Signal*, April 7, 1974, 4.

17. *Opelousas (LA) Clarion-News*, May 1, 1947, 1.

18. *Crowley Daily Signal*, November 17, 1949, 6.

19. *Shreveport (LA) Times*, May 14, 1954, 6B.

20. *Odessa (TX) American*, March 9, 1950, 13.

21. *Lake Charles (LA) Southwest Citizen*, June 8, 1950, 10.

22. *Shreveport Times*, May 14, 1954, 6B.

23. *Crowley Daily Signal*, March 6, 1950, 4.

24. *Crowley Daily Signal*, March 23, 1951, 6.

25. *Crowley Daily Signal*, March 23, 1951, 6.

3. JOHNNY ON THE SPOT

1. *Baton Rouge (LA) Morning Advocate*, April 11, 1951, 2-B.

2. *Andalusia (AL) Star*, May 20, 1948, 4.

3. *Andalusia Star*, May 20, 1948, 4.

4. *Crowley Daily Signal*, March 23, 1951, 6.

5. *Crowley Daily Signal*, November 27, 1951, 6.

6. *Life*, April 5, 1948, 117.

7. *Baton Rouge Morning Advocate*, April 11, 1951, 2-B.

8. *Lake Charles Southwest Citizen*, April 2, 1950, Section IV, 1.

9. *Crowley Post-Signal*, July 28, 2000, 28.

10. *Miami (FL) News*, April 10, 1959, 3C.

11. Bill Veeck, with Ed Linn, *Veeck—As in Wreck: The Autobiography of Bill Veeck* (Chicago: University of Chicago Press, 2001), 67.

12. *Lake Charles Southwest Citizen*, June 4, 1950, Section 4, 1.

13. *Corsicana (TX) Daily Sun*, July 7, 1950, 8.

14. *Crowley Daily Signal*, July 28, 2000, 23.

15. *Crowley Daily Signal*, June 23, 1950, 6.

16. *The Eagle* (Bryan, TX), July 19, 1950, 9.

17. *Beaumont (TX) Enterprise*, September 1950 (exact date and page number unavailable).

18. *Lake Charles Southwest Citizen*, May 28, 1950, Section 4, 1.

19. *Crowley Daily Signal*, March 23, 1951, 6.

20. *Crowley Daily Signal*, March 23, 1951, 6.

4. THE PEPPER POT LEAGUE

1. *New Iberia (LA) Daily Iberian*, September 15, 1985, 6.

2. *New Orleans (LA) Times-Picayune*, January 24, 1946, 13.

3. *Hattiesburg (MS) American*, June 16, 1942, 6.

4. *Opelousas (LA) Daily World*, June 26, 2000, 10.

5. *Crowley Post-Signal*, July 28, 2000, 10B.

6. *Crowley Post-Signal*, July 28, 2000, 10B.

7. *Palm Beach (FL) Post*, May 30, 1942, 7.
8. *Atlanta (GA) Constitution*, April 22, 1952, 12.
9. *Brooklyn (NY) Daily Eagle*, April 11, 1943, 26.
10. *Baltimore (MD) Evening Sun*, April 8, 1943, 33.
11. *Alexandria (LA) Town Talk*, May 30, 1942, 9.
12. *New Orleans Times-Picayune*, January 24, 1946, 13.
13. *New Orleans Times-Picayune*, November 1, 1946, 18.
14. *New York Daily News*, January 30, 1947, 61.
15. *Sporting News*, February 5, 1947, 10.
16. *New Orleans Times-Picayune*, January 30, 1947, 1.
17. *San Francisco Examiner*, October 31, 1946, 21.
18. *Sporting News*, February 5, 1947, 9.
19. *Crowley Daily Signal*, March 23, 1951, 6.

5. "LIGHTNING HAS HIT THIS BALLPARK"

1. *Crowley Daily Signal*, May 28, 1951, 6.
2. *Crowley Daily Signal*, May 29, 1951, 6.
3. *Crowley Daily Signal*, June 15, 1951, 6.
4. *Crowley Daily Signal*, June 15, 1951, 6.
5. *Crowley Daily Signal*, June 18, 1951, 1.
6. *Crowley Daily Signal*, June 18, 1951, 1.
7. *Crowley Daily Signal*, June 18, 1951, 1.
8. *Crowley Daily Signal*, June 18, 1951, 1.
9. *Alexandria Town Talk*, June 19, 1951, 12.
10. *Crowley Daily Signal*, June 18, 1951, 1.
11. *Crowley Daily Signal*, June 18, 1951, 1.
12. *Crowley Daily Signal*, June 18, 1951, 1.
13. *Crowley Daily Signal*, June 18, 1951, 1.
14. *Crowley Daily Signal*, August 17, 1951, 6.
15. *Crowley Daily Signal*, June 23, 1951, 6.
16. *Crowley Post-Signal*, July 28, 2000, 21B.

6. THE CONKER HITS TOWN

1. *New York Tribune*, March 15, 1921, 13.
2. *New York Tribune*, March 15, 1921, 13.
3. *Easton (MD) Star-Democrat*, May 19, 1939, 13.

4. *Easton Star-Democrat*, June 2, 1939, 8.

5. *Ottawa (Canada) Citizen*, June 4, 1940, 10.

6. *Sporting News*, August 11, 1948, 2.

7. *Sporting News*, August 11, 1948, 2.

8. *Sporting News*, August 11, 1948, 2.

9. *Sporting News*, August 11, 1948, 2.

10. David Pietrusza, *Baseball's Canadian American League* (Jefferson, NC: McFarland, 2006), 105.

11. Pietrusza, *Baseball's Canadian American League*, 105.

12. Pietrusza, *Baseball's Canadian American League*, 105.

13. *Easton Star-Democrat*, June 27, 1941, 6.

14. *Frederick (MD) Herald*, January 24, 1946, 6.

15. *St. Louis (MO) Star and Times*, February 27, 1946, 13.

16. *St. Louis Star and Times*, February 27, 1946, 13.

17. *St. Louis Star and Times*, February 27, 1946, 13.

18. *Houston (TX) Post*, March 14, 1946, Section II, 5.

19. *Houston Post*, March 29, 1946, Section II, 8.

20. *Lufkin (TX) Daily News*, August 21, 1946, 2.

21. *Crowley Post-Signal*, July 28, 2000, 20B.

22. *Crowley Daily Signal*, November 17, 1951, 1.

7. OH, HAPPY DAY!

1. *Crowley Post-Signal*, July 28, 2000, 15B.

2. *Saturday Evening Post*, July 28, 1951, 70.

3. *Asbury Park (NJ) Evening Press*, August 8, 1951, 13.

4. *Crowley Daily Signal*, June 28, 1952, 6.

5. *Dixie, New Orleans (LA) Times-Picayune States Roto Magazine*, July 13, 1952, 19.

6. *Dixie, New Orleans Times-Picayune States Roto Magazine*, July 13, 1952, 20.

7. *Dixie, New Orleans Times-Picayune States Roto Magazine*, July 13, 1952, 20.

8. *Dixie, New Orleans Times-Picayune States Roto Magazine*, July 13, 1952, 20.

9. *Dixie, New Orleans Times-Picayune States Roto Magazine*, July 13, 1952, 20.

10. *Dixie, New Orleans Times-Picayune States Roto Magazine*, July 13, 1952, 20.

11. *Alexandria Town Talk*, July 22, 1952, 12.

12. Joe DiMaggio, *Baseball for Everyone* (New York: Signet), 33.

8. MISSED OPPORTUNITY

1. *Crowley Daily Signal*, December 9, 1952, 6.
2. *Crowley Daily Signal*, December 9, 1952, 6.
3. *Sporting News*, January 7, 1953, 6.
4. *Crowley Daily Signal*, September 4, 1952, 2.
5. *Crowley Daily Signal*, January 16, 1953, 6.
6. *Crowley Daily Signal*, January 16, 1953, 6.
7. *Crowley Post-Signal*, July 25, 2002, 2A.
8. *Washington Post*, February 20, 1951, 17.
9. *Lamesa (TX) Daily Reporter*, March 5, 1951, 3.
10. *Abilene (TX) Reporter-News*, April 27, 1951, 6A.
11. *Amarillo (TX) Daily News*, June 5, 1951, 11.
12. *Abilene Reporter-News*, June 2, 1951, 7A.
13. *Paris (TX) News*, May 22, 1952, 11.
14. *Shreveport Times*, June 3, 1952, 18.
15. *Sporting News*, March 4, 1953, 15.
16. *Hattiesburg American*, May 22, 1953, 4.
17. *Delta-Democrat-Times* (Greenville, MS), April 6, 1953, 4.
18. *Fort Pierce (FL) News Tribune*, April 7, 1953, 5.
19. *Fort Pierce News Tribune*, April 7, 1953, 5.
20. *Panama City (FL) News-Herald*, June 9, 1953, 7.
21. *Blytheville (AR) Courier-News*, May 20, 1953, 6.
22. *Daily Herald* (Gulfport and Biloxi, MS), May 21, 1953, 28.
23. *Pantagraph* (Bloomington, IL), May 22, 1953, 16.
24. *Sporting News*, April 29, 1953, 2.
25. *Crowley Daily Signal*, January 24, 1953, 6.
26. *San Francisco (CA) Examiner*, June 1, 1951, 29.
27. *Crowley Daily Signal*, March 27, 1953, 6.
28. *Crowley Daily Signal*, April 4, 1953, 6.
29. *Brownsville (TX) Herald*, April 11, 1954, 11.
30. *Lake Charles (LA) American-Press*, May 11, 1954, 6.
31. *Baton Rouge Morning Advocate*, May 4, 1954, 2B.
32. *Baton Rouge Morning Advocate*, May 22, 1954, 4B.
33. *Reading (PA) Eagle*, May 10, 1970, 65.
34. *Crowley Post-Signal*, April 5, 1998, 10.

9. "THE COOPERSTOWN OF DIXIE"

1. *Crowley Daily Signal*, December 4, 1952, 6.
2. *Sporting News*, August 27, 1952, 35.
3. *Crowley Post-Signal*, July 28, 2000, 21B.
4. *Lamesa (TX) Daily Reporter*, March 23, 1950, 2.
5. *Sporting News*, November 6, 1946, 20.
6. *Crowley Daily Signal*, March 31, 1953, 9.
7. *Crowley Daily Signal*, April 18, 1953, 6.
8. *Beaumont (TX) Enterprise*, April 19, 1953, 1B.
9. *Alexandria (LA) Town Talk*, May 26, 1953, 11.
10. *Alexandria Town Talk*, May 26, 1953, 11.
11. *Crowley Daily Signal*, July 18, 1953, 6.
12. *Crowley Daily Signal*, August 6, 1953, 7.
13. *Beaumont Enterprise*, May 15, 1953, page number unavailable.
14. *Crowley Daily Signal*, August 29, 1953, 4.
15. *Crowley Daily Signal*, August 17, 1953, 6.
16. *Crowley Daily Signal*, September 18, 1953, 1.

10. THE WRITING WAS ON THE WALL

1. *Crowley Daily Signal*, October 9, 1947, 5.
2. *Albuquerque (NM) Journal*, January 3, 1954, 22.
3. *Albuquerque Journal*, January 3, 1954, 22.
4. *Crowley Daily Signal*, May 8, 1954, 4.
5. *Crowley Daily Signal*, May 8, 1954, 4.
6. *Crowley Daily Signal*, April 10, 1954, 4.
7. *Crowley (LA) Post-Signal*, July 28, 2000, 20B.
8. *Crowley Post-Signal*, July 28, 2000, 20B.
9. *Crowley Daily Signal*, July 16, 1954, 6.
10. *Crowley Post-Signal*, July 26, 2001, 2B.
11. *Crowley Daily Signal*, November 18, 1953, 6.
12. *Crowley Daily Signal*, November 16, 1954, 6.
13. *Crowley Daily Signal*, May 31, 1955, 6.
14. *Lake Charles American Press*, July 21, 1955, 1.
15. *Crowley Daily Signal*, June 6, 1955, 1.
16. *Crowley Daily Signal*, June 6, 1955, 1.
17. *Crowley Daily Signal*, June 6, 1955, 1.
18. *Crowley Daily Signal*, June 4, 1955, 9.

19. *Crowley Daily Signal*, June 4, 1955, 9.

20. *Crowley Daily Signal*, June 4, 1955, 9.

21. *Crowley Daily Signal*, May 17, 1955, 6.

22. *Crowley Daily Signal*, May 18, 1955, 6.

23. *Crowley Daily Signal*, June 6, 1955, 6.

24. *Crowley Post-Signal*, July 26, 2001, 2B.

25. *Crowley Post-Signal*, July 26, 2001, 2B.

26. *Daily Advertiser* (Lafayette, LA), August 31, 1955, 11.

27. *Daily Advertiser*, September 1, 1955, 14.

28. *Daily Advertiser*, September 4, 1955, 10.

29. *Crowley Daily Signal*, December 5, 1955, 6.

30. *Crowley Daily Signal*, December 5, 1955, 6.

11. THE KID AND THE OLD PRO

1. *New Iberian* (New Iberia, LA), May 29, 1954, 3.

2. *Charlotte (NC) News*, September 16, 1950, 2B.

3. *San Francisco Examiner*, June 12, 1965, 49.

4. Andre Dubus, *Broken Vessels* (Boston: David R. Godine, 1991), 25.

5. Dubus, *Broken Vessels*, 25–26.

6. Dubus, *Broken Vessels*, 26.

7. Dubus, *Broken Vessels*, 27.

8. *Lafayette (LA) Daily Advertiser*, February 14, 1954, 9.

9. *Lafayette Daily Advertiser*, July 8, 1951, 11.

10. *Lafayette Daily Advertiser*, July 8, 1951, 11.

11. *Lafayette Daily Advertiser*, July 8, 1951, 11.

12. *Lafayette Daily Advertiser*, July 8, 1951, 11.

13. *Lafayette Daily Advertiser*, March 30, 1954, 14.

14. *Lafayette Daily Advertiser*, March 30, 1954, 14.

15. *Atlanta (GA) Constitution*, December 15, 1954, 11.

16. *Atlanta Constitution*, March 31, 1956, 5.

17. Carl Erskine, *Tales from the Dodger Dugout* (Champaign, IL: Sports Publishing, 2001), 8.

18. *Detroit (MI) Free Press*, February 22, 1961, 27.

19. *Detroit Free Press*, February 22, 1961, 27.

20. "Roger Maris 1961—58th Home Run as called by Phil Rizzuto, WPIX-TV, 9/19/1961," *YouTube*, https://youtu.be/hiD7hqYSN1w.

21. *Detroit Free Press*, March 6, 1964, 1D.

12. A LEFTY FOR THE AGES

1. *Los Angeles Times*, July 19, 1966, Part III, 1.
2. *Los Angeles Times*, July 19, 1966, Part III, 1.
3. *Honolulu (HI) Star-Bulletin*, March 14, 1972, G1.
4. *Lowell (MA) Sun*, September 10, 1978, D5.
5. *Los Angeles Times*, June 24, 1965, B1.
6. Jim Bouton, with Leonard Shecter, *Ball Four*, twentieth anniversary edition (New York: Wylie, 1990), 282.
7. Bouton, *Ball Four*, 307.
8. *Los Angeles Times*, June 24, 1965, B1.
9. *Crowley Daily Signal*, December 17, 1955, 8.
10. *Sports Illustrated*, August 18, 1980, 25.
11. *Crowley Daily Signal*, July 15, 1956, 10.
12. *Los Angeles Times*, June 24, 1965, B1.
13. *Alexandria Town Talk*, November 15, 1956, 12.
14. *Boston Globe*, September 19, 1956, 47.
15. *Boston Globe*, September 19, 1956, 47.
16. *Sports Illustrated*, August 18, 1980, 25.
17. *Alexandria Town Talk*, November 15, 1956, 12.
18. *Kansas City (MO) Times*, January 10, 1958, 29.
19. *Kansas City Times*, March 25, 1958, 19.
20. *Kansas City Times*, March 25, 1958, 19.
21. *Los Angeles Times*, July 19, 1966, B1.
22. *Los Angeles Times*, July 19, 1966, B1.
23. Bouton, *Ball Four*, 460.

13. ALMOST ARMAGEDDON

1. *Pittsburgh (PA) Press*, November 23, 1955, 16.
2. *Boston Globe*, December 1, 1955, 36.
3. *Atlanta Constitution*, May 18, 1954, 10.
4. *Atlanta Constitution*, December 3, 1955, 3.
5. *Atlanta Constitution*, December 3, 1955, 1.
6. *Pittsburgh Press*, December 3, 1955, 1.
7. *Pittsburgh Press*, December 3, 1955, 1.
8. *Pittsburgh Press*, December 3, 1955, 3.
9. *Atlanta Constitution*, December 6, 1955, 1.
10. *Atlanta Constitution*, December 5, 1955, 14.

11. *Atlanta Constitution*, December 6, 1955, 10.

12. *Atlanta Constitution*, December 6, 1955, 10.

13. *Louisville (KY) Courier-Journal*, January 3, 1956, Section 2, 9.

14. *Pittsburgh (PA) Post-Gazette*, January 4, 1956, 43.

15. *Boston Globe*, February 5, 1956, 54.

16. *Atlanta Constitution*, December 3, 1955, 5.

17. *Atlanta Constitution*, May 26, 1954, 4.

18. *Sporting News*, March 31, 1954, 17.

19. *Atlanta Constitution*, April 19, 1954, 8.

20. Bruce Adelson, *Brushing Back Jim Crow* (Charlottesville and London: University Press of Virginia, 1999), 150.

21. Adelson, *Brushing Back Jim Crow*, 150.

22. Adelson, *Brushing Back Jim Crow*, 151.

23. *Pittsburgh (PA) Courier*, May 15, 1954, 5.

24. *Kansas City Times*, November 15, 1955, 29.

25. *Lake Charles American Press*, March 4, 1956, 16.

26. *Lake Charles American Press*, March 4, 1956, 16.

27. *Lake Charles American Press*, April 16, 1956, 6.

28. Felipe Alou, with Peter Kerasotis, *Alou: My Baseball Journey* (Lincoln and London: University of Nebraska Press, 2018), 33.

29. *Lafayette Daily Advertiser*, April 16, 1956, 11.

30. *Lake Charles American Press*, April 8, 1956, 30.

31. *Alexandria Town Talk*, April 27, 1956, 10.

32. *Lake Charles American Press*, April 8, 1956, 30.

33. Adelson, *Brushing Back Jim Crow*, 182.

34. *Baton Rouge Morning Advocate*, April 29, 1956, 1D.

35. *Baton Rouge Morning Advocate*, May 3, 1956, 4A.

36. *Crowley Daily Signal*, May 7, 1956, 8.

37. *Shreveport Times*, May 8, 1956, 9-B.

38. *Lake Charles American Press*, May 7, 1956, 6.

39. *Shreveport Times*, May 8, 1956, 9B.

40. *Pittsburgh Courier*, May 26, 1956, 40.

41. *Lafayette Daily Advertiser*, May 20, 1956, 11.

42. *Lafayette Daily Advertiser*, June 21, 1956, 16.

43. *Crowley Daily Signal*, September 12, 1956, 9.

44. *Pittsburgh Press*, July 17, 1956, 20.

45. *Pittsburgh (PA) Sun-Telegraph*, July 14, 1956, 14.

46. *Pittsburgh Sun-Telegraph*, July 14, 1956, 14.

14. THE UNWANTED VISITOR
NAMED AUDREY

1. *Crowley Daily Signal*, January 13, 1957, 5.
2. *Alexandria Town Talk*, January 15, 1957, 11.
3. *Orlando (FL) Evening Star*, May 7, 1957, 11.
4. *Orlando Evening Star*, May 7, 1957, 11.
5. *Crowley Daily Signal*, April 24, 1957, 4.
6. *Crowley Daily Signal*, May 12, 1957, 8.
7. *Crowley Daily Signal*, May 12, 1957, 8.
8. *Lafayette Daily Advertiser*, June 20, 1957, 2.
9. *Crowley Daily Signal*, June 26, 1957, 1.
10. *Alexandria Town Talk*, July 16, 1957, 9.
11. *Cincinnati (OH) Enquirer*, June 4, 1955, 15.
12. *Cincinnati Enquirer*, July 25, 1955, 30.
13. *Sporting News*, May 23, 1956, 14.
14. *Sporting News*, May 23, 1956, 14.
15. *Paducah (KY) Sun*, August 22, 1957, 9B.
16. *Crowley Daily Signal*, May 14, 1958, 8.
17. *Crowley Daily Signal*, May 14, 1958, 8.
18. *Crowley Daily Signal*, May 14, 1958, 8.

15. THE SHOWDOWN BEFORE THE STORM

1. *Alexandria Town Talk*, June 11, 1957, 10.
2. *Alexandria Town Talk*, August 1, 1957, 8.
3. *Alexandria Town Talk*, August 10, 1957, 8.
4. *Monroe (LA) Morning World*, August 18, 1957, 7.
5. *Birmingham (AL) News*, August 14, 1957, 34.
6. *Sporting News*, August 21, 1957, 48.
7. *Nashville Tennessean*, August 25, 1957, 2C.
8. Jim Bouton, with Leonard Shecter, *Ball Four*, twentieth anniversary edition (New York: Wylie, 1990), 26.
9. Bouton, *Ball Four*, 47.
10. *Shreveport (LA) Times*, August 23, 1961, 8A.
11. *Kansas City Times*, April 25, 1962, 13.
12. *Alabama (Montgomery) Journal*, April 25, 1962, 5C.
13. *Kansas City Times*, May 5, 1962, 25.
14. *Kansas City Times*, May 5, 1962, 25.

15. *The Record* (Hackensack, NJ), July 5, 1962, Section 4, 1.
16. *New York Daily News*, July 17, 1962, 44.
17. *Boston Globe*, March 15, 1963, 34.
18. *Boston Globe*, March 15, 1963, 34.
19. *Boston Globe*, March 15, 1963, 34.
20. *Boston Globe*, March 15, 1963, 34.
21. *Indianapolis (IN) News*, May 23, 1963, 42.
22. *Kansas City Times*, July 3, 1964, 17.

16. THE MANAGER WAS A CROOK

1. *Dublin (GA) Courier-Herald*, April 30, 1953, 8.
2. *Lake Charles American Press*, January 8, 1954, 10.
3. *Tallahassee (FL) Democrat*, January 23, 1954, 10.
4. *Tallahassee Democrat*, January 24, 1954, Section 2, 1.
5. *Tallahassee Democrat*, January 24, 1954, Section 2, 1.
6. *Tallahassee Democrat*, January 24, 1954, Section 2, 1.
7. *Tallahassee Democrat*, January 25, 1954, 6.
8. *Tallahassee Democrat*, January 25, 1954, 6.
9. *Tallahassee Democrat*, January 28, 1954, 8.
10. *Tallahassee Democrat*, January 27, 1954, 9.
11. *Tallahassee Democrat*, January 28, 1954, 8.
12. *Tallahassee Democrat*, January 28, 1954, 8.
13. *Tallahassee Democrat*, January 28, 1954, 8.
14. *Tallahassee Democrat*, January 29, 1954, 10.
15. *Tallahassee Democrat*, February 1, 1954, 6.
16. *Tallahassee Democrat*, February 1, 1954, 6.
17. *Tallahassee Democrat*, January 31, 1954, 9.
18. *Tallahassee Democrat*, April 4, 1954, 9.
19. *Tallahassee Democrat*, February 21, 1954, 25.
20. *Tallahassee Democrat*, April 11, 1954, Section 2, 1.
21. *Tallahassee Democrat*, April 8, 1954, 10.
22. *Tallahassee Democrat*, April 26, 1954, 8.
23. *Tallahassee Democrat*, May 2, 1954, Section 2, 1.
24. *Tallahassee Democrat*, May 27, 1954, 10.
25. *Tallahassee Democrat*, May 6, 1954, 10.
26. *Tallahassee Democrat*, May 6, 1954, 10.
27. *Tallahassee Democrat*, July 27, 1954, 8.
28. *Tallahassee Democrat*, July 27, 1954, 8.
29. *Tallahassee Democrat*, July 27, 1954, 8.

30. *Tallahassee Democrat*, July 27, 1954, 8.

31. *New Iberian* (New Iberia, LA), May 15, 1954, 3.

32. *Birmingham (AL) Post-Herald*, December 6, 1956, 44.

17. THE CONKER GOES BONKERS

1. *Long Beach (CA) Independent*, October 16, 1949, 37.

2. "Bear Tracks Greer," *A Ball Player's Son: Memoir by Dell Franklin*, *DellFranklin.com*, https://www.dellfranklin.com/a-ballplayers-son-chapter-16-bear-tracks-greer.html.

3. "Bear Tracks Greer."

4. Paul Hemphill, *Long Gone* (Chicago: Ivan R. Dee, 2002).

5. *Los Angeles Times*, April 3, 1945, A7.

6. *Kingsport (TN) Times*, February 4, 1946, 2.

7. *Tallahassee (FL) Democrat*, April 26, 1954, 8.

8. *Tallahassee Democrat*, May 12, 1954, 10.

9. *Houston (TX) Post*, March 10, 1946, Section 4, 1.

10. *Houston Post*, April 25, 1946, Section 2, 10.

11. *Allentown (PA) Morning Call*, November 10, 1946, 20.

12. *Allentown Morning Call*, November 24, 1955, 48.

13. *Allentown Morning Call*, November 22, 1955, 34.

14. *Houston Post*, May 12, 1946, Section 4, 3.

15. *Tampa (FL) Tribune*, January 21, 1948, 1.

16. *Tallahassee Democrat*, July 23, 1954, 8.

17. *Tallahassee Democrat*, July 23, 1954, 8.

18. *Sarasota (FL) Herald-Tribune*, November 21, 1955, 5.

19. *Miami (FL) Herald*, November 21, 1955, 1A.

20. *Miami Herald*, November 23, 1955, 4C.

21. *Miami Herald*, November 23, 1955, 4C.

22. *Miami Herald*, November 23, 1955, 4C.

23. *Miami (FL) Daily News*, November 21, 1955, 10A.

24. *Sarasota Herald-Tribune*, November 21, 1955, 5.

25. Conklyn Wells Meriwether Criminal M-2 document, Clerk of the Circuit and Country Courts, Monroe County, Florida.

26. Conklyn Wells Meriwether Criminal M-2 document.

27. Conklyn Wells Meriwether Criminal M-2 document.

28. Conklyn Wells Meriwether Criminal M-2 document.

29. *Miami Herald*, November 2, 1971, 2B.

30. *Miami Herald*, January 15, 1972, 1B.

31. *Miami Herald*, January 15, 1972, 1B.

32. *Miami Herald*, January 15, 1972, 1B.

18. RESTORE IT AND THEY WILL RETURN

1. *Crowley Daily Signal*, August 5, 1967, 5.
2. *Crowley Post-Signal*, July 9, 2000, 1–2.
3. *Crowley Post-Signal*, July 25, 2000, 1.
4. *Crowley Post-Signal*, July 28, 2000, 20B.
5. *Crowley Post-Signal*, July 28, 2000, 20B.
6. *Crowley Post-Signal*, July 28, 2000, 20B.
7. *Crowley Post-Signal*, July 26, 2001, 2B.
8. *Crowley Post-Signal*, July 26, 2001, 2B.
9. *Crowley Post-Signal*, July 26, 2001, 2B.
10. *Crowley Post-Signal*, July 26, 2001, 2B.
11. *Crowley Post-Signal*, July 25, 2002, 4B.
12. *Crowley Post-Signal*, July 25, 2002, 5B.
13. *Crowley Post-Signal*, July 26, 2001, 6B.
14. *Crowley Post-Signal*, August 26, 1986, 4.
15. *Crowley Post-Signal*, September 4, 1986, 4.
16. *Crowley Daily Signal*, June 18, 1951, 1.
17. *Crowley Daily Signal*, June 18, 1951, 1.
18. *Crowley Daily Signal*, June 18, 1951, 1.

APPENDIX B

1. *Crowley Post-Signal*, October 30, 2013, 2A.

INDEX

ABOUT THE AUTHOR

Gaylon H. White is the author of three books—*Left on Base in the Bush Leagues*, *Singles and Smiles*, and *The Bilko Athletic Club*—and coauthor, with Ransom Jackson, of *Handsome Ransom Jackson: Accidental Big Leaguer*. All four books were published by Rowman & Littlefield.

Called "one of the best sports books of 2014" by Bruce Miles of the *Chicago Daily Herald*, *The Bilko Athletic Club* is a blast from the past revolving around beer-loving, home run–hitting Steve Bilko and the 1956 Los Angeles Angels of the old Pacific Coast League

Handsome Ransom Jackson: Accidental Big Leaguer covers the career of Jackson, a two-time National League All-Star in the 1950s and the last Brooklyn Dodger to hit a home run. The book was a grand slam with Allen Barra of the *Chicago Tribune*, who wrote, "We can only hope that among today's players there's someone as sharp and funny as Handsome Ransom Jackson to remember them."

In 2018, *Singles and Smiles* received the Negro Leagues Research Committee's Robert Peterson Recognition Award, which was named after the author of the trailblazing book on black baseball *Only the Ball Was White*. *Singles and Smiles* traces the life of Artie Wilson, the greatest shortstop no one heard of—from Birmingham, Alabama, where he was born in 1920, to Portland, Oregon, where he lived for 55 years until his death in 2010, at the age of 90.

"Meticulously researched and compellingly presented, *Left on Base in the Bush Leagues* is the best book on 1950s Minor League Baseball ever, a milestone worthy of sharing the same bookshelf with *The Glory of*

Their Times," according to Jim McConnell, author of the critically acclaimed biography *Bobo Newsom: Baseball's Traveling Man.*

The Los Angeles–born White graduated in 1967, from the University of Oklahoma, with a bachelor's degree in journalism and broadcasting. He was a sportswriter for the *Denver Post, Arizona Republic,* and *Oklahoma Journal* before working nearly 40 years for such varied companies as Hallmark Cards, Inc., the Goodyear Tire & Rubber Company, Control Data Corporation, and Eastman Chemical Company.

At Eastman, White worked closely with industrial designers, and, in 2015, the Industrial Designers Society of America selected him as one of its 50 most notable members from the past half-century.

He and his wife, Mary, live in Kingsport, Tennessee. They have three children and seven grandchildren.

www.GaylonWhiteBaseball.com